Essential Welsh Gramm

Teach Yourself®

Essential Welsh Grammar

Christine Jones

For UK order enquiries: please contact Bookpoint Ltd,
130 Milton Park, Abingdon, Oxon, OX14 4SB.
Telephone: +44 (0) 1235 827720. Fax: +44 (0) 1235 400454.
Lines are open 09.00–17.00, Monday to Saturday, with a 24-hour
message answering service. Details about our titles and how to
order are available at www.teachyourself.com

For USA order enquiries: please contact McGraw-Hill
Customer Services, PO Box 545, Blacklick, OH 43004-0545, USA.
Telephone: 1-800-722-4726. Fax: 1-614-755-5645.

For Canada order enquiries: please contact McGraw-Hill
Ryerson Ltd, 300 Water St, Whitby, Ontario, L1N 9B6, Canada.
Telephone: 905 430 5000. Fax: 905 430 5020.

Long renowned as the authoritative source for self-guided
learning – with more than 50 million copies sold worldwide –
the **Teach Yourself** series includes over 500 titles in the fields of
languages, crafts, hobbies, business, computing and education.

British Library Cataloguing in Publication Data: a catalogue record
for this title is available from the British Library.

Library of Congress Catalog Card Number: on file.

First published in UK 2007 by Hodder Education, part of
Hachette Livre UK, 338 Euston Road, London, NW1 3BH.

First published in US 2007 by The McGraw-Hill Companies, Inc.

This edition published 2010, previously published as
Teach Yourself Welsh Grammar.

The **Teach Yourself** name is a registered trade mark of
Hodder Headline.

Typeset by MPS Limited, a Macmillan Company.

Printed in Great Britain for Hodder Education, an Hachette Livre
UK Company, 338 Euston Road, London NW1 3BH by
CPI Group (UK) Ltd, Croydon, CR0 4YY.

The publisher has used its best endeavours to ensure that the URLs
for external websites referred to in this book are correct and active
at the time of going to press. However, the publisher and the
author have no responsibility for the websites and can make no
guarantee that a site will remain live or that the content will remain
relevant, decent or appropriate.

Hachette Livre UK's policy is to use papers that are natural,
renewable and recyclable products and made from wood grown
in sustainable forests. The logging and manufacturing processes
are expected to conform to the environmental regulations of the
country of origin.

Impression number   10 9 8 7 6 5 4 3 2

Year   2014 2013 2012

Acknowledgements

I would like to thank all those at Hodder Education involved
with the production of this book for their support and guidance,
together with all their hard work. I would also like to thank my
students and colleagues at the University of Wales, Lampeter for
trying out many of the exercises and for their useful suggestions
and comments. Most of all I would like to thank my husband
Owen, our children Gwenllïan and Sioned and my mother, for
their patience, understanding and continued support.

In preparing this grammar, I have used information readily
available in a variety of sources such as Peter Wyn Thomas,
Gramadeg y Gymraeg, University of Wales Press, (1996); David
Thorne, *Gramadeg Cymraeg*, Gomer Press, (1996); Phylip Brake,
Cymraeg Graenus, Gomer Press, (1998) and Heini Gruffudd,
Cymraeg Da, Lolfa Press, (2000), together with a range of other
books. While remaining solely responsible for any weaknesses
or inaccuracies to be found here, I sincerely hope that this Welsh
grammar will be found to be a user-friendly and practical resource
for both adult learners of Welsh and those studying Welsh as a
second language in secondary school.

Credits

Contents

Meet the author

I am Head of the School of Welsh and Bilingual Studies at the University of Wales Trinity St David. A former Pro Vice-Chancellor, I have over twenty years' teaching experience in the university sector and have taught Welsh to adults since 1984. As well as producing academic articles and books on applied linguistics, sociolinguistics and dialectology, I have edited a range of books for adult learners and tutors. I am also an External Examiner for both Cardiff and Glyndŵr Universities and an advisor on publications for Welsh learners for the Welsh Assembly.

I have worked closely with Hodder Education over the last ten years and am the co-author of *Teach Yourself Welsh* (2000/2003), *Teach Yourself World Cultures: Wales* (2004) and *Teach Yourself Welsh Conversation* (2007) together with *Speak Welsh with Confidence* (2010) and *Complete Welsh* (2010). I am also the author of *Teach Yourself: Welsh Grammar* (2007), the first edition of this title.

Having learnt Welsh as a second language while at school, I feel that I can empathize with those learning the language through self-study, and hope my personal understanding and appreciation of the highs and lows of language learning are reflected in my books. I hope too that this jargon-free reference book, based on my experiences teaching grammar to learners of all levels and abilities, will help to show that Welsh grammar is not nearly as daunting as it may first appear!

Christine Jones

Only got a minute?

Welsh has a rich cultural heritage and is the oldest surviving language in Britain, with a history and a literature extending over 15 centuries. Over half a million people in Wales speak Welsh and many more outside of Wales too, particularly in the Chubut Province of Patagonia. Many of the 12 per cent of Welsh speakers now living in Wales but who were born elsewhere, have learnt the language either through self-study, online courses or by attending weekly night classes.

This user-friendly and jargon-free introduction to the key elements of Welsh grammar is designed for all those who, with or without the help of a teacher, need to study or revise all the essentials of Welsh grammar. A particular feature of the book is its two-fold approach to the language: it is communicative and grammatical in outlook. It contains plenty of examples of the grammar at work in the spoken language, but at the same time where appropriate, such as in relation to the verbs, the formal written forms are also listed.

You may not have used Welsh since your school days and be looking for a reference book both to strengthen your knowledge of grammar and improve your written skills, so as to improve your employment prospects. This book therefore should be useful to you as a reference book, as well as to those who are beginning to learn the language and wish to use it as a grammar exercise book. Night classes naturally cannot focus too much on the grammar and this book allows you to revise at your leisure and test yourself by means of a range of exercises at the end of every unit. All the answers are in the back of the book of course!

10 Only got ten minutes?

Welsh is the oldest language in Britain, with a history extending over 15 centuries. It is spoken by over half a million speakers in Wales, around 20 per cent of the population. Welsh is also spoken by unknown numbers in England, the United States of America, Australia and other parts of the world, including a small, bilingual Welsh-Spanish community which was established in Patagonia in 1865. For ten years this Welsh state was completely self-governing, with Welsh being the language of its own constitution, parliament and education. The colony in Patagonia was the first democracy in the world to give the vote to all people over the age of 18 and voting was by means of a secret ballot. Today around 8,000 people in Patagonia speak Welsh.

The Welsh originally called themselves *Brython* or *Brythoniaid* (British) and later after the invasion of Germanic tribes, *Cymry*, which means comrades or fellow countrymen. The same 'cym' element exists in the related form Cumberland, the former name of the county in northern England now called Cumbria. The English words Welsh and Wales derive from a Germanic name for foreigners or for people who have been influenced by the culture of the Roman Empire. There are similar related forms in other parts of the old Roman Empire which bordered on the lands of the Germanic speakers – the Wallons in Belgium, the Valais in Switzerland and the Welsch of the Italian Tyrol.

The Welsh language is derived from the Brythonic form of Celtic (also called British or Brittonic). Cornish and Breton are also descendants of Brythonic. Scottish and Irish Gaelic and Manx descend from the Goidelic branch of Celtic. Although there are many words in the Celtic languages which are very similar, the spoken Celtic languages today are not really mutually intelligible.

The evolution of Welsh from Brythonic is believed to have occurred by about AD 600. Around 1,000 Latin words were absorbed into the Brythonic language during the time of the Roman occupation and are still present in the language today, including *pysgod* (fish – from the Latin *piscis*) and *eglwys* (church – from the Latin *ecclesia*, cf. French *église*). Early Welsh evolved into Old Welsh, the language of Wales between the ninth and eleventh centuries, although very few examples of Welsh from this period have survived. One example is the *Computus Fragment* written about AD 920 which discusses the movements of the moon, providing evidence that Welsh was used in the tenth century to discuss scientific topics.

The term Middle Welsh is used to describe the language spoken from the twelfth to the fourteenth centuries. Welsh had evolved into the language of learning and culture in Wales. Manuscripts of the laws of Hywel Dda date from this period and are proof of a rich legal vocabulary in Welsh. Despite the influx of French and then English speakers from 1066 onwards, Wales remained a predominantly Welsh-speaking community throughout the Middle Ages.

The language between the fourteenth and sixteenth century is an example of Early Modern Welsh. While much literature was produced in Welsh during this period, the Welsh gentry were beginning to realize that learning English was advantageous. The Act of Union of 1536 went a step further, and the English language was declared to be the only language of the courts of Wales. Its intention was to get rid of the differences between Wales and England, thus creating a uniform administrative system run by a Welsh ruling class fluent in English. The language of the future was seen to be English, and by the eighteenth century the anglicization of the gentry was virtually complete.

Although excluded from state administration, Welsh remained the language of worship in Welsh churches. This was partly because of governmental fears that Wales would remain Catholic, thereby providing a sympathetic back-door through which Catholic nations like Spain could invade Britain, if religious material was not provided in a language understood by the majority of the population. An Act was therefore passed in 1563 commanding that Welsh translations of the Bible and Prayer Book be available by 1567. William Salesbury translated the Book of Common Prayer and New Testament in 1567, and William Morgan produced the complete Bible in 1588.

The translation of the Bible was a turning point for the language, in that it provided a model of correct written Welsh and introduced the beginnings of a standardised national language based on the language of the poets of the Middle Ages. Many books were published in the sixteenth and seventeenth centuries, demonstrating the richness of the language and its suitability as a medium of learning and religion. Interestingly, the first grammar book written in Welsh was produced in Milan by Catholic exile Gruffydd Robert in 1567!

During the eighteenth century a national revival was attempted by restoring Wales's ancient history and literature. Druids became fashionable and various theories about the origins of the Welsh language abounded, including one promoted by the Breton Paul-Yves, that the Welsh people were descended from Gomer, the grandson of Noah.

The Industrial Revolution also transformed the Welsh language, and as increasing numbers of Welsh speakers moved from rural areas into the towns, many cultural societies, choirs and debating societies were formed. Welsh became the language of mass communication and many new words were formed to meet the needs of the new age by men such as William Owen Pughe. Pughe wrote a grammar book based on his theory that grammar books should not describe a language as it is, but as it ought to be! He created a new set of verbs and plurals to eliminate irregularity in the language.

Nevertheless, more and more people were seeing Welsh as the language of the hearth and English the language for everywhere else. In 1846 an inspection of schools was carried out by three English barristers. Their report became known as *Brad y Llyfrau Gleision* (The Treason of the Blue Books) as it labelled standards in the schools as deplorable and laid the blame for the state of Welsh schooling on the Welsh tongue, 'the language of slavery'. The report stated, 'the Welsh language is a manifold barrier to the moral progress and commercial prosperity of the people'.

By 1847, only three out of 1,656 day schools in Wales taught any Welsh, and in 1852 the Inspector of Schools announced that it was 'socially and politically desirable' that the language be erased. In some schools a wooden board called the 'Welsh nok' was hung around the necks of children caught speaking Welsh; the last child to wear it at the end of the day would receive a beating. The 1870 Education Act made the English school system compulsory, and without the Sunday schools, it is possible that many children in Wales would not have been literate at all in Welsh.

Gradually during the twentieth century the tide began to turn, with Welsh-medium schools being established from the 1940s as a result of parental demand both among native speakers and non Welsh-speakers who wished their children to learn the language. On average 14.4 per cent of all secondary school pupils between the ages of 11 and 16 are now taught Welsh as a first language. Within that average there is of course great geographic diversity, but areas such as the valleys in South Wales show what potential there is for further growth and expansion. When two Welsh-medium primary schools opened in the anglicized Rhondda Valley in 1950, there were only 49 children receiving a Welsh-medium education. By September 2005 there were 1,385 pupils attending five Welsh-medium primary schools and a further 951 in the secondary school that serves the area. Five years on, the schools continue to grow and flourish. Without doubt the contribution of education to the reversal of language-shift in Wales has been considerable and one organisation that has played a significant part in this reversal process is *Mudiad Ysgolion Meithrin*, the Welsh Nursery School Movement founded in 1971.

Also key when discussing the twentieth century revival of the language is the Welsh Language Society (*Cymdeithas yr Iaith Gymraeg*), founded after a speech on the future of the Welsh language given by J Saunders Lewis in 1962 entitled *Tynged yr Iaith* (the Fate of the Language). *Tynged yr Iaith* called for the use of 'revolutionary methods' to preserve the language, and the society forced the English Parliament to pass the Welsh Language Act of 1967. This gave equal status to the Welsh language for the first time since 1536. A further Act passed in 1993 gave people in Wales the right to deal with public bodies in Welsh. *Cymdeithas yr Iaith Gymraeg* is also responsible for many symbols which have made the Welsh language a natural part of public life in the last half of the twentieth century. Their campaign of painting over English words on road signs led to the government introducing bilingual road signs. After considerable public pressure *Radio Cymru* and the Welsh language television channel *Sianel Pedwar Cymru*, which now transmits over 80 hours of Welsh-medium programmes per week, were established.

The Welsh language today is therefore in an encouraging position. For the first time since 1891, when a question on language was included on the census form, knowledge of the Welsh language is more widespread among children than it is among the population as a whole, and virtually all children at primary level in Wales have Welsh lessons. The 2001 census revealed that 16.3 per cent of the population can speak, read or write Welsh, up from 13.6 per cent in 1991. Around 28 per cent have some knowledge of Welsh, with the number of speakers estimated to be at least 20.5 per cent – the highest proportion since 1961. Reflecting the growth in Welsh-medium education, almost 38 per cent of children aged between three and fifteen can speak the language, an increase of 13.4 per cent since 1991. Also on the increase is the number of Welsh speakers now living in Wales who were born elsewhere. Many of the 12 per cent of Welsh speakers who were not born in Wales have learnt Welsh either through self-study courses, online courses or by attending classes.

This grammar is designed for all those of you who, with or without the help of a teacher, need to study or revise all the essentials of Welsh grammar. With the public sector in Wales legally bound to provide services in both Welsh and English, bilingual speakers are in particular demand in some employment areas. You may not have used Welsh since your school days and be looking for a reference book to strengthen your knowledge of Welsh grammar and to improve your written skills, so as to improve your employment prospects. This book should prove to be as useful to you as a reference book, as it will to those who are in the early stages of learning the language and wish to use it as a grammar exercise book. It allows you to revise at your leisure and test yourself by means of a range of exercises, at the end of every unit, with the answers in the back of the book.

Welsh has a particularly rich cultural heritage as this brief introduction has attempted to show. Since devolution and the establishment of the Welsh Assembly in 1999, the language has gone from strength to strength. A key priority in its recent revival has been to promote it as a community language, thereby raising its profile and facilitating its usage locally and causing new activities to be organized and existing activities coordinated. Understanding and speaking Welsh can open very many doors in relation to the social and cultural aspects of the language.

So why not give it a go!

How to use this book

A glossary of grammatical terms follows this section for easy reference whenever the explanation of a term is required. Each of the 27 units – with the exception of the first, which is slightly different – consists of the following sections:

- ▶ *Grammar in focus*
- ▶ *Author insight boxes*
- ▶ *Exercises*
- ▶ *Grammar in context*
- ▶ *End of unit diagnostic test*

The following is a suggestion as to how you might sensibly work through each unit:

Read through the **Grammar in focus** section, where the language point of the unit is explained together with examples translated into English. See if you can think of any further examples yourself. You may also find it useful to start making a list in a separate notebook of the new words you come across in the examples. In the **Author insight boxes** I try to help with those elements of Welsh grammar which are, in my opinion, difficult to grasp or which are essential for you to know in order to progress successfully.

Having studied and digested the structures, attempt the exercises that follow the explanations. These are designed to give you immediate practice of the grammar points, through a variety of activities. It may well be better not to write your answers into the book, so that you can return to the exercises at a later date to test yourself. At that point, try to do them without looking at the explanations, to see what you can remember.

Having done the exercises, look at the **Grammar in context** section, where you will find the structures of the unit illustrated in realistic texts such as dialogues, magazine and novel extracts, adverts and web pages. You will find some help with vocabulary and a few questions to guide you through comprehension of the texts.

Each unit concludes with a diagnostic test, to be attempted when you are content that you fully understand the unit and have undertaken the exercises. Completion of the test will help you assess whether or not you are ready to move on to the next unit.

As with *Complete Welsh*, the emphasis in this grammar is very much on the standard spoken forms and the exercises and tests clearly reflect this. However, wherever appropriate, for example in the units on verbal forms or pronouns, the formal written literary alternatives are also given, thereby adding a useful extra dimension for the advanced Welsh learner.

At the end of the book you will find a selection of common verb-noun stems and the full conjugations of the main irregular verbs. A **Taking it further** section contains a selection of useful language websites and additional advice and this is followed by the **Key to the exercises**.

There are clear explanations of the structures of the Welsh language, although, to ease comprehension and therefore progress, grammatical terminology has been kept to a minimum. Note, however, the following abbreviations, which are used several times within the book:

NW	a word or form used in North Wales
SW	a word or form used in South Wales
AM	a word which causes an aspirate mutation
NM	a word which causes a nasal mutation
SM	a word which causes a soft mutation

Glossary of grammatical terms

Grammar is nothing to fear! Many people have an aversion to the word itself, as they may remember bad experiences of early (dull) learning or consider it generally difficult or 'irrelevant'. However it is impossible to learn a language without studying the grammar, in whatever guise that might be. Grammar is simply the building blocks which, once linked together, make up the framework of the language, enabling you to do something more than simply churn out stock phrases parrot fashion. The main basic terms are explained simply below, with examples in English. You can refer back to these notes at any time while you are studying.

accents these are written marks above letters which affect how that letter is pronounced, or at what point the word should be stressed (emphasized) when spoken. An accent can also be used sometimes in Welsh to differentiate between two words with identical spelling but with different meaning e.g. **gêm** *game*, **gem** *gem*. See Unit 1 for more on accents in Welsh.

adjectives adjectives give more information about nouns, e.g. *A **naughty** dog. The **interesting** book. That house is **old**.*

adverbs adverbs provide additional information about how, where or when an action takes place. In English they often, but not always, end in *-ly*, e.g. *He drove home **slowly**. They arrive **tomorrow**.*

auxiliary in Welsh this refers to a verb used in conjunction with a verb-noun to give it a tense and a person, e.g. **gwneud** in the sentence **Gwnes i fwyta sglodion i swper.** *I ate chips for supper.* (Lit. *I did eat*).

cardinal numbers numbers one, two, three, etc.

clause a unit of speech which is less than a sentence, but usually contains at least a subject and a verb.

colloquial a more casual, familiar style of spoken speech.

comparative when we make comparisons we use the comparative form of the adjective. In English this generally means adding *–er* to the adjective or putting *more* in front of it. This dress is *longer* than the other one. A few common adjectives in Welsh such as **good da** and **bad drwg** have irregular comparative forms as explained in Unit 6.

conjugation this term is used to describe the changing formation of a verb according to person, number, tense, etc.

conjunction conjunctions are words joining two clauses in a sentence, e.g. *but, because, and.*

definite article English has a definite article namely *the* and an indefinite article *a / an / some*. Welsh has a definite article which is **y** (preceding a consonant), **yr** (preceding a vowel) and **'r** after a vowel, but there is no equivalent to the indefinite article in Welsh.

demonstratives the words used for pointing things out – *this, that, these, those.*

gender in English, gender is usually linked to male and female persons or animals, so, for example, we refer to a man as *he* and to a woman as *she*. Objects and beings of an indeterminate sex are referred to as having *neuter* gender. So, for example, we refer to a chair as *it*. In Welsh, nouns referring to female persons are feminine and those referring to male persons are masculine. But all nouns in Welsh are either masculine or feminine and this has nothing to do with sex. **Ffenestr** *window* and **cadair** *chair* are feminine, while **drws** *door* and **cwpwrdd** *cupboard* are masculine.

idiom an expression or saying which is not easily directly translated into another language and often does not relate to normal rules of grammar.

imperative the imperative is the form of the verb used to give directions, instructions, orders or commands: *Turn left at the bottom of the street. Go and tell him at once.*

impersonal forms formal forms which convey the general action of the verbs to which they are added, without specifying who or what is doing the action: *A meeting will be held tomorrow night. Welsh was spoken in the classroom.* See Unit 25.

indicative mood the normal form of the verb used for straightforward statements, questions and negatives.

infinitive the form of the verb found in the dictionary (see also verb-noun below).

interrogative any verb form used in making questions as opposed to positive (affirmative) statements or negatives.

irregular verbs verbs which do not behave according to a set pattern. In Welsh there are only a small number of irregular verbs.

mutation a change in the initial consonant of a word under particular circumstances, for example, **c > g** after the preposition **o**. **Dw i'n dod o Gymru.** *I come from Wales.* See Unit 2 for full details of mutation changes in Welsh.

negative the expression of ideas such as no, not, never, no one, etc.

nouns nouns are words that refer to a person, a place or an object. Definite nouns refer to a specific thing or person as opposed to a general one, e.g. *the girl, the family, Prince Charles*. An indefinite noun is a noun used in a general sense, which doesn't refer to any individual or specific thing.

number the term is used to indicate whether something is *singular* or *plural*. See **singular**.

object the object in a sentence is the thing or person that is at the 'receiving end' of the action of a verb. For example, in the sentence, *the baby drank milk*, *milk* is the direct object. In Welsh the direct object of a conjugated verb (also known as a short form verb) takes the soft mutation if possible: **Yfodd y babi laeth. Llaeth** (*milk*) is mutated to **laeth**.

ordinal number first, second, third, etc.

passive a sentence construction in which the subject is the receiver and not the doer of the action: *She was elected to the council.*

periphrastic any tense of a verb that is expressed in the long form, not by endings on the verb itself, but by the use of an auxiliary. e.g. **Roedd hi'n canu** *She was singing*. This uses the verb 'to be' rather than putting the ending on **canu – canai**.

person a means of identifying the relationship of something to the speaker. The first person is the speaker: *I, we*, the second person is the one spoken to: *you*, while the third person is the one spoken about: *he, she, they*.

personal pronouns these refer to persons, e.g. *I, you, he, she,* etc. See **pronouns**.

phrase a group of words which together have some meaning but do not contain a verb, e.g. *after supper, in the class*.

possessives words showing ownership or possession, *my car, our dog*.

prepositions words used to relate a noun or a pronoun to some other part of the sentence, e.g. *of*, *at*. Welsh contains a number of *compound prepositions* that consist of two elements, e.g. **o gwmpas** *around*. See Unit 15 for further examples.

pronouns words like *he, they, we* often used to replace a noun that has already been mentioned, e.g. *My **mother** (noun) has moved to England. **She** (pronoun) is very happy in her new home.*

sentence a group of words, with a beginning, an end and a finite **verb** (see below), which has a meaning. A sentence may have any number of separate clauses, but one of these will be the main clause, which can make sense in its own right as a sentence. e.g. *She wants to learn Welsh. If you go now, you will find him working in the shed.*

singular the terms singular and plural are used to make the contrast between 'one' and 'more than one', e.g. *cat/cats, child/children.*

stem the part of a noun, verb, etc. to which endings are added.

subject the subject of a sentence is that which does the action of the verb. For example in the sentence *The girl sang a song,* **the girl** is the subject as it is she who is doing the singing.

subjunctive mood a separate set of verb endings for use in certain situations such as *if* clauses, or with expressions of doubt.

syllable this is part of a word containing one, two or more letters so that we can divide up the word as we say it.

superlative the superlative is used for the most extreme version of a comparison. In English this generally means adding *-est* to the adjective or putting *most* in front of it. *This jacket is the **most** comfortable.* See Unit 6 for a detailed discussion on Welsh superlative forms.

....

tense an indication within the form of the verb as to when an action happened in relation to the speaker. e.g. *He sang* (past). *They are going now* (present). *We will call tomorrow* (future). *I was thinking of leaving* (imperfect). Don't worry too much about the actual terminology – concentrate on learning which verb ending to use in what circumstances.

....

verbs verbs are action or doing words which usually come first in a Welsh sentence. e.g. *He drank. We sang.* Verbs can also denote a physical or mental state. e.g. *I knew.* A sentence must have a verb in a 'finite' form – which tells you what the action is, who is doing it and at what point in time. Words that describe actions, but do not tell you who is doing the action or when it occurred are called **verb-nouns** in Welsh e.g. *to sleep, to live.*

....

1

The Welsh alphabet and pronunciation

In this unit you will learn:
- **The Welsh alphabet and how to pronounce it**
- **Accents and stress in Welsh**
- **Double consonants in Welsh**

Welsh is often described as a phonetic language, which means that you say something the way it looks. Once you have learnt the basics of spelling and pronunciation, you should be able to deduce relatively easily how the majority of words are said. This introductory chapter is designed to give you some guidance on the language as preparation for the work you will do in this book, but for further detailed assistance on how to speak Welsh you will need a coursebook with accompanying audio material. This grammar is particularly designed to be used in conjunction with *Complete Welsh* (2010) which concentrates on teaching you to understand and speak Welsh as it is spoken today. Like *Complete Welsh* this grammar emphasizes the spoken forms, but the literary written alternatives are also cited where appropriate, such as in the list of verbal forms. Unlike the other units, there are no exercises with this reference unit, although a short self-diagnostic test is included to ensure that you understand the basics before moving on.

The alphabet

The 29 letters of the Welsh alphabet are:

a, b, c, ch, d, dd, e, f, ff, g, ng, h, i, j, l, ll, m, n, o, p, ph, r, rh, s, t, th, u, w, y

The letters **b, d, j, m, n, p, s, t** and **th** are pronounced as in English. Some of the letters which are pronounced differently from English include:

c	always a hard sound, pronounced as in the English word *car*. Example: **coleg** (*college*)
ch	as in the Scottish word *loch*. Example: **chwech** (*six*)
dd	as in the English word *the*. Example: **ddoe** (*yesterday*)
f	as in the English word *violin*. Example: **fel** (*like*)
ff	as in the English word *off*. Example: **ffa** (*beans*)
g	as in the English word *grand*. Example: **gwaith** (*work*)
ng	as in the English word *gang*. Example: **rhwng** (*between*)
ll	place tongue to say the *l* in the English word *land* and then blow. Example: **llaeth** (*milk*)
ph	as in the English word *physical*. Example: **ei phen** (*her head*)
r	as in the English *red* but rolled more. Example: **roced** (*rocket*)
rh	place tongue to say the *r* in the English word *red* and blow. Example: **rhif** (*number*)

As in English, vowels – **a, e, i o, u, w, y** – can be either long or short:

a	short as in the English word *cat*
	long as in the English word *car*
e	short as in the English word *met*
	long as in the English word *pear*
i	short as in the English word *bit*
	long as in the English word *feel*

o	short as in the English word *hot*
	long as in the English word *bore*
u	short as in the English word *bin*
	long as in the *ee* in *seen*
w	usually pronounced as in the English word *moon*, following **g**
	it is usually pronounced as in the English word *went*
y	has two sounds *ee* or *i* in the final syllable or in words
	of one syllable and *uh* in the preceding syllables: **dyn**
	(*man*) pronounced deen; **mynydd** (*mountain*) pronounced
	'muhnithe'; **dynion** (*men*) pronounced 'duhneeon'

Take care when looking words up in a dictionary. **Ng** for example can cause confusion. **Anghofio** (*to forget*) comes before **amynedd** (*patience*) although **n** comes after **m**.

Vowel combinations

ae, ai and **au** are pronounced as in the English word *aisle*. Examples: **Cymraeg** (*Welsh*), **Llundain** (*London*), **mwynhau** (*to enjoy*)

ei and **eu** are pronounced as in the English word *way*. Examples: **eithaf** (*quite*), **neu** (*or*)

oe, oi and **ou** are pronounced as in the English word *boy*. Examples: **poeth** (*hot*), **rhoi** (*to give / to put*), **cyffrous** (*exciting*)

ew is pronounced as *eh-oo*. Example: **tew** (*fat*)

aw is pronounced like the *ou* in the English word *cloud*. Example: **llawn** (*full*)

ow is pronounced as in the English *oh*. Example: **brown** (*brown*)

Stress

Generally the stress is placed on the penultimate syllable in Welsh, although there are certain exceptions such as:

- ▶ a few verbs with **ym** in the first syllable
  ymweld   *to visit*   ymroi   *to apply oneself*

- ▶ a number of adverbs and prepositions
  erioed   *ever / never*   heblaw   *beside(s)*

- ▶ several English borrowed words
  apêl   *appeal*   carafán   *carafan*

English borrowed words are also occasionally stressed on the antepenultimate syllable:

paragraff   *paragraph*   **pol**isi   *policy*

Accents

Most words in Welsh do not usually need a written accent. When it does occur, the written accent is generally used to enable words to be correctly stressed when they have deviated from the usual stress pattern, as in the word **carafán** above. The three accents to be found in Welsh are:

1 The acute accent (´) found on the letter **a**.
2 The grave accent (`) found on **i** and **o**.
3 The circumflex (ˆ) found on any vowel to emphasize its length.

The diaeresis (¨) is used to show that a particular vowel is pronounced separately rather than forming a dipthong with the vowel next to it. The sound of the vowel itself does not alter.

copïau   *copies*   storïau   *stories*

Double consonants

The only double consonants you will find in Welsh are **nn** and **rr**. These occur primarily after a short vowel between the penultimate and final syllable:

ennill   *to win*   torri   *to break*   cynnydd   *progress*

You will however find many exceptions to this rule:

penderfynu   *to decide*   crynu   *to shiver*

When the stress moves as a result of the addition of a syllable, one of the double consonants is dropped:

enillais   *I won*   cynyddu   *to progress*
cyrraedd   *to arrive*   cyrhaeddais i   *I arrived*

The best way to learn how to spell correctly is by practice and that includes reading in the language and noting down new words as you acquire them. Let's move on to the rest of the book therefore to do just that…

Test yourself

Translate the following into Welsh, taking note of what you have read about accents and double consonants.

1	a house	**6**	to be surprised
2	to disappear	**7**	a stone
3	you arrived	**8**	appeal
4	to hate	**9**	to pray
5	a smile	**10**	to increase

2

Mutations

In this unit you will learn:
* *The soft, nasal and aspirate mutations and when to use them*

Grammar in focus

In the Celtic languages, certain consonants are subject to change at the beginning of words. These letter changes are known as mutations and while they may appear daunting at first, the main rules are usually mastered relatively quickly. In Welsh, the mutation system as it is known, only affects nine consonants in all.

Insight

Don't worry about the mutations too much! What is important, especially orally, is that you practise using the language. No one will criticise you if you don't get every mutation correct.

The soft mutation

This is the most common mutation affecting all nine consonants referred to above:

Original consonant	Soft mutation	Example	Meaning
c	g	car > ei gar	*car > his car*
t	d	tad > ei dad	*father > his father*
p	b	pen > ei ben	*head > his head*

Original consonant	Soft mutation	Example	Meaning
b	f	bord > ei ford	*table > his table*
d	dd	dwylo > ei ddwylo	*hands > his hands*
g	disappears	gardd > ei ardd	*garden > his garden*
m	f	mam > ei fam	*mother > his mother*
ll	l	llong > ei long	*ship > his ship*
rh	r	rhaff >ei raff	*rope > his rope*

It occurs in a wide range of instances which, as well as being listed here, will be referred to in the appropriate units in the book.

1 Feminine singular nouns after the definite article **y** (*the*) except for those beginning with **ll** and **rh**.
y (*the*) + merch (*girl*) = y ferch   *the girl*

2 Adjectives after feminine singular nouns.
cath (*cat*) + bach (*small*) = cath fach   *small cat*

3 Nouns after adjectives.
hen (*old*) + pobl (*people*) = hen bobl   *old people*
unig (*only*) + plentyn (*child*) = unig blentyn   *only child*

4 A noun used as an adjective after a feminine singular noun.
llwy (*spoon*) + cawl (*soup*) = llwy gawl   *soup spoon*

5 Feminine singular nouns after **un** (*one*) except for those beginning with **ll** and **rh**.
un + merch (*girl*) = un ferch   *one girl*

6 Adjectives after **un** when **un** refers to something feminine, except for those beginning with **ll** and **rh**.
un + talentog (*talented*) = un dalentog   *a talented one*

7 **Dau** (*two* – masc.) and **dwy** (*two* – fem.) after **y**.
y ddau, y ddwy   *the two of them / both of them*

8 After **dau** and **dwy**.

dau + bachgen (*boy*) = dau fachgen   *two boys*

dwy + menyw (*woman*) = dwy fenyw   *two women*

9 Ordinal numbers when they are feminine after the definite article **y**. The feminine noun it precedes also mutates softly.

y + trydedd (*third*) + merch = y drydedd ferch   *the third girl*

10 A noun denoting time or measure used as an adverb.

Gweithiodd hi'n galed ddydd   *She worked hard day and*
a nos.   *night.*

Insight

This mutation can be difficult to grasp. I tell my students to think of the word **pob**, which is generally more familiar as **bob** in phrases such as **bob nos**. Always think of familiar examples that you know and use automatically, as this will help you to understand less familiar examples of the same construction.

11 After the prepositions – **am** (*for*), **ar** (*on*), **at** (*to*), **dan** (*under*), **dros** (*over*), **drwy** (*through*), **heb** (*without*), **i** (*to*), **o** (*of*), **wrth** (*by*), **gan** (*by*), **hyd** (*until*).

heb + cymorth (*help*) = heb gymorth   *without help*

12 After the personal pronouns **dy** (*your*), **ei / 'i**, (*his / him*), **i'w** (*to his*).

dy + menig (*gloves*) = dy fenig   *your gloves*

i'w + tŷ (*house*) = i'w dŷ   *to his house*

13 Nouns and verbs after **'th**, (*your / you*) and **fe'th** (*introductory word + you + verb*).

gyda'th (*with your*) + rhieni   *with your parents*
  (*parents*) = gyda'th rieni

fe'th glywais (clywed = *to hear*)   *I heard you*

14 Nouns after **pa** (*which*), **pa fath** (*what kind of*), **rhyw** (*some, certain*), **unrhyw** (*any*), **amryw** (*several*), **cyfryw** (*such*).

pa + lliw (*colour*) = pa liw?   *which colour?*

amryw + llyfrau (*books*) = amryw lyfrau   *several books*

15 Nouns when addressing.

bore da (*good morning*) + plant   *good morning*
  (*children*) = bore da blant   *children*

16 Nouns after **dacw** (*there he / she / it is*), **dyna** (*there they / that is / those are*), **dyma** (*here is / are*).

dyma + cadair (*chair*) = dyma gadair   *here's a chair*

17 Nouns after **sut** (*what sort of*).

sut + bwyd (*food*) = sut fwyd?   *what sort of food?*

18 Nouns and adjectives after the predicative **yn** except for those beginning with **ll** and **rh**.

yn + cyfoethog (*rich*) = yn gyfoethog
yn + tlawd (*poor*) = yn dlawd

19 Nouns, adjectives and verb-nouns after the conjunction **neu** (*or*). A verb-noun is the form of the verb as it is in the dictionary, i.e. the infinitive.

cyfoethog neu dlawd   *rich or poor*
merch neu fachgen   *girl or boy*

20 The direct object of a short form of the verb.

Gwelais i (gweld = *to see*) + ceffyl   *I saw a horse.*
  (*a horse*) = Gwelais i geffyl.
Bwytodd e (bwyta = *to eat*) + bisgïen   *He ate a biscuit.*
  (*a biscuit*) = Bwytodd e fisgïen.

21 Question forms of the short form of the verb, regardless of whether or not they follow the interrogative particle **a**, normally found in the literary language.

Werthoch (gwerthu = *to sell*)   *Did you sell the*
  chi'r car?   *car?*
A ddaw (dod = *to come*) i'r sioe?   *Will he come to*
                               the show?

22 Verbs after **ni** (*not*), **na** (*not*) and **oni** (*if not*), except those beginning with **t, c** and **p** which take the aspirate mutation.

y plant (*children*) na ddaw   *the children who will*
                                                        not come

oni ofynnodd (gofyn = *to ask*) hi?   *didn't she ask?*

23 Verbs beginning a negative sentence in the spoken language where **ni** is omitted, except those starting with **t**, **c** and **p**, which take the aspirate mutation.
Fwytodd (bwyta = *to eat*) e mo'r swper.   *He didn't eat the*
                                                             supper.

24 Verbs after the relative pronoun **a** (*whom / which / that*).
Dyna'r fenyw a alwodd   *There's the woman who*
  (galw = *to call*) y bore 'ma.   *called this morning.*

25 Verbs after **a** (*whether*).
Dw i ddim yn gwybod a ddaw   *I don't know whether she*
  hi i'r parti.   *will come to the party.*

Insight

A common error in sentences such as the example given here is to use **os** rather than **a**, as **os** of course translates as 'if' – 'I don't know if she will come to the party'. However, if the English word 'whether' can be used rather than 'if', then **a** is needed, not **os**.

26 Verbs after the interrogative pronouns, **beth** (*what*) and **pwy** (*who*).
Beth ddigwyddodd? (digwydd = *to happen*)   *What happened?*

27 Adjectives after the adverbs **rhy** (*too*), **lled** (*quite*), **gweddol** (*fairly*), **go** (*quite*), **pur** (*quite*).
rhy + rhwydd (*easy*) = rhy rwydd   *too easy*
go + da (*good*) = go dda   *quite good*

28 Adjectives after the adverb **mor** (*so*) and equative **cyn** (*as*) except those beginning with **ll** and **rh**.
mor + brwnt (*dirty*) = mor frwnt   *so dirty*

29 A repeated adjective.

yn dawel, dawel   *very quietly* (lit. *quietly, quietly*)

30 After an intervening word or phrase which causes a break in the normal order of words.

Mae yn yr ysgol lawer o blant.   *There is in the school a lot of children.*

The expected word order would be:

Mae llawer o blant yn yr ysgol.   *There are a lot of children in the school.*

31 After **y naill** (the one), **ychydig** (*a few*), **holl** (*all*), **y fath** (*such*), **ambell** (*some*), **aml** (*many*).

y fath + lle (*place*) = y fath le   *such a place*

ambell + gwaith (*times*) = ambell waith   *sometimes*

The nasal mutation

The nasal mutation affects six of the consonants listed above as indicated in the chart below:

Original consonant	Nasal mutation	Example	Meaning
c	ngh	car > fy nghar	*car > my car*
t	nh	tad > fy nhad	*father > my father*
p	mh	pen > fy mhen	*head > my head*
b	m	bord > fy mord	*table > my table*
d	n	dwylo > fy nwylo	*hands > my hands*
g	ng	gardd > fy ngardd	*garden > my garden*

1 Nouns and verb-nouns after the personal pronoun **fy** (*my*).

fy + brawd (*brother*) = fy mrawd

Mae fy mrawd a fy nhad yn dod i fy mharti.   *My brother and my father are coming to my party.*

2 Nouns after **yn** (*in*).

yn + Caerdydd (*Cardiff*) = yng Nghaerdydd
Dw i'n byw yng Nghaerdydd.   *I live in Cardiff.*
yn + Pen-y-bont ar Ogwr (*Bridgend*) = ym Mhen-y-bont ar Ogwr
Mae e'n byw ym Mhen-y-bont ar Ogwr.   *He lives in Bridgend.*

Note how **yn**, when meaning *in*, changes to **yng** in front of
words beginning with **c** or **g** and to **ym**, when meaning *in*, in
front of words beginning with **p** or **b**.

Insight

Memorize phrases not individual consonant changes –
for example learn **yng Nghaerdydd,** rather than just the
mutation; it will then be easier to apply the rule to other
place names.

3 **Blynedd** (*years*), **blwydd** (*year*) and **diwrnod** (*day*) after **pum**
(*five*), **saith** (*seven*), **wyth** (*eight*), **naw** (*nine*), **deg / deng** (*ten*),
deuddeg / deuddeng (*twelve*), **pymtheg / pymtheng** (*fifteen*),
deunaw (*eighteen*), **ugain** (*twenty*) and its compound forms,
can (*hundred*).

Roedd Gwenllïan yn ddeuddeg mlwydd oed ym mis Medi.	*Gwenllïan was twelve years old in September.*
Arhosodd yno am saith niwrnod.	*He stayed there for seven days.*

While there is a tendency to no longer mutate **diwrnod** in
spoken Welsh following the above numbers, in written formal
Welsh the mutation remains.

Note also that **tair mlynedd** (*three years*) and **chwe mlynedd**
(*six years*), while heard in spoken Welsh, are incorrect.
The correct forms are **tair blynedd** and **chwe blynedd**
(see Unit 10).

The aspirate mutation

The aspirate mutation affects only three consonants:

Original consonant	Aspirate mutation	Example	Meaning
c	ch	car > ei char	*car > her car*
t	th	tad > ei thad	*father > her father*
p	ph	pen > ei phen	*head > her head*

1 Nouns and verb-nouns after **ei / 'i** (*her*), **i'w** (*to her*).
   ei + ceffyl (*horse*) = ei cheffyl   *her horse*
   i'w + teulu (*family*) = i'w theulu   *to her family*

2 Nouns, verb-nouns and verbs after **a** (*and*).
   ci (*dog*) + a + cath (*cat*) = ci a chath   *cat and dog*
   papur (*paper*) + a + pensil (*pencil*) = papur   *paper and pencil*
   a phensil

3 Nouns and verb-nouns after the prepositions **â** (*with*), **gyda** (*with / in the company of*), **tua** (*about*).
   â + pleser (*pleasure*) = â phleser   *with pleasure*
   gyda + caniatâd (*permission*) = gyda   *with permission*
   chaniatâd

4 After **tri** (*three*) and **chwe** (*six*).
   tri + cais (*try*) = tri chais   *three tries*
   chwe + peint (*pint*) = chwe pheint   *six pints*

5 Nouns and verb-nouns after **na** (*nor*).
   llyn (lake) + na + coedwig (*forest*) = llyn   *lake nor forest*
   na choedwig

6 Adjectives after **tra** (*very*).
   tra + cyfoethog (*rich*) = tra chyfoethog   *very rich*

7 Verbs beginning with **c, p, t** after **ni** (*not*), **na** (*that / who...not*) and **oni** (*if not*).

Ni chafodd (cael = *to have*) e ginio.	*He didn't have supper.*
Fe oedd y dyn na thalodd (talu = *to pay*) am ei fwyd.	*He was the man that didn't pay for his food.*

8 Verbs beginning with **c, p, t** at the start of a negative sentence in the spoken language where **ni** is omitted.

Phryna (prynu = *to buy*) i mo'r car yfory.	*I won't buy the car tomorrow.*

Aspirate h

h is added in front of a vowel:

1 Before nouns and verb-nouns after **ei / 'i** (*her*), **ein / 'n** (*our / us*), **eu / 'u** (*their / them*).

ei + arwain (*to lead*) + hi = ei harwain hi	*to lead her*
eu + eglwys (*church*) + nhw = eu heglwys nhw	*their church*

2 Nouns and verb-nouns after **i'w** (*to her / to their / to them*).

i'w + eglwys (*church*) + hi = i'w heglwys hi	*to her church*

> **Insight**
>
> Certain dictionaries give mutated forms. If they don't, think carefully as to whether or not the word you are looking for could be mutated.

Words that don't mutate!

1 Personal names.

i Bethan not i Fethan	*for Bethan*

2 Non-Welsh place names.

o Birmingham not o Firmingham	*from Birmingham*

One common exception is Paris.

ym Mharis	*in Paris*

Welsh place names outside of Wales nevertheless are subject to mutation.

i Lundain – *to London*   i Gaeredin – *to Edinburgh*

3 Borrowed words especially those beginning with **g**.
grant, gêm (*game*), garej

4 Several common miscellaneous words such as **pan** (*when*)
mae (*is / are*), **byth** (*ever / never*), **mor** (*so*), **lle** (*where*),
tua (*towards / about*).

5 Words that are already mutated such as **beth** (*what*) or
dros (*over*) and **druan** (*poor thing*).
Beth sy'n bod â Jenny druan?   *What's the matter with Jenny poor thing?*

Exercises

A Translate the following phrases, remembering to mutate where
appropriate.
  1 my relatives
  2 heaven and hell
  3 in Bangor
  4 two dogs
  5 father or son
  6 the fourth century
  7 her comb
  8 cats and rabbits
  9 to their school
  10 old books

B There are three mutation related errors in the following
paragraph. What are they?
  Fy enw i yw Gillian. Dw i'n byw yn Nhreorchy ac dw
  i'n dysgu Cymraeg mewn dosbarth nos yn Nhonypandy.
  Dw i'n hoffi dysgu Cymraeg. Mae fy tad yn siarad tipyn
  o Gymraeg ond mae fy mam yn Saesnes o Lerpwl yn

wreiddiol. Dw i'n weithio mewn swyddfa yng Nghaerdydd. Dw i'n hoffi fy ngwaith ond mae rhaid i fi weithio oriau hir a does dim llawer o amser rhydd gyda fi. Pan fydd amser gyda fi, dw i'n hoffi nofio a cerdded. Ar ddydd Sul dw i'n hoffi mynd am dro hir gyda fy nghi Sam.

Grammar in context

Can you spot and explain the mutations in the following adverts from a local paper?

> **LLOGI CESTYLL NEIDIO**
> Beth am roi hwyl a sbri i'r parti?!
> Cestyll bownsio tu mewn neu'r tu allan
> Prisiau o £35 y dydd
> Nifer o gestyll â themâu gyda llithren
> Dosbarthiad am ddim o fewn 15 milltir
> Ffôn 01269 850051

> **SIOP Y PENTAN**
> Y dewis gorau o lyfrau,
> casetiau a chardiau Cymraeg
> Y Farchnad Newydd
> Caerfyrddin
> Ffôn 01267 235044

Test yourself

Translate the following sentences, remembering to mutate where appropriate.

1 I come from Bangor originally, but I live in Cardiff now.
2 Did you pay a lot of money for the ring?

3   He ate two chocolate cakes at lunchtime.
4   The little girl wasn't listening to her teacher.
5   Remember to take a piece of paper and a pencil with you.
6   We will be in Bridgend for the weekend visiting Sue's family.
7   Have you got time to call in the garage next door to the clothes shop?
8   It's difficult to know whether I will get another chance.
9   He was the student who missed the lecture on Welsh literature.
10 The weather was awful and we had rain all day every day for a fortnight.

3

The article

In this unit you will learn:
- **How to say** a, an, some **and** any **in Welsh**
- **The words for** the (the definite article) **in Welsh and when to use them**

Grammar in focus

The indefinite article

In Welsh, there is no equivalent to *a, an* and *some*, known as the indefinite article in English. This means:

▶ *dog* and *a dog* are exactly the same – **ci**
▶ *apple* and *an apple* are exactly the same – **afal**

I've got a dog.	Mae ci gyda fi.
There was an apple in his pocket.	Roedd afal yn ei boced.

Some and *any* are used with plural nouns as article substitutes in English, but once again they have no Welsh equivalent and are therefore omitted in translation.

*Did you have **some fruit** for supper?*	Gawsoch chi **ffrwythau** i swper?
*I haven't **any books** on Welsh grammar.*	Does dim **llyfrau** gyda fi ar ramadeg Cymraeg.

However when *some* and *any* do hold a particular meaning in a sentence then they do have to be translated.

Some children in the class are good while others are naughty.	Mae **rhai** plant yn y dosbarth yn dda tra bod eraill yn ddrwg.

Rhai is always followed by a plural noun and doesn't cause mutation.

Rhyw is always followed by a singular noun and causes a soft mutation.

Mae rhyw fenyw wedi ysgrifennu ato fe yn gofyn am help i ddod o hyd i Jim.

Some woman (or other) has written to him asking for help to find Jim.

Any in such circumstances is translated as **unrhyw** and also causes a soft mutation.

Any book would be a great help.	Byddai unrhyw lyfr yn help mawr.

The definite article

The full form of the definite article (*the*) in Welsh is **yr**, which is used in front of vowels and **h**.

Roedd yr afal yn flasus.	*The apple was tasty.*
Diflanodd yr hwyaden.	*The duck disappeared.*

Y is used in front of consonants and singular feminine nouns, except for those beginning with **ll** and **rh,** which take the soft mutation if appropriate (see Unit 2).

y ferch *the girl*   y bachgen *the boy*   y ci *the dog* 'r is used after a vowel:

Dw i'n casáu'r bwyd yn y   *I hate the food in the refectory.*
  ffreutur.

Singular feminine nouns mutate following **'r** but once again those beginning with **ll** and **rh** are exempt.

> ## Insight
> Remember that **mae** followed by **y/yr** becomes **mae'r**.
>
> Mae'r plant wedi anghofio eu   *The children have forgotten*
>   gwaith cartref.   *their homework.*

Uses of the definite article
y / yr is used with:

- ▶ the names of certain countries.
  Yr Alban   *Scotland*   Yr Eidal   *Italy*

- ▶ A selection of Welsh place names.
  Y Barri   *Barry*   Y Fenni   *Abergavenny*

- ▶ The names of some mountains and seas.
  Yr Wyddfa   *Snowdon*   y Môr Tawel   *the Pacific Ocean*

- ▶ The seasons and certain holidays.
  yr haf   *summer*   y Pasg   *Easter*

- ▶ The name of a language in place of the word *iaith*.
  y Gymraeg   *Welsh*   yr Wyddeleg   *Irish*

- ▶ Certain illnesses.
  y ffliw   *flu*   y frech goch   *measles*

▶ Several phrases where there is no definite article in the corresponding English phrase.

yn y gwaith	*in work*	yn yr ysgol	*in school*
yn yr eglwys	*in church*	i'r gwely	*to bed*
gyda'r trên	*by train*	ar y bws	*by bus*

▶ Certain titles.

yr Athro Watcyn Jones   *Professor Watcyn Jones*

▶ Unlike in English, names of rivers in Welsh do not normally include the definite article, although as in English, the word **afon** (*river*) can prefix the name of the river.

Hafren   *the Severn*   Afon Tywi   *the river Towy*

▶ The definite article is included in one or two cases.

Yr Iorddonen   *the Jordan*   Y Fenai   *the Menai Straits*

▶ It is also used in certain phrases denoting price, measure, etc.

dau ddeg ceiniog y tro	*20 pence a go*
tri deg saith milltir i'r galwyn	*37 miles a gallon*
saithdeg milltir yr awr	*70 miles an hour*

Exercise

Place the correct form of the definite article in the sentences below and translate them.

1 Mae .... ffilm wedi dechrau.
2 Aethon nhw i .... pwll nofio cyn cinio.
3 Gwelais i fe gyda .... ferch o'r swyddfa.

4 Roedd ……. oriau'n hir iawn.
5 Gwerthon ni ddau geffyl i ……. dyn o Gaerfyrddin.
6 Aeth ……. amser yn rhy gyflym yn anffodus.
7 Fy hoff adeg o'r flwyddyn yw …… hydref.
8 Mae hi'n hoffi …… rhaglenni am hanes Cymru.
9 Enillodd e lawer o wobrau yn …… Eisteddfod.
10 Faint o lythrennau sydd yn …… wyddor Gymraeg?

Grammar in context

The events diary below comes from the Welsh monthly community newspaper *Y Lloffwr* to be found in the Towy Valley, West Wales. There are over 50 Welsh language community newspapers such as this printed in Wales every month.

MEDI

16–18 Gŵyl yn y Parc. Tair noson awyr agored o gerddoriaeth wych o'r sioeau, cerddoriaeth glasurol a chorau ym Mharc Dinefwr, Llandeilo.

23 Cyngerdd yng Nghanolfan Gymdeithasol Llangadog gyda Bois y Castell i ddechrau am 7.30 pm. Elw'r noson at Gapel Providence, Llangadog.

24 Cwmni Drama'r Mochyn Du yn Neuadd Bro Fana, Ffarmers.

1 As well as classical music and choirs, what else can be enjoyed in Dinefwr Park between 16–18 September?
2 Who is performing in the concert in Llangadog?
3 The drama company performing in Ffarmers on 24 September have an unusual name. How would you translate it into English?

Test yourself

Correct the following sentences.

1 Daethon nhw i aros gyda ni yn ystod gwyliau Nadolig.
2 Aethon ni i Bala i weld ein modryb.
3 Yr Afon Hafren yw'r afon hiraf yng Nghymru.
4 Roedd hi wedi cael ffliw ddwywaith yn ystod y gaeaf.
5 Aeth e a'i wraig i fyw yn Eidal.
6 Mae'r Afon Teifi yn afon boblogaidd gyda physgotwyr.
7 Mae y plant eisiau mynd i Sbaen yn y haf.
8 Ydych chi'n gwybod a aeth e ar fws?
9 Aeth Siân i waith y wythnos diwethaf yn teimlo'n drist iawn.
10 Mae rhyw ferched yn trefnu cyngerdd dros Basg i godi arian i'r achos.

4

Nouns

In this unit you will learn:
- *Masculine and feminine words in Welsh*
- *How to form plurals in Welsh*
- *How to say that something belongs to someone or something*

Grammar in focus

Nouns refer to people, places or things and can be singular or plural, specific (*y coleg*) or non-specific (*coleg*).

Gender

Most nouns in Welsh are either masculine or feminine. A small number have different genders in different parts of Wales.

cinio	*lunch*	clust	*ear*
munud	*minute*	rhyfel	*war*
braich	*arm*	cyngerdd	*concert*

Names of male persons and male animals are masculine, while names of female persons and female animals are feminine. As already demonstrated in Unit 3, feminine singular nouns unlike masculine nouns, take the soft mutation after the definite article, namely *the*.

y tad	*the father*	y fam	*the mother*
y bachgen	*the boy*	y ferch	*the girl*
y ceffyl	*the horse*	y gaseg	*the mare*

Adjectives mutate after feminine singular nouns, but not after masculine singular nouns.

| tad-cu caredig | *a kind grandfather* | mam-gu garedig | *a kind grandmother* |
| hwrdd mawr | *a big ram* | dafad fach | *a small sheep* |

Special forms of some adjectives and numbers are used with feminine singular nouns (see Units 5 / 12).

| car gwyn | *a white car* | cath wen | *a white cat* |
| dau fachgen | *two boys* | dwy ferch | *two girls* |

A small number of nouns have two meanings – one is masculine in gender, the other feminine.

noun	masculine		feminine	
math	y math hwn	*this kind*	y fath	*such*
man	yn y man	*presently*	yn y fan	*immediately*
gwaith	y gwaith	*the work*	unwaith	*once (time / turn)*
golwg	yn y golwg	*in sight*	yr olwg	*appearance*

The feminine forms of masculine nouns can be formed by:

▶ Turning the masculine ending **–wr** into **–wraig**.

| myfyriwr | *student* | myfyrwraig |
| cyfreithiwr | *lawyer* | cyfreithwraig |

▶ Adding **–es** to the masculine noun.

| plismon | *policeman* | plismones |
| actor | *actor* | actores |

▶ Sometimes this involves a vowel change:

athro	*teacher*	athrawes
Cymro	*Welshman*	Cymraes

▶ Turning the ending **–yn** into **–en**.

merlyn	*pony*	merlen
hogyn	*boy* (NW)	hogen (NW)

Many nouns can refer to male and female persons – these nouns are masculine in gender.

meddyg	*doctor*	baban	*baby*
darlithydd	*lecturer*	swyddog	*officer*

Pobl (*people*), although a feminine singular noun, is collective in meaning.

person arall   *another person*   pobl eraill   *other people*

Adjectives following **pobl** will mutate because it is a feminine singular noun.

Roedden nhw'n bobl
garedig iawn.   *They were very kind people.*

Insight

As noted above, **pobl**, although singular, is plural in meaning and therefore is often followed by a plural adjective as discussed in Unit 5.

pobl ifainc   *young people*

Pobl has a plural form, **pobloedd** *(peoples)* which you may come across occasionally.

Classification by gender

It is impossibile to classify all masculine and feminine nouns according to definite rules as there are so many exceptions.

However, the days of the week, the months, seasons and points of the compass are masculine, while the names of countries, languages, towns, rivers and trees are generally feminine.

In the case of abstract nouns, the following endings occur in masculine nouns:

–ad, –adur, –aint, –awd, –deb, –der, –did, –dod, –dra, –edd, –er, –had, –i, –iad, –iant, –id, –in, –ineb, –ioni, –ni, –og, –rwydd, –waith, –wm, –wch, –wr, –yd, –ydd, –yn

| henaint | *old age* | haelioni | *generosity* |
| blinder | *tiredness* | iechyd | *health* |

While the following endings occur in abstract feminine nouns:

–ach, –aeth, –as, –eb, –eg, –ell, –en, –es, –fa, –igaeth, –wraig, –yddes

| cyfrinach | *secret* | cyfrifanell | *calculator* |
| barddoniaeth | *poetry* | meddygfa | *surgery* |

Common exceptions to the above rule are:

| hiraeth | *longing* | gwasanaeth | *service* |
| gwahaniaeth | *difference* | pennaeth | *chief* |

which are all masculine singular nouns.

Insight

As gender is not always obvious from the ending of a word, nouns should be learnt together with their gender. You can check this in the Welsh–English section of a dictionary where *nf* or *nm* is placed after the Welsh word. Some dictionaries use the Welsh equivalent – e.b. (**enw benywaidd** – *feminine noun*) and e.g. (**enw gwrywaidd** – *masculine noun*).

Number

Unfortunately there is no uniform way of forming plurals in Welsh and, as with gender, the easiest way is to learn the plural forms of the nouns when learning the singular.

Two main principles are involved in the formation of plurals in Welsh: these are the adding of endings and internal vowel change. These principles are used separately and together. There are eight ways in which the plural can be formed:

1 By adding one of the following plural endings:
–au, –iau, –ion, –on, –i, –ydd, –oedd, –iaid, –od

| afal | *apple* | afalau | ysgol | *school* | ysgolion |
| pentref | *village* | pentrefi | anifail | *animal* | anifeiliaid |

By far the most common of these is **–au**.

2 By changing one or more vowels of the original noun in some way.

| llygad | *eye* | llygaid | iâr | *hen* | ieir |
| ffon | *stick* | ffyn | castell | *castle* | cestyll |

3 By adding a plural ending and changing one or more vowels.

| buwch | *cow* | buchod | mab | *son* | meibion |
| Sais | *English-man* | Saeson | cawr | *giant* | cewri |

4 By dropping the singular endings **–yn** or **–en**.

| mochyn | *pig* | moch | llygoden | *mouse* | llygod |
| seren | *star* | sêr | pysgodyn | *fish* | pysgod |

5 By dropping the singular endings **–yn** and **–en** and making a vowel change.

| deilen | *leaf* | dail | plentyn | *child* | plant |

6 By replacing **–yn** and **–en** with a plural ending.

| blodyn | *flower* | blodau | cwningen | *rabbit* | cwningod |

7 By replacing **–yn** and **–en** with a plural ending and making a vowel change.

cerdyn *card* cardiau   miaren *bramble* mieri

8 Nouns denoting persons and professions ending in **–wr**, or **–iwr** are replaced with **–wyr** in the plural, while those ending in **–ydd** change to either **–yddion** or **–wyr**.

dysgwr	*learner*	dysgwyr
myfyriwr	*student*	myfyrwyr
cyfieithydd	*translator*	cyfieithwyr
golygydd	*editor*	golygyddion

There are however a large number of nouns that do not fit tidily into the above categories. For example:

ci	*dog*	cŵn	brawd	*brother*	brodyr
gŵr	*man*	gwŷr	tŷ	*house*	tai
llaw	*hand*	dwylo	chwaer	*sister*	chwiorydd

Often abstract nouns and foods have no plural form.

caredigrwydd	*kindness*		te	*tea*
caws	*cheese*		bara	*bread*

On the other hand, some nouns have more than one plural.

llythyr	*letter*	llythyron	llythyrau
mynydd	*mountain*	mynyddoedd	mynyddau
darlith	*lecture*	darlithiau	darlithoedd

In certain instances, the two plurals have a different meaning.

bron	bronnau	*breasts*
	bronnydd	*hills*
llwyth	llwythau	*tribes*
	llwythi	*loads*
pryd	prydiau	*times*
	prydau	*meals*

pwys	pwysau	*weights*
	pwysi	*pounds*
dosbarth	dosbarthiadau	*classes*
	dosbarthau	*categories*

Expressing belonging

Insight

Genitive noun phrases as described below sometimes can cause difficulty for those learning the language. Study the section below carefully and whenever you come across them in your reading, for example in novels for Welsh learners, think about how they would read in English. Remember, never translate literally: *y + o'r* is incorrect in Welsh!

When one noun is dependent on the noun which precedes it in order to show belonging or ownership, this is known as a **genitive noun phrase**. This is expressed in English by either **'s** or **s'** or **of**.

John's book   *the capital of Wales*

In Welsh there is only one way of forming the genitive – all English sentences containing **'s** or **s'** must be rephrased in the long form.

John's book   *the book of John*

The and **of** are then removed:

John's book   llyfr John

Similarly:

the capital of Wales   prifddinas Cymru

The only remains between the nouns if the second noun is definite. *The* is always removed at the beginning of a genitive noun phrase:

*the mother of **the** young boy*	mam **y** bachgen ifanc
Not:	**y** fam **o'r** bachgen ifanc
the shop window = the window of the shop	ffenestr **y** siop
Not:	**y** ffenestr **o'r** siop
*the father of **a** young girl*	tad merch ifanc
Not:	**y** tad **o** ferch ifanc

The same ruling applies if more than two nouns are involved.

ffeil gwaith cartref y prifathro	*the headmaster's homework file*
cynnwys siop y pentref	*the contents of the village shop*
mab cyfreithwraig ifanc	*the son of a young lawyer*

Exercises

A Give the feminine forms of the following masculine nouns.

ceffyl	bachgen
athro	telynor
tafarnwr	asyn
hwrdd	Sais
ysgrifennydd	siaradwr

B With or without the help of a dictionary, decide whether the following nouns are masculine or feminine.

haelioni	porfa
cariad	barddoniaeth
derwen	gaeaf
seren	Cymru

C Translate the following genitive noun phrases.
   1 the old school hall
   2 the future of the Welsh language
   3 Mair's first home
   4 the policeman's sister's daughter
   5 the children of the Third World

Grammar in context

The following piece comes from the online magazine for Welsh learners, produced by ACEN, and tells of the life story of Gwrtheyrn, after whom Nant Gwrtheyrn in North Wales was named. Nant Gwrtheyrn, on the Lleyn Peninsula, has been the home of the Welsh Language and Heritage Centre since 1978. Translate the singular nouns given below and find their plurals in the extract.

dyn	llaw
milwr	plentyn
gwraig	derwydd
arweinydd	

Pan aeth y Rhufeiniaid, gadawon nhw Brydain yn nwylo stiwardiaid lleol. Yn ôl un stori, roedd Gwrtheyrn y Nant yn un o'r stiwardiaid. Roedd y '*superbus tyrrannus*' hwn yn byw yn Ne Prydain yn ardal Caint yn gynnar yn y 5ed ganrif. Roedd e eisiau cadw eraill rhag dod i mewn i'w ardal ac, fel y Rhufeiniaid o'i flaen, penderfynodd gael help milwyr cyflog o Germania a Sacsonia. Rhoiodd e Ynys Thanet ger Hastings iddyn nhw a'u harweinwyr Hors a Hengist. Yn fuan, dechreuon nhw ddod â'u gwragedd a'u plant drosodd ac un ohonyn nhw oedd Alys Rhonwen, merch Hengist. Syrthiodd Gwrtheyrn mewn cariad â hi ac roedd e eisiau ei phriodi. Ond, roedd Alys yn ferch i'w thad a threfnodd hi ginio un noson a rhoi dynion Hors a Hengist a dynion Prydain i eistedd bob yn ail o gwmpas bwrdd. Yn sydyn, ar ganol y cinio, cododd pob un o ddynion Germania a thrywanu'r Prydeiniwr drws nesaf iddo a chyllell. Dihangodd Gwrtheyrn, ei deulu a'i dderwyddon.

QUICK VOCAB	**Caint**	*Kent*
	cadw rhag	*keep / prevent from*
	bob yn ail	*every other one*
	trywanu	*to stab*
	dianc (dihang–)	*to escape*

Test yourself

Translate the paragraph below into Welsh. It contains several genitive noun phrases, along with a selection of masculine, feminine and plural nouns.

Heledd, the daughter of my Welsh tutor, moved into the village some weeks ago. She lives in the house next door to the village hall. She says that her neighbours have been very kind to her. There are lots of holiday homes in the village. Many people from large towns and cities visit the village in the summer. They come in large cars which fill the narrow roads. English is the language of the village in the summer, but in winter it is Welsh. It is good to see another Welsh person moving into the village. Heledd is a Mathematics teacher in our local secondary school.

5

Adjectives

In this unit you will learn:
- **The position of adjectives in a sentence**
- **The plural forms and their uses**
- **The feminine forms and when to use them**

Grammar in focus

Adjectives are words which describe, or give additional information about, nouns and pronouns.

Position

Adjectives in Welsh are usually placed after the noun they are describing. They do not mutate after masculine singular nouns or plural nouns, however they do take the soft mutation after a feminine singular noun.

car coch	*a red car*
myfyrwyr gweithgar	*hardworking students*
cân brydferth	*a beautiful song*
rhaglen ddiddorol	*an interesting programme*

Adjectives also do not mutate when they are preceded directly by verb-nouns, namely the basic dictionary form of the verb, which makes no reference to tense or person.

| canu da | *good singing* | actio cryf | *strong acting* |

The following adjectives only occur before the noun, causing it to mutate softly.

ambell	*occasional*	prif	*principal, chief*
amryw	*several*	rhyw	*some*
cryn	*considerable*	unrhyw	*any*
hoff	*favourite*	ychydig	*little / few*
holl	*all / whole*	y fath	*such*
pa	*what / which*		

Roedd cryn gyffro yn y pentref ar ôl iddyn nhw glywed y newyddion.	*There was considerable excitement in the village after they heard the news.*
Does dim syniad 'da fi pa lyfr i'w ddewis.	*I have no idea which book to choose.*
Doeddwn i erioed wedi gweld y fath lanastr yn fy mywyd!	*I had never seen such a mess in my life!*

The following adjectives also precede the noun, but do not cause soft mutation.

peth	*some / a small amount*
pob	*every*
sawl	*several*
rhai	*some / a few*

Roedd peth Cymraeg gyda fy nhad-cu.	*My grandfather knew some Welsh. (lit. There was some Welsh with my grandfather.)*
Mae rhai tiwtoriaid newydd yn dysgu ar y cwrs eleni.	*There are a few new tutors teaching on the course this year.*

A small number of adjectives can be placed either before or after the noun. Their meaning varies according to their position. Those placed in front of the noun cause soft mutation.

	before the noun	**after the noun**
gwahanol	*various*	*different*
gwir	*genuine*	*true*
hen	*old*	*ancient*
mân	*minor*	*small*
prin	*scarcely*	*rare*
unig	*only*	*lonely*
union	*exact*	*straight*

Aeth gwahanol bobl i weld a
oedden nhw'n gallu helpu.

*Various people went to see
whether they could help.*

Dim ond un neu ddau o fân
bethau sydd ar ôl i'w gwneud
nawr.

*There's only one or two minor
things left to do now.*

Ein bwthyn ni oedd yr unig
fwthyn yn y cwm.

*Our cottage was the only cottage
in the valley.*

Insight

When **hen** precedes the noun it may express either disgust or
endearment, regardless of age.

Yr un hen stori yw hi bob tro.   *It's always the same old story.*

Sut mae'r hen ddyn erbyn hyn?   *How's the old fellow by now?*

When **pur** is an adjective meaning *pure*, it follows the noun as in
aur pur (*pure gold*). When it is an adverb meaning *fairly* or *very* it
precedes the adjective as in **pur dda** (*very good*). Ll and **rh** do not
mutate after the adverb **pur**.

Number

Some adjectives possess plural forms that can be used instead of
the singular after plural nouns. Many of these plural adjectives are
formed by adding –**ion** or –**on**, or by changing a vowel, or by both
changing a vowel and adding –**ion** or –**on**.

The most common plural forms of adjectives to be heard in the spoken language are:

budr	budron	*dirty*	byr	byrion	*short*
bychan	bychain	*small*	coch	cochion	*red*
cryf	cryfion	*strong*	dewr	dewrion	*brave*
du	duon	*black*	glas	gleision	*blue/green*
gwyn	gwynion	*white*	hir	hirion	*long*
ifanc	ifainc	*young*	ieuanc	ieuainc	*young*
mawr	mawrion	*big*	trwm	trymion	*heavy*

Although there is an increasing tendency to select the singular form of the adjective, rather than the plural, with a plural noun:

llygaid mawr	*big eyes*	llygaid mawrion

one important exception to this is **arall** *(an)other*. The plural form of the adjective, namely **eraill**, is *always* used with a plural noun.

dosbarth arall	*another class*
dosbarthiadau eraill	*other classes*
y dyn arall	*the other man*
y dynion eraill	*the other men*

Due to its collective meaning, the feminine singular noun, **pobl** (*people*) is frequently followed by a plural adjective. As noted in Unit 4, **eraill** not **arall** follows **pobl** in all instances.

| pobl ifainc | | *young people* |
| pobl ifainc eraill | | *other young people* |

Plural forms of the adjective are also commonly used as nouns denoting classes of persons or kinds of animals.

tlawd	y tlodion	*the poor*
cyfoethog	y cyfoethogion	*the rich*
dall	y deillion	*the blind*
ffyddlon	y ffyddloniaid	*the faithful*
meddw	y meddwon	*the drunk*
enwog	yr enwogion	*the famous*
marw	y meirw	*the dead*

Gender

Only a few adjectives in Welsh now possess a feminine form that is used regularly in everyday speech. These are formed:

▶ By replacing the vowel **y** with **e**

gwyn	gwen	*white*	gwyrdd	gwerdd	*green*
melyn	melen	*yellow*	bychan	bechan	*small*
byr	ber	*short*	cryf	cref	*strong*

▶ By replacing the vowel **w** with **o**

| crwn | cron | *round* | trwm | trom | *heavy* |
| llwm | llom | *bare* | tlws | tlos | *beautiful* |

▶ By replacing the vowel **i** with **ai**

| brith | braith | *speckled* |

Insight

Ireland is often known as The Emerald Isle. In Welsh this is **Yr Ynys Werdd** – **ynys** being a feminine singular noun. If an adjective has a feminine form, that form (mutated) is generally used with a feminine singular noun. Other common combinations include:

| torth wen | *a white loaf* | stori fer | *a short story* |

The masculine form of the adjective is generally selected in the predicate. The predicate is the part of the sentence which tells us something about the subject.

Mae'r ferch yn dlws.   *The girl is pretty.*
Roedd y fenyw'n gryf.   *The woman was strong.*

Exercises

A Complete the sentences below using the words in the box. Remember to mutate either the noun or adjective where appropriate.

> ber, diddorol, gwahanol, unig, sawl, melen, meirw,
> hoff, peth, hen

1 Roedd ei dad yn .... plentyn.
2 Gwelon ni raglen .... iawn ar hanes y wlad.
3 Beth yw dy .... bwyd?
4 Dim ond .... pobl sy'n mynd yno nawr yn anffodus.
5 Oes llawer o actorion .... yn y ddrama?
6 Mae .... dysgwr newydd yn y dosbarth y tymor 'ma.
7 Prynais i ffrog .... ar gyfer y briodas.
8 Oedd .... bisgedi ar ôl 'da nhw?
9 Byddai'r .... yn troi yn eu beddau.
10 Ysgrifennodd hi stori .... ar gyfer y gystadleuaeth.

B In the wordsearch grid over the page find:
  i the following feminine adjectives:
    cref, cron, ber, gwen

  ii the following plural adjectives:
    gleision, ifainc, trymion, duon

```
G  L  E  I  S  I  O  N  D  A
A  D  U  S  R  R  M  I  U  H
C  C  R  E  F  D  A  L  O  B
R  T  B  Ll I  F  A  I  N  C
O  L  E  G  A  N  C  F  E  S
N  O  I  M  Y  R  T  O  W  G
D  N  O  M  I  N  E  W  G  Th
```

Grammar in context

Below is a review of the novel for Welsh learners *Chwarae Mig*.
Does the reviewer like the book? Pick out two adjectives to support
your answer. What is her opinion of the series *Nofelau Nawr*?

NOFELAU NAWR: CHWARAE MIG

Mae *Chwarae Mig* gan Annes Glynn yn nofel deimladwy ac mae
llawer o themâu ynddi hi, fel perthnasau, teimladau dirgel a hud y
foment. Dyn ni'n dilyn pedwar o bobl ifainc sy'n teithio i Barcelona
am wyliau a dyn ni'n gweld pam fod un llun gan Dalí mor bwysig i'r
prif adroddwr Alaw.

Roeddwn i'n meddwl bod *Chwarae Mig* yn llyfr diddorol ac mae'n
gyfoes hefyd ac mae wedi ei ysgrifennu mewn arddull eithaf syml.
Mae'n addas i ddysgwyr sydd wedi bod yn astudio am tua dwy
flynedd ac mae geirfa ar waelod pob tudalen a nodiadau yn y cefn.
Dyma nofel wych arall gan Gomer mewn cyfres ardderchog.

Alyson Tyler
gwales.com

Test yourself

Translate the following into Welsh using the appropriate adjectival form.

1 a white dress
2 the only lonely child
3 considerable tension
4 the Society of the Blind
5 a simple sentence
6 old rusty cars
7 my brother's favourite programme
8 with a heavy heart
9 the poor
10 Arthur and the Round Table

6

....

Comparatives and superlatives

In this unit you will learn:

- *How to form equative adjectives:* **mor hardd â** (*as beautiful as*)
- *How to compare adjectives:* **yn harddach na / yn fwy hardd na** (*more beautiful than*)
- *The formation of superlatives:* **y harddaf / y mwyaf hardd** (*the most beautiful*)

Grammar in focus

Comparison of regular adjectives

There are four degrees of comparison in Welsh:

Absolute	e.g.	**cryf**	*strong*
Equative	e.g.	**mor gryf (â / ag)**	*as strong (as)*
Comparative	e.g.	**cryfach (na / nag)**	*stronger (than)*
Superlative	e.g.	**cryfaf**	*strongest*

Adjectives following **mor** take the soft mutation, with the exception of those begining with **ll** and **rh**. In literary Welsh, **cyn** is sometimes used rather than **mor** and **–ed** is added to the adjective itself. **Cyn** also causes a soft mutation, but not to **ll** or **rh**.

mor gryf â   cyn gryfed â

Mor can also be used without **â / ag** to mean *so*. **Mor** itself never mutates.

Mae hi'n dwym.	*It's hot.*
Mae hi mor dwym.	*It's so hot.*
Mae hi'n ferch mor bert.	*She's such a pretty girl.* (lit. *she's so pretty a girl.*)

Â and **na** cause the consonants they precede to take the aspirate mutation. **Ag** and **nag** are used in front of vowels.

mor gryf â cheffyl	*as strong as a horse*
yn wynnach nag eira	*whiter than snow*

As in the second example above, the final **n** and **r** are often doubled when an ending is added (see Unit 1).

gwyn *white*   gwynnach *whiter*   byr *short*   byrrach *shorter*

Some adjectives change an **–w–** or an **–aw–** to **–y–** and **–o–** respectively as they add the ending **–ach** and **–af**.

tlawd *poor*   tlotach *poorer*   trwm *heavy*   trymaf *heaviest*

When the endings **–ach** and **–af** are added to words which end in **b**, **d** or **g**, these letters harden to **p**, **t** and **c**.

gwlyb *wet*	gwlypach *wetter*	gwlypaf *wettest*
drud *expensive*	drutach *more expensive*	drutaf *most expensive*
teg *fair*	tecach *fairer*	tecaf *fairest*

Every adjective can also be compared periphrastically, i.e. by placing **mor** (*as*), **mwy** (*more*), **mwyaf** (*most*) before it and this is often the case orally.

Absolute	e.g.	**cyfforddus**	*comfortable*
Equative	e.g.	**mor gyfforddus (â)**	*as comfortable (as)*

Comparative	e.g.	**mwy cyfforddus (na)**	*more comfortable (than)*
Superlative	e.g.	**mwyaf cyfforddus**	*most comfortable*

> ## Insight
>
> Learners often ask which system they should use, and I would recommend that you use the periphrastic method in the case of adjectives longer than two syllables as in the example above, but **–ach** etc. in most other instances. This system is more traditionally Welsh, but the periphrastic system should also be used with some adjectives formed from nouns.
>
> | **gwynt** | **gwyntog** | **mor wyntog** |
> |---|---|---|
> | *wind* | *windy* | *so windy* |

Unlike **mor**, there is *no* mutation after **mwy** and **mwyaf**. *How...* with adjectives is **pa mor** not **sut**.

Pa mor gyfforddus ydy'r gadair newydd?	*How comfortable is the new chair?*

Note that after a feminine singular noun, the comparative and superlative forms of the adjective mutate softly.

Dw i erioed wedi gweld gardd bertach.	*I've never seen a prettier garden.*
Mae hi'n mynd i brynu'r ffrog fwyaf lliwgar.	*She's going to buy the most colourful dress.*

In English, when only two people or things are compared, the comparative degree is used, however in Welsh it is the superlative that is used in this context.

Hi yw'r fwyaf gweithgar o'r ddwy chwaer.	*She's the more industrious of the two sisters.*

In the above example the adjective is used as a definite noun and, since the noun is feminine, soft mutation occurs.

Irregular comparison

A few common adjectives have irregular formations:

Absolute	Equative	Comparative	Superlative
da *good*	cystal *as good*	gwell *better*	gorau *best*
drwg *bad*	cynddrwg *as bad*	gwaeth *worse*	gwaethaf *worst*
mawr *big*	cymaint *as big*	mwy *bigger*	mwyaf *biggest*
bach *small*	mor fach / cyn lleied *as small*	llai *smaller*	lleiaf *smallest*
uchel *high*	mor uchel / cyfuwch *as high*	uwch *higher*	uchaf *highest*
isel *low*	mor isel *as low*	is *lower*	isaf *lowest*

When used adverbially, the equative forms of the irregular adjectives mutate softly.

Doeddwn i ddim yn bwriadu bwyta gymaint.	*I didn't intend eating so much.*

As can be seen from the above example, **cymaint** can mean *so much / many* as well as *so big*. **Cyn lleied** can also mean *so little / few* as well as *so small*. As already indicated, **mwy** and **mwyaf** mean *more* and *most* as well as *bigger* and *biggest* while **llai** and **lleiaf** can also be used to mean *less* and *least*.

Roedd cyn lleied o bobl yn y gynulleidfa.	*There were so few people in the audience.*
Bydd mwy o bobl yna nos yfory, ond llai nag y llynedd dw i'n ofni.	*There will be more people there tomorrow night, but less than last year I'm afraid.*

To say a phrase such as *the (more) the better*, the construction **gorau + po + superlative** can be used. Adjectives mutate softly after **po**. (See Unit 27).

| Gorau po fwyaf o blant sydd yna. | The more children there the better. |
| Gorau po leiaf o bobl sy'n cefnogi'r syniad. | The less people supporting the idea the better. |

Insight

Proverbs are a good source of irregular comparative and superlative forms, and the use of such sayings will help broaden your vocabulary considerably.

| Gwell dysg na golud | Better education than wealth |
| Gorau arf, arf dysg | The best weapon is the weapon of education |

Several adjectives, which orally have a tendency to form their degrees of comparison like regular adjectives, have irregular forms in more formal written Welsh. These include:

Absolute	Equative	Comparative	Superlative
hen *old*	cyn hyned	hŷn	hynaf
ieuanc *young*	cyn ieuenged	ieuengach	ieuengaf
ifanc *young*	cyn ifanced	iau	ieuaf
hawdd *easy*	cyn hawsed	haws	hawsaf
anodd *difficult*	cyn anhawsed	anos	anhawsaf
agos *close*	cyn nesed	nes	nesaf
hir *long*	cyhyd	hwy	hwyaf

A yw Cymraeg cyn hawsed â Sbaeneg?	Yr oedd ei frawd yn iau na fi.
Ydy Cymraeg mor hawdd â Sbaeneg?	Roedd ei frawd e'n ifancach na fi.
Is Welsh as easy as Spanish?	*His brother was younger than me.*

(For a discussion on verb forms in the formal written language see Unit 17 onwards.)

Exercises

A Match up the Welsh sentences with the corresponding English versions.

1. Roedd hi mor dwym yn yr ysbyty.
2. Dyw e ddim cystal â'i frawd.
3. Mae cymaint 'da fi i'w wneud.
4. Pa mor hir fydd y wers?
5. Oedd cyn lleied â hyn yma neithiwr?
6. Doeddwn i ddim mor fodlon yr ail dro.

a How long will the lesson last?

b I wasn't so willing the second time.

c Were there as few as this here last night?

d He isn't as good as his brother.

e I've got so much to do.

f It was so warm in the hospital.

B Form sentences *in the comparative degree* in accordance with the example given below.

Sbaen   sych   Cymru

Mae Sbaen yn sychach na Chymru.

1 Abertawe	mawr	Aberystwyth
2 Yr Wyddfa	uchel	Y Preselau
3 Owen Glyndŵr	enwog	William Morgan
4 Gwenllïan	drwg	Bronwen
5 Gomer	trwm	Watcyn
6 Wrecsam	tlawd	Caerdydd

C Look at the pictures and decide whether each statement is True or False.

1. A yw'r ferch dalaf.
2. C yw'r car drutaf.
3. B yw'r gath dewaf.
4. C yw'r dyn cryfaf.
5. A yw'r mynydd uchaf.
6. B yw'r wlad oeraf.
7. A yw'r ci lleiaf.
8. C yw'r plentyn ifancaf.

Grammar in context

Having read the horoscope extract below, answer the following questions:

1 Are those born under the sign of Capricorn going to experience more misfortune in the weeks to come?

2 To whom should they be particularly kind during this time?

> **Yr Afr**
> **22 Rhagfyr – 20 Ionawr**
>
> Mae'r gwaethaf drosodd! Mae eich bywyd yn mynd i wella gan fod Pluto y blaned sy'n rheoli eich arwydd, mewn sefyllfa ffafriol. Mae lwc a rhamant mawr ar y ffordd. Mae'n bosib iawn y byddwch chi'n newid swydd neu'n symud tŷ – neu'r ddau, cyn diwedd 2010. Ond cofiwch fod yn garedig tuag at eich teulu a'ch ffrindiau, yn enwedig y rhai sy'n ifancach na chi.

Test yourself

Fill in the gaps in each sentence below by using the appropriate form of the adjective given in brackets.

1 Fy chwaer yw'r un........................ yn y teulu. (*talkative*)

2 Dywedodd Lili bod ei char yn .... char ei thad. (*fast*)

3 Roedd yr uned hon yn .... 'r uned ddiwethaf. (*easy*)

4 Mae e ...., mae e'n ymarfer bob nos. (*hardworking*)

5 Sali yw'r .... ohonoyn nhw i gyd. (*naughty*)

6 Mae'r gacen hon .... gallwn i fwyta darn arall! (*tasty*)

7 Doeddwn i ddim yn teimlo .... ar ôl bwyta rhywbeth. (*good*)

8 Mae'r llyfr hwn yn ddiflas, oes un .... gyda chi? (*exciting*)

9 Dyw e ddim .... fi. (*strong*)

10 P'un yw'r sir .... yng Nghymru? (*wet*)

7

Adverbs

In this unit you will learn:
- *How to give more information concerning actions or conditions*
- *How to use* byth *and* erioed (*ever / never*)
- *Some useful everyday adverbial expressions*

Grammar in focus

Adverbs are words which provide additional information about verbs, adjectives or other adverbs. They tell us how, when, where, why or to what extent an action takes place.

Formation

As in English, many adverbs are formed from adjectives e.g. *quiet – quietly*, although others are words in their own right. Sometimes whole phrases are used as adverbs, e.g. **yn ôl pob tebyg** – *more than likely*.

Adverbs of manner

These adverbs tell us *how* an action was performed. Virtually all of them are formed by placing **yn** in front of the adjective. With the exception of those beginning with **ll** or **rh**, all preceded by **yn** mutate softly.

gofalus	*careful*	yn ofalus	*carefully*
cyflym	*quick*	yn gyflym	*quickly*
rhamantus	*romantic*	yn rhamantus	*romantically*

Cerddodd hi i'r ysgol **yn araf**. *She walked to school <u>slowly</u>.*

Adverbs of time

These adverbs tell us *when* an action was performed.

Gwelon ni nhw **ddydd Sadwrn diwethaf**. *We saw them <u>last Saturday</u>.*

Dw i'n gweithio yno **bob nos**. *I work there <u>every night</u>.*

As can be seen above, these adverbs mutate softly. However, there are exceptions. One such exception is **llynedd** (*last year*) which is really **y llynedd**. Another is **byth** (*never / ever*) which does not mutate, as **fyth** is added to the comparative form of the adjective to express *even* or *even more*.

Roedd e'n dlotach fyth wedi bod yng Nghaerdydd am benwythnos. *He was even poorer having been in Cardiff for the weekend.*

Bore (*morning*) mutates with a day of the week, but not in the following instances:

Bore 'ma (*this morning*), **bore ddoe** (*yesterday morning*), **bore yfory** (*tomorrow morning*), **bore drannoeth** (*the morning after tomorrow*). **Prynhawn** (*afternoon*) however does mutate.

Aeth y plant i'r dref fore Sadwrn. *The children went to town on Saturday morning.*

Bydd y plant yn mynd i'r dref brynhawn yfory. *The children will go to town tomorrow afternoon.*

Byth ac erioed

Both **byth** and **erioed** mean *never* and *ever*, but they are used in different circumstances and are not interchangeable.

Byth refers to actions that are ongoing. It is used with the present, imperfect, future and conditional tense.

Paid byth â gwneud hynny eto!	*Don't ever do that again!*
Fyddai fe byth yn deall.	*He would never understand.*

Byth can also occasionally be used with a verb in the past tense, if referring to a specific time in the future.

Chlywais i mohoni hi byth wedyn.	*I never heard from her again.*

Erioed refers to completed actions and is used with all **wedi** tenses.

Ydy'r ferch honno erioed wedi bod i'r dosbarth?	*Has that girl ever been to the class?*

It is also used with the past tense.

Atebon nhw erioed?	*Did they ever answer?*
Fues i erioed yn yr Alban.	*I have never been to Scotland.*

Adverbs of place

These adverbs tell us *where* something happened.

yma	*here*	adref	*homewards*
yna	*there*	gartref	*at home*
yn ôl	*back*	uchod	*above*
ymlaen	*ahead*	isod	*below*
i mewn	*in*	i fyny	*upwards*
drosodd	*over*	gyferbyn	*opposite*

Rhaid i fi fynd adref.	*I must go home.*
	(i.e. in the direction of home)
Mae e gartref.	*He is at home.*
Trowch y llyfr drosodd.	*Turn the book over.*

> **Insight**
>
> Do note the difference between **adref** and **gartref** as shown
> in the previous examples. Also remember the noun **cartref**
> meaning *home*, used frequently in house names. Colloquially
> do not be surprised if you hear **gartref** used where
> grammatically you would expect **adref** – this is very common.

When locating objects in relation to the speaker, the following
forms are used:

dyma *here is / are*	Dyma'r plant.	*Here are the children.*
dyna *there is / are*	Dyna ford.	*There's a table.*
dacw *there is / are*	Dacw'r eglwys.	*There is the church.*

Note that when used with an indefinite noun – that is one preceded
by *a*, *an*, or *some* – all three of these adverbs cause a soft mutation.

Dyna can also mean *that's* or *how*.

Dyna fendigedig!	*How wonderful! / That's wonderful!*
Dyna chi.	*There you are.* (i.e. that's it.)

Adverbs of degree

Certain adverbs are used to modify adjectives.

Maen nhw'n hen **iawn.**   *They're <u>very</u> old.*

Several such adverbs precede the adjective that they modify:

digon	*enough*	pur	*very, fairly*
lled	*fairly*	cymharol	*comparatively*
llawer	*considerably*	gweddol	*fairly*
hollol	*totally*	go	*rather*
rhy	*too*	eithaf	*quite*
cwbl	*completely*	gwir	*truly*
tra	*extremely*	hynod	*extremely*

Rhy, lled, cymharol, cwbl, hollol, gweddol, go, pur and **hynod** cause a soft mutation.

Mae'r lluniau yn gymharol rad.	*The pictures are comparatively cheap.*
Dw i'n credu fod hynny'n syniad hollol dwp.	*I think that that is a totally stupid idea.*

Tra causes an aspirate mutation.

Roedd ei fam yn dra charedig.	*His mother was extremely kind.*

A small number of adjectives are used adverbially and are linked to the main adjective by an **o**.

arbennig o dda	*particularly good*
ofnadwy o wael	*awfully bad*

Stative adverbs

A stative adverb is one expressing an unchanging condition or state. In Welsh, there are several which follow the pattern **ar + noun / verb:**

ar agor	*open*	ar gau	*closed*
ar dân	*on fire*	ar ddihun	*awake*
ar frys	*in a hurry*	ar fai	*at fault*
ar gael	*available*	ar werth	*for sale*
ar glo	*locked*	ar wahân	*separate*
ar goll	*lost*	ar ben	*at an end / over*

Bydd y siop ar gau am wythnos.	*The shop will be closed for a week.*
Roedd y frwydr ar ben.	*The battle was over.*

Some common adverbial phrases

fel arfer	*usually*	ac eithrio	*with the exception of*
hyd yn oed	*even*	o leiaf	*at least*
chwarae teg	*fair play*	gwaetha'r modd	*unfortunately*
ar y llaw arall	*on the other hand*	siŵr o fod	*probably*
ar y cyfan	*on the whole*	erbyn hyn	*by now*
mewn gwirionedd	*as a matter of fact*	gyda llaw	*by the way*
beth bynnag	*anyway*	wedi'r cyfan	*after all*
yn ogystal	*as well*	dim ond	*only*
yn arbennig	*particularly*	yn enwedig	*especially*

Does dim llawer o amser gyda fi beth bynnag.	*I haven't got much time anyway.*
Mae hyd yn oed y plant wedi colli diddordeb.	*Even the children have lost interest.*

Insight

Due to space constraints, paper dictionaries frequently do not list adverbial phrases such as those displayed above. Take particular note of these therefore, as like idioms they enrich your vocabulary and make your use of the language more natural. Tags such as **chwarae teg** or **mewn gwirionedd** provide valuable thinking time when responding to native speakers!

Exercises

A Translate the following sentences into Welsh.
1 He ran quickly over to the shop.
2 The work was too hard for me.

3 They should have finished by now.
4 I was on my way home when I saw him.
5 That is fairly easy to do.
6 They will be going tomorrow morning unfortunately.
7 Go to see if the car is locked. (**chi** form)
8 The film was particularly slow.

B Fill in the gaps below, using either BYTH or ERIOED.
1 Doedd e .... wedi bod yn Sbaen.
2 Fyddwn ni .... yn ddigon da.
3 Welodd hi .... gymaint o blant mewn un ystafell.
4 Doeddwn i .... yn gwybod yr ateb i'r cwestiynau.
5 Fydden nhw .... yn fodlon i'r plant fynd i nofio.
6 Dw i .... wedi darllen y nofel.

Grammar in context

Read the following extract from an interview with the Welsh TV presenter and former international marathon runner Angharad Mair and list the adverbs cited in her reply.

Roeddech chi'n mynd i gystadlu yng Ngemau'r Gymanwlad yn 1998 ond cawsoch chi anaf. Oeddech chi'n siomedig?

Roeddwn i'n ofnadwy o siomedig. Roedd siawns gyda fi i gael medal... Ond dyna ni. Mae bywyd fel hynny – rhai pethau da a rhai pethau drwg. Erbyn hyn, dw i'n gallu edrych yn ôl gydag atgofion hynod o felys....

Dw i'n gallu edrych yn ôl a gweld beth wnes i o'i le – ymarfer gormod. Roeddwn i'n rhy awyddus.

QV		
Gemau'r Gymanwlad	*Commonwealth Games*	
o'i le	*wrong*	

Test yourself

A Is the use of **byth / erioed** correct or incorrect in the sentences below?

1 Dw i byth yn ei gweld hi nawr.
2 Welon ni mohono fe erioed wedyn.
3 Dych chi byth wedi clywed beth ddigwyddodd iddo fe?
4 Welais i erioed y fath beth.
5 Fyddet ti byth yn gallu ei wneud e i gyd.

B Translate into Welsh the following dialogue, which contains several adverbs.

John:	The film was awfully bad.
Julie:	I thought it was particularly interesting.
John:	Your eyes were shut during most of it!
Julie:	They were not, that's a lie! I'm never going to the cinema with you again.
John:	I hope you will be in a better temper next Saturday.
Julie:	I've had enough, I'm going home. Goodnight!

8

....

Personal pronouns

In this unit you will learn:
- **The various forms of the personal pronouns** *I, you, he, my, yours, his,* **etc. and how and when to use them**
- **How to form the reflexive pronouns** *myself, yourself,* **etc. in Welsh**

Grammar in focus

A pronoun is a word like *he, they* and *we*, used to replace a noun. In Welsh, personal pronouns are divided into two groups – **independent pronouns**, which as their name suggests, stand on their own and **dependent pronouns** which are dependent on another word in a sentence.

Independent pronouns

These can be sub-divided into three classes:

1 simple
2 reduplicated
3 conjunctive

Simple
1	fi (SW) mi (NW)	*I / me*	ni	*we / us*
2	ti	*you*	chi	*you*

3 fe / e (SW)   *he / him*   nhw *they / them*
    fo / o (NW)
    hi   *she / her*

In formal written Welsh **ef, chwi** and **hwy** are used in place of **fe, chi**
and **nhw**. **E / o / hi** are also used to translate *it*, the choice depending
on the grammatical gender of the word in question in Welsh.

Mae'r llyfr yn anodd.   *The book is difficult.*
Mae e'n rhy galed i fi.   *It is too hard for me.*

Hi is used when describing the weather or time.

Mae hi'n gynnar.   *It's early. / She's early.*

Simple independent pronouns are used in the following
circumstances:

- ▶ Without a verb, when responding to questions.
  Pwy aeth i'r parti?   Fi.
  Who went to the party? *I (did).*

- ▶ After conjunctions or connecting words.
  Roedd Dafydd a hi yno *She and Dafydd were there*
    trwy'r nos.   *all night.*

- ▶ In emphatic sentences.
  Fi sy'n iawn wrth gwrs. *Of course it's <u>me</u> who's correct.*

- ▶ In identification sentences.
  Fe yw'r tiwtor newydd. *He's the new tutor.*

- ▶ After prepositions which do not decline e.g. **gyda** (*with*),
  â (*with*), **heblaw** (*with the exception of*).
  Roedd pawb wedi anghofio *Everyone except me had*
    heblaw fi.   *forgotten.*

- ▶ As the object of short form verbs.
  Yfais i fe'n gyflym iawn. *I drank it very quickly.*

Reduplicated

1	myfi	*I / me*	nyni	*we / us*
2	tydi	*you*	chwychwi	*you*
3	efe / efô	*he / him*	hwynt-hwy	*they / them*
	hyhi	*she / her*		

Reduplicated pronouns are more emphatic than simple pronouns and occur primarily in literature. While it is important to recognize them, you are unlikely to encounter them often in the spoken language. In the spoken language they are pronounced as follows:

1	y fi	y ni
2	y di	y chi
3	y fe / y fo	y nhw
	y hi	

To form the negative, **nid** is placed in front of the pronoun:

Nid y fe oedd y broblem.   *It wasn't him who was the problem.*

The stress normally occurs on the final syllable.

Conjunctive

1	finnau	*I / me*	ninnau	*we / us*
	minnau (NW)			
2	tithau	*you*	chithau	*you*
3	yntau	*he / him*	nhwthau	*they / them*
	hithau	*she / her*		

In formal written Welsh **chwithau** and **hwythau** are used in place of **chithau** and **nhwthau**.

Conjunctive pronouns are used:

▶ For emphasis.
  Rhaid i yntau wybod beth   *He must know what*
    ddigwyddodd.   *happened.*

▶ For contrast or balance.

Aethon ni i'r Bala ac aeth hithau i'r Barri.

We went to Bala and she went to Barry.

▶ In order to convey the idea of *also / too*.

Aethon ninnau i'r Eidal ar ein gwyliau eleni.

We went to Italy on our holidays this year too.

Insight

Two useful phrases you will hear frequently are **a finnau** *(me too)* and **na finnau** *(me neither)*.

Dw i ddim yn hoffi gyrru ar y draffordd.

Na finnau.

I don't like driving on the motorway.

Me neither.

Reciprocal greetings are another good example of the conjunctive at work.

Blwyddyn Newydd Dda!

Ac i chithau.

Happy New Year!

And to you.

Dependent pronouns

These can be divided into:

1 prefixed pronouns
2 auxiliary pronouns
3 infixed pronouns

Prefixed pronouns

1	fy	*my*	ein	*our*
2	dy	*your*	eich	*your*
3	ei	*his / her*	eu	*their*

These are used:

▶ In front of a noun or verb-noun to show possession. Mutation
   occurs after the singular forms.

fy + nasal mutation	fy nghar (i)	*my car*
dy + soft mutation	dy gar (di)	*your car*
ei + soft mutation	ei gar (e)	*his car*
ei + aspirate mutation	ei char (hi)	*her car*

As detailed in Unit 2, aspirate **h** is placed in front of a vowel before
nouns and verb-nouns after **ei / 'i** (*her*), **ein / 'n** (*our*) and **eu / 'u**
(*their*).

ei heglwys (hi)	*her church*
ein hysgol (ni)	*our school*
eu hafalau (nhw)	*their apples*

The auxiliary pronouns in brackets, which are described in more
detail below, are frequently omitted in formal written Welsh.

Ei, eu, ein and **eich** are abbreviated after a vowel.

Emma yw enw'i cheffyl hi.	*Her horse is called Emma.*
Mae'ch llyfr chi'n ddiddorol iawn.	*Your book is very interesting.*

In a row of nouns, the pronoun is used before every noun.

Collodd ei swydd, ei deulu, ei	*He lost his job, family,*
dŷ a'i gar.	*house and car.*

▶ As the object of a verb-noun.

Dw i eisiau ei weld (e).	*I want to see him.*
Doedden nhw ddim yn gallu	*They couldn't remember*
ei chofio (hi).	*her.*

The mutation patterns are the same as those above. Once again
the auxiliary pronouns discussed below and presented in brackets

above, are included in speech, but frequently omitted in formal writing.

Auxiliary pronouns

1	i	*I / me*	ni	*we / us*
	fi			
2	ti / di	*you*	chi	*you*
3	fe / e	*he / him*	nhw	*they / them*
	fo / o			
	hi	*she / her*		

In formal Welsh **ef, chwi** and **hwy** are once again used in place of **fe, chi** and **nhw**. Auxiliary pronouns occur:

▶ For emphasis after nouns and verb-nouns when the prefixed pronoun has already been used.

dy arian di	*your money*
Wyt ti wedi'u dysgu nhw?	*Have you learnt them?*

▶ After the personal forms of verbs and prepositions.

cysgon nhw	*they slept*
chwaraeon ni	*we played*
arni hi	*on her / it*
amdano fe	*about him / it*

Infixed pronouns

These may be used either as possessives or as direct object forms. The possessive and direct object forms are the same apart from the 3rd person.

POSSESSIVES

1	'm (h)	*my*	'n (h)	*our*
2	'th (SM)	*your*	'ch	*your*
3	'i / 'w (SM – *masc.*)	*his*	'u / 'w (h)	*their*
	'i / 'w (AM + h – *fem.*)	*her*		

Infixed possessive pronouns are used after the following words.

a (*and*), â (*with*), i (*to*), o (*of / from*), gyda / efo (*with*), tua (*towards*), na (*neither / nor / than*).

Note the mutations and the addition of **h** shown above. After **i**, **'w** is used both with the third person singular and plural.

Rhoion ni'r arian i'w thad hi.	*We gave the money to her father.*
Es i yno â'm brawd i.	*I went there with my brother.*
Daeth neb o'n hysgol ni.	*No-one came from our school.*

DIRECT OBJECT FORMS

These are used after **fe / mi** which introduces a verb and **a** (*who / which*) to indicate the object of the verb. They also follow the negative pre-verbal particles **ni, na** (*not*) and the conjunctions **pe** (*if*) and **oni** (*unless / if not*). **–s** (rather than **'i**) is used with **ni, na, oni** and **pe**. Note the mutations.

1	'm (h)	*me*	'n (h)		*us*
2	'th (SM)	*you*	'ch		*you*
3	'i (h) / –s (*neg.*)	*him / her*	'u (h) / –s (*neg.*)		*them*

Fe'i hawgrymaf heno.	*I will suggest it tonight.*
Dyna'r ferch a'm trawodd i.	*That's the girl who hit me.*
Nis clywais.	*I did not hear him / her / it.*
Oni'ch gwelaf, ffoniaf nos yfory.	*Unless I see you, I will phone tomorrow night.*

Reflexive pronouns

1	fy hun / fy hunan	*myself*	ein hun / ein hunain	*ourselves*
2	dy hun / dy hunan	*yourself*	eich hun / eich hunan	*yourself*
			eich hun / eich hunain	*yourselves*

3 ei hun / ei hunan *himself /* eu hun / eu *themselves*
                          herself hunain

Insight

In spoken southern Welsh one is more likely to use **yn hunan** or **fy hunan** rather than **fy hun**. **Fy** in general is often pronounced colloquially as **yn** and is followed by a soft mutation in certain dialects in south Wales.

fy mam   **yn fam**   *my mother*

Reflexive pronouns are used in the following circumstances:

▶ For emphasis with the meaning *self*.
Roedd y plant eu hunain wedi   *The children themselves had*
  gwneud y bwyd i gyd.   *made all the food.*

▶ For emphasis with the meaning *own*.
Talodd e am y llyfr gyda'i arian *He paid for the book with*
  ei hun.   *his own money.*

▶ As an object of a verb.
Clywais i ei bod hi wedi brifo   *I heard that she'd hurt*
  ei hunan neithiwr.   *herself last night.*

In a small number of cases, the reflexive element is contained in the **ym** at the start of the verb concerned and the use of **hun / hunan** is incorrect:

Dyw'r plant ddim yn hoffi golchi eu hun. – **incorrect**
The children don't like washing themselves.

Dyw'r plant ddim yn hoffi ymolchi. – **correct**

▶ Idiomatically in the sense of *on my own*:
ar fy mhen fy hun(an)   *on my own*
ar dy ben dy hun(an)   *on your own*

ar ei ben ei hun(an)	*on his own*
ar ei phen ei hun(an)	*on her own*
ar ein pennau ein hun(ain)	*on our own*
ar eich pen eich hun(an)	*on your own* (*sing.*)
ar eich pennau eich hun(ain)	*on your own* (*plural*)
ar eu pennau eu hun(ain)	*on their own*
Hoffwn i fyw ar fy mhen fy hun mewn tŷ mawr yn y wlad.	*I would like to live on my own in a big house in the country.*

Exercises

A Replace the nouns in the sentences below with pronouns.
1 Mae Rhys yn cysgu'n drwm.
2 Clywodd Mrs Davies y stori ar y newyddion.
3 Roedd hi eisiau darllen y llyfr.
4 Dwedon nhw eu bod nhw'n mynd i dalu Siân.
5 Dyma ŵr Mrs Williams.
6 Nid Angharad oedd ar fai.
7 Mae Cerys a Lowri'n mynd.
8 Ydyn nhw wedi bwyta'r gacen i gyd?

B Translate the following.
1 Did you go to hear the concert?
2 He lived with my brother.
3 She's the new teacher in the school.
4 Dafydd was the only child who didn't answer me.
5 What's her dog called?
6 We too must help more around the house.
7 He helped us in the morning and them in the afternoon.
8 How are your parents? (*fam.*)
9 They went over to her house this morning.
10 I've lived on my own for years now.

Grammar in context

Eleri is describing a family photograph to a friend. Can you work out:

1 Who is Steffan?
2 What is the name of Elen and Mared's mother?
3 When did Julie's father die?
4 Who wants to move to France?
5 What is Eileen and Dafydd's problem?

> Dyna fy mam a'm tad ar y dde ac mae fy mrawd Steffan y tu ôl
> iddyn nhw. Ei wraig e Julie a dynnodd y llun. Mae dau o blant
> gyda nhw, Elen a Mared. Mae Elen yn ddeg a Mared yn saith.
> Dyna nhw o flaen eu mamgu, Eileen, mam Julie. Bu farw tad
> Julie pan oedd hi yn yr ysgol gynradd. Y dyn arall yn y llun yw
> Dafydd, partner Eileen – maen nhw eisiau symud i Ffrainc i fyw
> ond dyn nhw ddim yn gallu gwerthu eu tŷ nhw ar hyn o bryd.

Test yourself

Rewrite the sentences below, changing all pronouns from the
singular to the plural/formal, and making any other necessary
changes as appropriate.

1 Mae fy mhlant wedi hen adael y nyth.
2 Aeth Steffan a'th frawd i'r cyfarfod.
3 Fe'm ganwyd yn Lloegr.
4 Daeth hi yn ei char ei hun.
5 Oeddet ti'n hapus yn byw yno ar dy ben dy hun?
6 Ni'th welaf yr wythnos nesaf.
7 Ble mae ei hysgol hi?
8 Dylai hithau ddeall y sefyllfa.
9 Tydi yw'r Pennaeth.
10 Fe'i harestiwyd yn syth.

9

Further pronouns and pronominalia

In this unit you will learn:
- *How to form questions using interrogative pronouns*
- *How to point out things and people using demonstrative pronouns*
- *How to use many of the miscellaneous words and phrases in Welsh which resemble or function as pronouns and are known as pronominalia*

Grammar in focus

Interrogative pronouns

The interrogative pronouns are **pwy?** (*who?*) and **pa?** (*what? / which?*). **Pwy** refers only to people, while **pa** combines with nouns and adjectives to form interrogative phrases e.g.

pa beth?	is contracted to beth?	*what?*
pa bryd?	is contracted to pryd?	*when?*
pa le?	is contracted to ble?	*where?*
pa faint?	is contracted to faint?	*how many?*
pa sut?	is contracted to sut?	*how?*
pa un?	is contracted to p'un?	*which one?*
pa rai?	no contraction	*which ones?*

Interrogative pronouns cause mutation in certain instances:

Verbs mutate softly after **beth, faint** and **pwy,** but not after **pryd, pam** or **ble.**

Beth ddigwyddodd?	*What happened?*
Faint ddaeth?	*How many came?*
Pryd galwodd hi?	*When did she call?*

Nouns mutate softly after **sut** and **pa.** Verbs do not mutate after **sut.**

Sut ferch?	*What sort of girl?*
Sut talon nhw am y bwyd?	*How did they pay for the food?*

Pa + noun + verb also mutates.

Pa lyfr ddarllenaist ti?	*What book did you read?*

Insight

Take care with the translation of *who/who is*. A common error is to use **pwy** together with **sy** in the middle of the sentence.

Pwy sy'n gwybod yr ateb?	*Who knows the answer?*
Iwan yw'r bachgen sy'n gwybod yr ateb.	*Iwan is the boy who knows the answer.*

not Iwan yw'r bachgen pwy sy'n gwybod yr ateb.

The use of **sy** in such instances is discussed in Unit 24. **Pwy** is used only where a question is intended. When it occurs after a noun at the beginning of a sentence, it means *whose.*

Pwy sy wedi ysgrifennu'r gerdd honno?	*Who has written that poem?*
Cerdd pwy yw honno?	*Whose poem is that?*

Interrogative pronouns are negated by placing **na** before the verb. **Na** causes **t**, **c** and **p** to take the aspirate mutation and **b**, **d**, **g**, **m**, **ll** and **rh** the soft mutation. **Nad** rather than **na** is used in front of a vowel.

Sut na chlywais i?	*How didn't I hear?*
Pam nad yw e'n fodlon siarad â nhw?	*Why isn't he willing to speak to them?*

More informally, **ddim** can be placed after the negative verb.

Pam dwyt ti ddim eisiau helpu?	*Why don't you want to help?*

(= pam nad wyt ti eisiau helpu?)

Demonstrative pronouns

This, *that*, *these* are what is known as demonstrative pronouns. Masculine forms refer to masculine nouns, feminine forms refer to feminine nouns and neuter forms are used when referring to something abstract such as news, events, ideas, thoughts, etc.

masculine	feminine	neuter
hwn (*this*)	hon	hyn
hwnnw (*that*)	honno	hynny

These pronouns are used in the following circumstances:

▶ In place of a noun.

Ci Sara yw hwn.	*This is Sara's dog.*
Honno oedd y ferch.	*That was the girl.*
Wyt ti'n credu hynny?	*Do you believe that?*

When replacing plural nouns **rhai** is used with **hyn** and **hynny** i.e. **y rhai hyn** (*these*), **y rhai hynny** (*those*). These are generally contracted to become **y rhain** (*these*), **y rheini / y rheiny** (*those*). Note the use of the definite article with these forms.

Mae'r rhain yn well na'r lleill.	*These are better than the others.*
Doedd y rheiny ddim yn flasus iawn.	*Those weren't very tasty.*

▶ In place of an adjective. Note once again the use of the definite article before the noun. **(Y)ma** and **(y)na** are also used in spoken Welsh in this context.

y ci hwn / yma	*this dog*
y ferch honno / 'na	*that girl*
y llyfrau hynny / yna	*those books*

Insight

Hwnna, as opposed to **hwnnw**, is often heard in speech, as is **honna** rather then **honno**.

Ble mae hwnna wedi mynd?	*Where has that gone?*

Many common expressions contain **hyn** or **hynny**.

ar hyn o bryd	*at the moment*
erbyn hynny	*by then*
bob hyn a hyn	*every now and again*
o hyn ymlaen	*from now on*
hyd yn hyn	*up until now*
hyn oll	*all this*
o ran hynny	*for that matter*

Pronominalia

Many words or phrases in Welsh are pronominal in nature. That is they resemble pronouns in the way that they are used. These include:

Cilydd (*each other*)

The basic form is **ei gilydd** which literally means *his partner* or *companion*, but is best translated as *each other* or *one another*. **Ei gilydd** is used in all instances except where the context implies *us* or *you*. In such instances **ein gilydd** or **eich gilydd** is used. All three forms are abbreviated after vowels:

Gofynnwch y cwestiynau i'ch gilydd.	*Ask each other the questions.*
Roedden nhw'n gwrthod siarad â'i gilydd.	*They were refusing to speak to one another.*

Gyda'i gilydd, which literally means *with his partner,* is used in Welsh to mean *together.*

Aethon nhw ar wyliau gyda'i gilydd.	*They went on holiday together / with each other.*

Note that there is no such form as **eu gilydd.**

There are several useful phrases and idioms which contain **ei gilydd** such as:

at ei gilydd	*on the whole*
rhywbryd neu'i gilydd	*some time or other*
rhywbeth neu'i gilydd	*something or other*
fel ei gilydd	*alike / both*
Bydd plant ac oedolion fel ei gilydd yn mwynhau'r ffilm hon.	*Both children and adults will enjoy this film. / Children and adults alike will enjoy this film.*

Naill ... y llall / arall (*the one ... the other*)

Naill may be used as a pronoun or an adjective.

▶ As a pronoun.

Arhosodd y naill gartref ac aeth y llall i weld y ffilm.	*The one stayed at home while the other went to see the film.*

▶ As an adjective.
   When used as an adjective, **naill** causes a soft mutation to the noun it precedes and **arall** is used to mean *other* after the second noun.

| ar y naill law ... ar y llaw arall. | *on the one hand ... on the other hand.* |
| Cafodd y naill ferch lyfr gan Siôn Corn a chafodd y ferch arall degan. | *The one girl had a book from Father Christmas and the other girl had a toy.* |

Naill may also be used without **y llall / arall**.

| Rhoiodd e naill hanner y gacen i'w chwaer. | *He gave his sister one half of the cake.* |

Naill ai ... neu are common conjunctions meaning *either ... or*

Rhyw (*some*) unrhyw (*any*)

Pronouns containing **rhyw** and **unrhyw** include **rhywun** (*someone*), **rhywbeth** (*something*), **unrhyw un** (*anyone*) and **unrhyw beth** (*anything*). **Rhywun** also has a plural form **rhywrai** (*some people*). Both **rhyw** and **unrhyw** cause a soft mutation.

| Dyn nhw ddim wedi gwneud unrhyw waith eto. | *They haven't done any work yet.* |

Rhyw mutates itself at the beginning of an adverbial expression of time, place or manner.

| Bydd rhywun yn cwyno ryw ddydd dw i'n siŵr. | *Someone will complain one day I'm sure.* |

Amryw means several and is followed by a plural noun.

| Mae hi wedi cyhoeddi amryw lyfrau i ddysgwyr. | *She has published several books for learners.* |

A common phrase containing **rhyw** is **fel y cyfryw** (*as such*).

| Maen nhw wedi gorffen y gwaith, fel y cyfryw. | *They've finished the work, as such.* |

Peth (*some*), **ambell** (*a few*), **sawl** (*several*)

You will have already seen the use of **peth** as an interrogative pronoun in its mutated form **beth?** (**pa beth?**). It can also be used to mean *a little* or *some*.

Mae peth bwyd ar ôl.   *There is some food left.*

It is often used idiomatically:

o dipyn i beth   *little by little*
da o beth   *good thing*

Ambell meaning *a few* and **sawl** meaning *several* are followed by a singular noun. **Ambell** causes a soft mutation.

Daeth ambell blentyn yn ôl   *A few children came back crying.*
    yn crio.
Cynhaliwyd sawl cyngerdd ar   *Several concerts were held on the*
    yr un noson.   *same night.*

Insight

Ambell is occasionally seen followed by **i**: **ambell i unigolyn** (*a few individuals*). This is incorrect, as no **i** is needed. Remember, for example, the common phrase **ambell waith** (*sometimes*).

Likewise no **o** is necessary following **amryw,** as sometimes occurs.

amryw fechgyn *several boys* <u>not</u> **amryw o fechgyn**

Holl, oll, i gyd (*all*), **hollol** (*entirely*)

Holl is used in front of a noun after a pronoun or the definite article and causes a soft mutation.

yr holl fwyd   *all the food*

Oll is used after a noun and after a pronoun.

y myfyrwyr oll	*all the students*
Roedden nhw oll yno.	*They were all there.*

I gyd is placed after a definite noun.

y plant i gyd   *all the children*

Hollol meaning *altogether* or *entirely* causes the adjective it precedes to mutate softly.

Mae'r cyfieithiad yn hollol gywir. *The translation is entirely correct.*

Pawb (*everyone*), **pob** (*every*)

Pawb was originally singular in meaning, but when a personal pronoun is used in place of it, it is regarded as plural.

Oedd pawb yno?	*Was everyone there?*
Oedden.	*Yes (they were).*

Pob meaning *every* is used an an adjective and is followed by a noun or pronoun equivalent.

pob un   *everyone*   pob dim   *everything*

The mutated form **bob** is found in several adverbial phrases and idioms.

bob yn un	*one by one*
bob yn ddau	*two by two*
bob yn dipyn	*bit by bit*
bob yn ail	*every other*

Pob + noun can be adjectival, qualifying a preceding noun.

Esgidiau pob dydd   *everyday shoes*

If the noun is feminine then **pob** will mutate:

cot bob dydd   *everyday coat*

Exercises

A Match up the common Welsh expressions 1–10 with the English a–j.

1	o ran hynny	**a**	a good thing
2	ar y naill law	**b**	as such
3	at ei gilydd	**c**	for that matter
4	o dipyn i beth	**d**	all this
5	bob hyn a hyn	**e**	bit by bit
6	fel y cyfryw	**f**	on the one hand
7	bob yn dipyn	**g**	on the whole
8	da o beth	**h**	every now and again
9	hyn oll	**i**	sometime or other
10	rhywbryd neu'i gilydd	**j**	little by little

B Give the correct form of **this** in the blanks below:
1 Cwblhewch y ffurflen ....
2 Ydy .... yn syniad da?
3 Bydd y llyfr .... yn help.
4 .... yw'r nofel orau yn y siop!
5 Roedd e wedi gwneud .... ddoe.

C Give the correct form of **that** in the blanks below:
1 Pwy oedd y dyn ....?
2 .... oedd y fenyw.
3 Mam Mererid yw ....
4 Roedd ....'n ateb da.
5 Roedd y rhaglen ....'n siomedig iawn.

Grammar in context

The advert below for a Welsh novel contains several sentences that include an interrogative pronoun. Translate these sentences into English. Can you also spot a demonstrative pronoun?

Hefyd yng Nghyfres NOFELAU NAWR
COBAN MAIR
gan Gwyneth Carey
Pwy fyddai'n magu plant?
Mae rhywun yn poeni mwy amdanyn nhw wrth iddyn nhw dyfu.
Sut bydd Ann yn ymdopi â bywyd coleg?
Pam mae gŵr Mair mor awyddus iddi hi newid?
Beth yw rhan Glenys yn hyn i gyd?
Ydy'r ateb yn y goban..?
£3.50
ISBN 185902 783 0

Test yourself

Translate the following sentences.

1 He's got some work to do before the end of the week.
2 This present is my favourite one.
3 On the whole the performance was excellent.
4 She's the teacher who helps Catrin with her maths.
5 They went to the swimming pool together.
6 I can remember being sent to bed every night at nine o'clock.
7 Any child would love that.
8 Why isn't Eluned happy to go on her own?
9 There are several good pubs in the village.
10 How many paid the full price?

10

Noun clauses

In this unit you will learn:
- **About forming noun clauses in Welsh** (*I know that it's easy*)
- **How to emphasize a particular point using** mai **or** taw
- **About using noun clauses with** efallai / hwyrach (*maybe*)

Grammar in focus

Noun clauses

A sentence generally contains at least one verb. Sentences containing more than one verb can be split into main clauses and sub-clauses. A noun clause is the subject or object of a verb in the main clause.

Present tense
Dw i'n credu   bod / fod y llyfr yn ddiddorol iawn.
I think   *that the book is very interesting.*

Although **bod / fod** in such instances can be thought of as *that*, it shouldn't be considered a direct translation as it is possible to leave the *that* out of the English sentence and it will still make sense.

I think the book is very interesting.

However in Welsh **bod / fod** is an integral part of the sentence, taking the place of **mae**.

Dw i'n credu + Mae'r llyfr yn ddiflas.
I believe + The book is boring.
Dw i'n credu bod y llyfr yn ddiflas.
I believe that the book is boring.

The concise form **credaf** could also have been used.

Credaf fod y llyfr yn ddiflas.

While **bod / fod** are interchangeable with the verb-noun, after a concise form of the verb **fod** is generally used.

Insight

A common mistake among learners is to include both **bod/ fod** and **mae** when constructing present tense noun clauses.

Dw i'n credu bod mae'r llyfr yn ddiflas – <u>This is incorrect!</u>

Imperfect tense
In noun clauses in the imperfect tense **bod / fod** takes the place of **roedd**.

Roedd e'n gobeithio	+	Roedd digon o amser gyda fe.
He was hoping		*He had enough time.*
Roedd e'n gobeithio bod		*He was hoping (that) he had*
digon o amser gyda fe.		*enough time.*

Insight

The construction of noun clauses in the imperfect tense as described above, can be difficult to comprehend. There is a natural tendency to include **roedd**, loosely translated as *was*, in the middle of the sentence.

Oeddet ti'n gwybod bod roedd dy fam wedi galw ddoe? – <u>This is incorrect!</u>

Oeddet ti'n gwybod bod dy fam wedi galw ddoe? – <u>Correct!</u>

Did you know that your mother called yesterday?

Future and conditional tenses

When the verb in the noun clause is future or conditional in tense the noun clause is introduced by **y** + verb or **yr** in front of a vowel.

Dwedon nhw	+	Bydd e'n cyrraedd yfory.
They said	+	*He will be arriving tomorrow.*
Dwedon nhw y bydd e'n cyrraedd yfory.		*They said (that) he will be arriving tomorrow.*
Clywais i y bydden nhw'n canu yn y cyngerdd.		*I heard (that) they would be singing in the concert.*
Dw i'n deall yr aiff y gwynt cyn hir.		*I understand (that) the smell will go before long.*

Past tense

When the verb in the noun clause is in the past tense the following construction is used: **i** + subject + verb-noun

When the subject is a pronoun, the appropriate forms of **i** are used. Note the soft mutation to the verb-noun.

Mae e'n meddwl	+	Gwnaethon nhw'n dda.
He thinks	+	*They did well.*
Mae e'n meddwl iddyn nhw wneud yn dda.		*He thinks (that) they did well.*
Dw i'n deall i dad Mair alw neithiwr.		*I understand that Mair's father called last night.*

Negative noun clauses

Informally the noun clause is negated simply by adding the negative particle **ddim**.

Dw i'n gwybod bod John ddim yn hapus yn ei swydd newydd.	*I know that John isn't happy in his new job.*
Dych chi'n credu fydd hi ddim yn gwybod?	*Do you think that she won't know?*

In formal written Welsh such clauses are expressed by **na** (**nad** before a vowel) before the verb. In the case of the verb *to be*, in the present tense, this will be **yw** or **ydynt,** depending on whether the subject is singular or plural.

Dw i'n gwybod nad yw John yn hapus yn ei swydd newydd.

Na causes the aspirate mutation to the verb it precedes if it begins with **t, c** or **p** and soft mutation in the case of **b, d, g, ll, rh** or **m.**

Wyt ti'n siŵr na chuddiodd   *Are you sure that Dafydd*
   Dafydd siwmper Nia?   *didn't hide Nia's jumper?*
Deallon ni na fyddai Della yn   *We understood that Della*
   dod i'r dosbarth y tymor nesaf.   *wouldn't be coming to the*
                              class next term.

Peidio â is also used sometimes to express the negative in the past tense.

Roeddwn i'n meddwl iddo beidio â   *I thought that he didn't*
   chwblhau'r gwaith mewn pryd.   *complete the work in time.*

This could also be written in Welsh using **na.**

Roeddwn i'n meddwl na chwblhaodd e'r gwaith mewn pryd.

Prefixed pronouns and *bod*

Personal forms of the noun clause are formed by combining the prefixed pronouns (see Unit 8) and **bod.**

fy mod i   *that I am / was*
dy fod ti   *that you are / were*
ei fod e   *that he is / was*
ei bod hi   *that she is / was*
ein bod ni   *that we are / were*
eich bod chi   *that you are / were*
eu bod nhw   *that they are / were*

Dw i'n deall.	+	Maen nhw'n symud i Ffrainc.
I understand.		*They are moving to France.*
Dw i'n deall eu bod		*I understand that they are*
nhw'n symud i Ffrainc		*moving to France*

Often in speech the prefixed pronoun is omitted, but the mutation remains.

Roedd e'n credu mod i'n crio.   *He thought that I was crying.*

That … has / had is translated using **wedi**.

Doedden nhw ddim yn gwybod	*They didn't know that I'd learnt*
fy mod i wedi dysgu'r gerdd	*the poem already.*
yn barod.	

The negative is formed in speech simply by placing **ddim** after the auxiliary pronoun.

Bydden nhw'n gwybod dy fod	*They'd know that you aren't*
ti ddim o ddifri.	*serious.*
Dw i'n gobeithio eich bod chi	*I hope that you haven't wasted*
ddim wedi gwastraffu eich	*your time.*
amser.	

Once again **na(d)** is used in the case of the formal written negative.

    Bydden nhw'n gwybod nad wyt ti o ddifri.

Noun clauses with *mai / taw*

When emphasizing a noun or the first word of a sub-clause, the sub-clause is introduced with **mai** rather than **bod / fod**. **Taw** is also used informally in South Wales in place of **mai**.

Roedd e'n meddwl mai <u>athrawes</u>	*He thought that you were a*
oeddet ti.	<u>*teacher*</u>.

Without such emphasis, this would be translated as:

Roedd e'n meddwl dy fod ti'n athrawes.

Dw i'n gwybod taw <u>Elen</u> fydd yn dysgu yfory.	*I know that it's <u>Elen</u> who will be teaching tomorrow.*
Dwedon nhw taw <u>Dylan</u> ddylai fynd.	*They said it's <u>Dylan</u> who should go.*

Note the soft mutation to the short form of the verb in the examples above caused by the omitted relative clause **a** (*who / which / that*) as described in Unit 24.

Negative

The negative is formed by using **nad** in place of **mai** or **taw**.

Mae e'n gwybod nad <u>John</u> fydd yn ei ddysgu fe eleni.	*He knows that it won't be <u>John</u> who will be teaching him this year.*

Insight

Remember not to think of the negative as **nid** in this case. A frequent error is to translate the sentence above as:

Mae e'n gwybod mai nid John fydd yn ei ddysgu fe eleni. – <u>This is incorrect!</u>

Efallai

Noun clauses are used in exactly the same way as already described, with the same mutations, after **efallai** (*perhaps*). In certain areas, particularly in North Wales, an alternative **hwyrach** is used rather than **efallai**.

Efallai ei fod e'n anghywir. (not **mae**)	*Perhaps he might be incorrect.*

Efallai na fydd amser gyda nhw.	*Perhaps they might not have time.*
Hwyrach y bydden nhw'n fodlon.	*Perhaps they would be willing.*
Efallai taw yn y <u>parti</u> mae e.	*Perhaps he's in the <u>party</u>.* (emphatic)

Exercises

A Fill in the gaps in the sentences below with the appropriate form of the noun clause.

1 Dw i'n credu eich .... chi'n iawn.

2 Dwedodd e .... chi oedd yn dysgu heno.

3 Clywais i .... byddan nhw'n cyrraedd cyn swper.

4 Mae e'n deall dy .... ti'n mynd yn gynnar.

5 Sylwais i .... chanodd Meleri yn y perfformiad neithiwr.

6 Wyt ti'n credu .... byddai hynny'n gwneud gwahaniaeth?

B Start each of the following sentences with **efallai** as shown in the example:

Mae hi'n dost.   Efallai ei bod hi'n dost.

In the case of a negative sentence use **na / nad**.

1 Bydd e'n gwybod.

2 Rwyt ti'n iawn.

3 Fyddan nhw ddim yma mewn pryd.

4 Cei di'r llythyr yn y post yfory.

5 Clywodd hi'r plant eraill yn siarad ar ôl y parti.

Grammar in context

Tyddewi – rhai ffeithiau

Read the following extract about St Davids in Pembrokeshire from the magazine *Lingo* for Welsh learners and answer the questions below:

Mae hanner miliwn o bobl yn mynd i ardal Tyddewi bob blwyddyn ar eu gwyliau neu am y dydd. Mae 300,000 o bobl yn mynd i'r Eglwys Gadeiriol.

Maen nhw'n dweud fod y Brenin Arthur wedi glanio ar draeth Tyddewi ac roedd môr-leidr enwog o'r enw Barti Ddu yn dod o Sir Benfro.

Erbyn heddiw, mae llawer o artistiaid yn dod yma. Maen nhw'n credu bod y golau yn dda iawn.

Mae llawer o bobl wedi symud yma o'r tu allan ac mae llawer o Saesneg yma. Ond mae'r bobl yn siarad a dysgu Cymraeg yma hefyd ac yn 2002 daeth yr Eisteddfod Genedlaethol i Dyddewi.

1 Who is said to have landed on St Davids' beach?
2 Why do artists like the area?
3 Why was 2002 an important year?

Test yourself

Translate the following questions or sentences into Welsh.

1 Have they heard that Luned has lost her job?
2 They were sure that Alun had called the police.
3 Maybe I should have asked him.

4 She knows that I have finished the book.
5 Had you heard that the Vicar was on holiday?
6 Maybe they didn't dance to the last record.
7 He should realize that going without food isn't the answer.
8 We hoped that we would get the chance to do it again.
9 Maybe they were growing vegetables for the local market.
10 I thought that she'd moved to London.

11

....

Conjunctions

In this unit you will learn:
- *The role of common conjunctions*
- *Subordinate conjunctions and their uses*

Grammar in focus

Conjunctions connect words, clauses or sentences and show the relationship between them.

Common conjunctions

A (*and*)

A is used before consonants including **h** and causes the word it precedes to take the aspirate mutation, if it begins with **t, c** or **p**. **A** also causes **gan** and **gyda** (*with / by*) to take the aspirate mutation, particularly in formal written Welsh.

te a choffi	*tea and coffee*
coffi a the	*coffee and tea*
a chyda llaw	*and incidentally*
Aeth Sioned i'r dref a phrynodd hi ffrog newydd.	*Sioned went to town and she bought a new dress.*

Ac is placed in front of a word beginning with a vowel.

| Roedd y ffrog yn wyrdd ac oren. | *The dress was green and orange.* |

There are however certain exceptions to the above rule – one of which is that **ac** is always placed before **mae** and **roedd**.

| Mae e'n artist talentog iawn ac mae e'n dysgu Cymraeg mewn dosbarth nos. | *He's a very talented artist and he's learning Welsh in a night class.* |

Insight

Other common exceptions containing *and* include:

ac fel	*and as*
ac felly	*and therefore*
ac mewn	*and in*
ac nid	*and not*
ac sydd	*and which is*
ac roedden nhw	*and they were*
ac mor	*and so*
ac wedyn	*and then*

Do note however that *and also* is **a hefyd**, not **ac hefyd** as is sometimes seen, due to the indirect influence of the above exceptions.

Na (*nor*)

Na follows a similar pattern to **a** – it is used before consonants and causes aspirate mutation of **c, p, t**. It is replaced by **nac** in front of a vowel.

| Dw i ddim yn bwyta pysgod na chig coch. | *I don't eat fish or red meat.* |
| Dyw'r plant ddim yn bwyta orennau nac afalau. | *The children don't eat oranges or apples.* |

Ond (*but*)

Mae hi'n dod ond mae hi'n teimlo'n eithaf blinedig heno.	*She's coming but she feels quite tired tonight.*

Note also the use of **ond** in the phrase **dim ond** (*only*).

Dim ond dau ddiwrnod oedd gyda ni.	*We only had two days.*

Neu (*or*)

Neu causes a soft mutation when it is followed by a verb-noun (the form of the verb as it is in the dictionary, without reference to tense or person), an adjective or a noun.

rhedeg neu gerdded	*run or walk*
glas neu binc	*blue or pink*
Atebwch naill ai cwestiwn 1 neu gwestiwn 2.	*Answer either question 1 or question 2.*

When it is followed by a conjugated form of the verb (i.e. a verb form with an ending attached to it), there is no mutation.

Dawnsiwch i ni neu can**wch** eich hoff gân.	*Dance for us or sing your favourite song.*

Subordinate conjunctions

A number of conjunctions, and prepositions used as conjunctions, are used to introduce various adverbial clauses. Adverbial clauses tell us how, why, when, where, or to what extent an action takes place.

Time conjunctions
These include:

ar ôl (i)	*after*	**tra (bod)**	*while*
cyn (i)	*before*	**hyd**	*until, as long as*

erbyn (i)	*by the time*	**pan**	*when*
ers (i)	*since*	**wedi (i)**	*after*
wrth (i)	*as, while*	**nes (i)**	*until*

Gofynnodd y plant i'w gweld nhw wedi iddo fe fynd.	*The children asked to see them after he had gone.*
Dw i ddim wedi bod yn ôl ers i fi adael y coleg.	*I haven't been back since I left college.*

Note that **i** declines (see Units 15 / 16) with pronouns, as in the first example above, and that the verb-noun always takes the soft mutation in such a construction.

Doedd neb ar ôl yn yr ystafell ddosbarth erbyn iddo fe orffen siarad.	*There was no one left in the classroom by the time he finished speaking.*

The verb-noun mutates even if it doesn't immediately follow **i**.

Doedd neb ar ôl yn yr ystafell ddosbarth erbyn i Mr Jones yr athro orffen siarad.

Y, or **yr** in front of a vowel, is used to introduce adverbial clauses in the future and imperfect tenses following **cyn**, **erbyn**, **hyd** and **nes**.

Byddwn ni'n gorffen cyn y daw eich rhieni.	*We will finish before your parents come.*

Byddan nhw yma erbyn y
byddwch chi'n barod.

*They will be here by the time
you're ready.*

Cyn, erbyn and **nes** can also be used with **bod** rather than **i**.
The meaning remains the same.

Dylwn i lanhau'r tŷ cyn bod fy mam i'n dod.

Dylwn i lanhau'r tŷ cyn i fy
mam i ddod.

*I should clean the house before
my mum comes.*

Tra is followed by **bod** not **i** and does not cause a mutation.
Y / yr is not used after **tra**.

Mae hi'n aros yn Llundain tra
bod ei gŵr hi yn yr ysbyty.
Cofiwch alw tra byddwch chi
yn yr ardal.

*She is staying in London while
her husband is in hospital.*
*Remember to call when you are
in the area.*

Pan is followed directly by the verb in every tense and causes soft
mutation. **Yw / ydy** is the third person singular form which follows
pan when referring to a specific time.

Gadewch i ni ei holi hi nawr
pan yw'n gyfleus.
Symudwn ni pan fydd y tŷ'n
barod.

*Let's ask her now when it is
convenient.*
*We will move when the house
is ready.*

The negative can be expressed in speech by the affirmative
construction + **ddim**.

Fi fydd yn cael y bai pan fydd e
ddim yna.

*It's me who will get the blame
when he won't be there.*

It can also be expressed by **na** or **nad** in front of a vowel. This is
always the case in formal written Welsh. **Na** causes the verb it
precedes to mutate softly unless it begins with **t, c** or **p,** in which
case it takes the aspirate muation.

Roedd Delyth yn siomedig iawn pan na ofynnodd Ceri iddi ddod i'r parti.

Delyth was very disappointed when Ceri didn't ask her to come to the party.

Reason conjunctions
These include:

achos (bod) *because*
oherwydd (bod) *because*

am (bod) *as* (SM after **am**)
gan (bod) *as* (SM after **gan**)

Roeddwn i'n grac achos bod popeth wedi mynd.
Gan dy fod ti'n gallu canu, dylet ti gystadlu heno.

I was angry because everything had gone.
As you can sing, you should compete tonight.

In the case of other tenses, **y / yr** is placed before the verb.

Clywith e yfory oherwydd y byddan nhw'n galw yn ei dŷ e ar ôl brecwast.

He will hear tomorrow because they will be calling at his house after breakfast.

The negative is expressed by **ddim** or **na / nad**. **Na** causes the verb it precedes to mutate softly unless it begins with **t, c** or **p,** in which case it takes the aspirate mutation.

Cwynodd Mair oherwydd na chyrhaeddodd yr ambiwlans mewn pryd.
Esboniodd y tiwtor eto am nad oedd y plentyn yn deall.

Mair complained because the ambulance didn't arrive in time.

The tutor explained again as the boy didn't understand.

Purpose conjunctions
These include:

er mwyn (i) *in order to / that*

fel (bod) *so that*

Dewch draw er mwyn i fi gael gweld y lluniau.

Come over so that I can see the pictures.

In the case of **fel, y / yr** can be placed before the relevant form of **bod**.

Dw i eisiau aros tan yfory fel y bydd digon o amser gyda fi.

I want to wait until tomorrow so that I've got enough time.

Contrast conjunctions
These include:

er (bod) *although*

tra (bod) *whereas*

Er ei fod e'n ifanc iawn, mae'n chwaraewr ardderchog.
Er nad yw e'n hen iawn, mae'n chwaraewr ardderchog.
Mae hi'n swnllyd iawn tra bod ei chwaer yn dawel iawn.

Although he's very young, he's an excellent player.
Although he isn't very old, he's an excellent player.
She's very noisy whereas her sister is very quiet.

Result conjunctions
These include:

fel (bod) *so that*

felly *so / therefore*

Roedd hi eisiau aros tan y diwedd fel bod cyfle gyda hi i siarad â phawb.
Maen nhw'n dod ar y trên, felly maen nhw'n gobeithio cyrraedd cyn deg.
Hoffai adael yn syth fel na fydd cyfle ehangu ar y ddadl.

She wanted to stay until the end so that she had the opportunity to talk to everyone.
They're coming on the train, so they are hoping to arrive before ten.
He would like to leave at once so that there won't be an opportunity to expand upon the argument.

Conditional conjunctions
These include:

os   *if*
pe   *if*

oni bai   *unless*
rhag ofn   *in case*

For a discussion on the differences between **os** and **pe** see Unit 27. **Os** is used in the indicative mood while **pe** is used with the subjunctive of **bod** to express doubt or uncertainty.

Os wyt ti'n rhydd, rho wybod i mi.	*If you are free, let me know.*
Pe byddwn i'n gwybod, byddwn i'n dweud wrthoch chi.	*If I knew, I would tell you.*

Oni bai and **rhag ofn** can be followed by **i** or **bod**. The meaning remains the same.

Dw i wedi ysgrifennu nodyn rhag ofn i ti anghofio.

Dw i wedi ysgrifennu nodyn rhag ofn dy fod ti'n anghofio.	*I've written a note in case you forget.*

Exercise

Choose the correct common conjunction to place in the gaps below, remembering to make any other changes to the sentences as appropriate. Translate the completed sentences into English.

1 Mae'n hwyr .... mae'n rhaid i fi orffen y gwaith cyn mynd i'r gwely.
2 Roedd hi'n fwy o actores .... ei chwaer.
3 Byddaf yn mynd yfory .... yn dod yn ôl ddydd Llun.
4 Dw i'n llai nerfus yn y car nawr .... oeddwn i.
5 Gwelodd hi'r plentyn .... daeth ar y daith.
6 Rhaid i fi fynd .... casglu'r plant.
7 Dylwn i ffonio .... ei fod e siŵr o boeni.
8 Dw i'n adnabod teulu'r priodfab yn well .... teulu'r briodferch.
9 Ysgrifennodd e ata i bob wythnos .... ffoniodd e unwaith y mis.
10 Mae un awr .... dwy'r wythnos yn ddigon.

Grammar in context

Read the advert below for a pub in Brecon, Mid-Wales.

Chwarae Teg

Bar : Bwyd : Gwely a Brecwast

Cynigion arbennig ar gyfer gwely a brecwast a swper nos
Mynediad i'r anabl, parcio a chyfleusterau

Dim pŵl: dim dartiau:
dim ond bwyd da,
cwrw da ac amser da

21 Y Watton, Aberhonddu, Powys, LD3 7ED
Ffôn: 01874 624555

1 Is it possible to stay in the pub?
2 What three things can Chwarae Teg offer its customers according to this advert?

Test yourself

Translate the following sentences into Welsh, using the appropriate subordinate conjunctions.

1 Write everything down in case you forget.
2 He will be there when he's ready.
3 She is miserable because the weather is so awful.
4 As it was early, he called to see his mother.
5 It will be too late by the time the bus comes.

6 Even though he hadn't learnt a lot, he'd enjoyed the experience.
7 I'd better go now, so that I'm there before the children.
8 They came, although Owen was feeling ill.
9 Ellie looked after the children in order for me to do a bit of work.
10 We won't go unless you come too.

12

....

Numerals

In this unit you will learn:
- *Cardinal numbers: how to say and write* one, two, *etc. in Welsh*
- *Ordinal numbers* (first, second, *etc.) and their use in Welsh*
- *How to form multiplicative numbers* (once, twice, *etc.)*

Grammar in focus

There are two ways of counting in Welsh: one which counts in tens (decimal system) and the other in twenties. The decimal system outlined below is the one generally used today among younger speakers, while the system of counting in twenties is still popular among older, native speakers.

Cardinal numbers – the decimal system

0	dim	9	naw
1	un	10	deg
2	dau / dwy (*fem.*)	11	un deg un
3	tri / tair (*fem.*)	12	un deg dau / dwy
4	pedwar / pedair (*fem.*)	13	un deg tri / tair
5	pump	14	un deg pedwar / pedair
6	chwech	15	un deg pump
7	saith	16	un deg chwech
8	wyth	17	un deg saith

18	un deg wyth	90	naw deg
19	un deg naw	97	naw deg saith
20	dau ddeg	100	cant
21	dau ddeg un	108	cant ac wyth
30	tri deg	150	cant pum deg
32	tri deg dau	200	dau gant
40	pedwar deg	209	dau gant a naw
43	pedwar deg tri	300	tri chant
50	pum deg	1,000	mil
54	pum deg pedwar / pedair	2,000	dwy fil
60	chwe deg	3,100	tair mil un cant
65	chwe deg pump	4,610	pedair mil chwe chant a deg
70	saith deg		
76	saith deg chwech	1,000,000	miliwn
80	wyth deg	2,000,000	dwy filiwn
86	wyth deg chwech		

Un causes a mutation to feminine singular nouns.

un gath *one cat*   un ci *one dog*

Numbers *two*, *three* and *four* have both masculine and feminine forms. Feminine forms are used with feminine nouns.

dwy gath *two cats*   pedair cadair *four chairs*
un deg pedair o eglwysi   *fourteen churches*

It is incorrect to mutate the feminine forms **tair** and **pedair** after the definite article, (**y, 'r**). Both **dwy** and **dau** however mutate after the definite article. **Dwy** and **dau** also cause a soft mutation.

y ddwy fenyw   *the two women*   y ddau ddyn   *the two men*
y tair merch   *the three girls*   y pedair ysgol *the four schools*

Pum and **chwe**, as opposed to **pump** and **chwech**, are used in front of nouns.

pum dyn   *five men*   chwe merch   *six girls*

Chwe causes an aspirate mutation, as does **tri**.

chwe choes   *six legs*   tri chwpan   *three cups*

Insight

A singular noun generally follows ten or less while number +
o + a plural noun is the normal rule in the case of numbers
greater than ten.

saith desg   *seven desks*
un deg un o longau   *eleven ships*
tri deg o dudalennau   *thirty pages*

Feminine forms are used where appropriate.

un deg tair o gathod   *thirteen cats*
dau ddeg dwy o fuchod   *twenty-two cows*

Cant is a masculine noun whereas **mil** and **miliwn** are feminine.
Can rather than **cant** is placed in front of nouns.

can mil o bunnoedd   *a hundred thousand pounds*

The first ten numbers after any hundred use **a** (*and*) or **ac** (*before a
vowel*). Those after do not.

cant ac un   *hundred and one*
dau gant a chwech   *two hundred and six*
tri chant pedwar deg   *three hundred and forty*

Cardinal numbers – the '20' system

The '20' system is the norm when referring to a number of years
and age as well as when telling the time. All three of these topics
are discussed in greater detail in Unit 13.

Numbers 1–10 are the same as in the decimal system.

11	un ar ddeg	30	deg ar hugain
12	deudddeg	31	un ar ddeg ar hugain
13	tri / tair ar ddeg	32	deuddeg ar hugain
14	pedwar / pedair ar ddeg	33	tri / tair ar ddeg ar hugain
15	pymtheg	40	deugain
16	un ar bymtheg	44	pedwar / pedair a deugain
17	dau / dwy ar bymtheg	45	pump a deugain
18	deunaw	50	hanner cant
19	pedwar / pedair ar bymtheg	56	hanner cant a chwech
20	ugain	60	trigain
21	un ar hugain	70	deg a thrigain
22	dau / dwy ar hugain	77	dau / dwy ar bymtheg a thrigain
23	tri / tair ar hugain	80	pedwar ugain
24	pedwar / pedair ar hugain	88	wyth a phedwar ugain
25	pump ar hugain	90	deg a phedwar ugain
26	chwech ar hugain	99	pedwar / pedair ar bymtheg a deg a phedwar ugain
27	saith ar hugain	111	cant ac un ar ddeg
28	wyth ar hugain		
29	naw ar hugain		

This is also the system used with money:

pymtheg punt	*fifteen pounds*
pedair ceiniog ar ddeg	*fourteen pence*
tair punt ar hugain	*twenty-three pounds*

As indicated above, the noun is placed after the first number in the '20' system.

tair merch ar hugain	*twenty-three girls*
chwe chadair ar hugain	*twenty-six chairs*

Ordinals

Ordinals beyond *tenth* are not used very frequently apart from in dates (see Unit 13)

1st	cyntaf	16th	unfed ar bymtheg
2nd	ail	17th	ail ar bymtheg
3rd	trydydd / trydedd (*fem.*)	18th	deunawfed
4th	pedwerydd / pedwaredd (*fem.*)	19th	pedwerydd / pedwaredd ar bymtheg
5th	pumed	20th	ugeinfed
6th	chweched	21st	unfed ar hugain
7th	seithfed	22nd	ail ar hugain
8th	wythfed	23rd	trydydd / trydedd ar hugain
9th	nawfed	24th	pedwerydd / pedwaredd ar hugain
10th	degfed	25th	pumed ar hugain
11th	unfed ar ddeg	26th	chweched ar hugain
12th	deuddegfed	27th	seithfed ar hugain
13th	trydydd / trydedd ar ddeg	28th	wythfed ar hugain
14th	pedwerydd / pedwaredd ar ddeg	29th	nawfed ar hugain
		30th	degfed ar hugain
15th	pymthegfed	31st	unfed ar ddeg ar hugain

Cyntaf is placed after the noun and mutates softly after a feminine singular noun.

y wers gyntaf   *the first lesson*
y ddarlith gyntaf   *the first lecture*

All other ordinals come before the noun.

y trydydd llun	*the third picture*
y chweched ebost	*the sixth email*

Ail causes all nouns following it to mutate.

yr ail gar	*the second car*
yr ail geffyl	*the second horse*

After the definite article, ordinals preceding feminine nouns mutate softly. The feminine noun itself also takes the soft mutation.

y drydedd bennod	*the third chapter*
y bumed raglen	*the fifth programme*

Masculine ordinals and masculine nouns do not mutate after the definite article.

y Trydydd Byd	*the Third World*
y pedwerydd car	*the fourth car*

As is the case with cardinals, the noun is placed after the first element.

y pedwerydd plentyn ar bymtheg	*the nineteenth child*
y drydedd salm ar hugain	*the twenty-third psalm*

Multiplicatives

Once, twice, etc are formed by using the word **gwaith**.

unwaith	*once*
dwywaith	*twice*
tair gwaith	*three times*
pedair gwaith	*four times*
pum gwaith	*five times*

unwaith ar bymtheg	*sixteen times*
dwywaith ar hugain	*twenty-two times*
canwaith	*a hundred times*

Insight

Tair gwaith has a literary alternative, namely **teirgwaith**, while the literary form of **deg gwaith** *(ten times)* would be **deng gwaith**. Other numbers containing **tri** or **deg** follow a similar pattern.

| tair gwaith ar ddeg | teirgwaith ar ddeg | *thirteen times* |

Note also the following idiomatic phrases.

ar unwaith	*at once*
unwaith yn rhagor	*once again*
unwaith neu ddwy	*once or twice*
does dim dwywaith amdani	*there is no doubt about it*
sawl gwaith	*many times*

Exercises

A Using the decimal system, write out the answers to the sums below in full.

17 + 3 =	357 − 30 =
29 + 6 =	200 − 101 =
7 + 5 =	78 − 8 =
44 + 13 =	17 − 15 =
104 + 12 =	1 − 1 =

B Fill the gaps in the sentences below.
1 Fe yw (3 + Cadeirydd) y Bwrdd.
2 Fy hoff salm yw'r (24 + salm).
3 Roedd y (5 + pennod) yn arbennig o drist.
4 Canais i'r (2 + cân) ddwywaith.
5 Hi oedd y (11 + merch) i orffen y marathon.

6 Gwelais i'r (3 + rhaglen) yn y gyfres neithiwr.
7 Aethan nhw ar eu gwyliau yn ystod (1 + wythnos) fis Awst.
8 Roedd hi'n bwrw eira am y (4 + dydd) yn olynol.

Grammar in context

Using the decimal system, write down the rugby scores of those in the Principality Premier Division on the first Saturday of the 2009/10 season.

Llanymddyfri	42	Bedwas	12
Pontypridd	13	Casnewydd	31
Llanelli	15	Pontypŵol	12
Glyn Ebwy	43	Cross Keys	17
Quinns Caerfyrddin	21	Aberafan	38
Castell Nedd	23	Glamorgan Wanderers	3
Abertawe	48	Caerdydd	18

Test yourself

Decide whether the statements below are written correctly or not. If they are not, correct what is wrong with them.

1	*three girls*	tri merched
2	*the third book*	y trydydd llyfr
3	*twenty-seven people*	saith ar ugain o bobl
4	*the second question*	yr ail cwestiwn
5	*the fourteenth house*	y pedwerydd ar ddeg tŷ
6	*three times a week*	tair gwaith yr wythnos
7	*the seventh programme*	y seithfed raglen
8	*the first answer*	y cyntaf ateb
9	*forty pounds*	deugain punt
10	*eighteen*	tri a phymtheg

13

Time

In this unit you will learn:
- *The days of the week, months and seasons of the year*
- *How to express dates, times and ages in Welsh*
- *Some other useful time expressions*

Days of the week

dydd Sul	*Sunday*
dydd Llun	*Monday*
dydd Mawrth	*Tuesday*
dydd Mercher	*Wednesday*
dydd Iau	*Thursday*
dydd Gwener	*Friday*
dydd Sadwrn	*Saturday*

To say 'on' a particular day mutate **dydd** softly.

Dw i'n mynd i'r ffair ddydd Mawrth.	*I'm going to the fair on Tuesday.*

If you go there every Tuesday without fail then **ar** (*on*) is added.

Dw i'n mynd i'r ffair ar ddydd Mawrth.	*I go to the fair on Tuesdays.*

If you go in the evening, substitute **nos** for **dydd**.

Dw i'n mynd i'r ffair ar nos Wener.	*I go to the fair on Friday evenings.*
Dw i'n mynd i'r ffair nos Fercher.	*I'm going to the fair Wednesday night.*

Note the soft mutation following **nos** as it is a feminine singular noun.

Months of the year

mis Ionawr	*January*	mis Gorffennaf	*July*
mis Chwefror	*February*	mis Awst	*August*
mis Mawrth	*March*	mis Medi	*September*
mis Ebrill	*April*	mis Hydref	*October*
mis Mai	*May*	mis Tachwedd	*November*
mis Mehefin	*June*	mis Rhagfyr	*December*

The inclusion of the word **mis** (*month*) is optional.

The seasons

y gwanwyn	*spring*	yr hydref	*autumn*
yr haf	*summer*	y gaeaf	*winter*

Special dates

Nos Galan	*New Year's Eve*
Dydd Calan	*New Year's Day*
Gŵyl Santes Dwynwen	*Welsh St Valentine's (25th January)*
Dydd Sant Folant	*St Valentine's Day*
Dydd Gŵyl Ddewi	*St David's Day (1st March)*
Dydd Gwener y Groglith	*Good Friday*
Y Pasg	*Easter*
Sul y Pasg	*Easter Sunday*
Calan Mai	*May Day*
Gŵyl y Banc	*Bank holiday / Public holiday*

Y Sulgwyn	*Whitsun*
Calan Gaeaf	*Halloween*
Noson Guto Ffowc	*Guy Fawkes' Night*
Noswyl Nadolig	*Christmas Eve*
Dydd Nadolig	*Christmas Day*
Y Nadolig	*Christmas*
Gŵyl San Steffan	*Boxing Day*

Dates

Masculine ordinal numbers (see Unit 11) are used with dates.

yr ail ar hugain o Ionawr	*the 22nd of January*
y pedwerydd o Fawrth	*the 4th of March*
y cyntaf o Fehefin	*the 1st of June*
y deunawfed o Fedi	*the 18th of September*
yr unfed ar ddeg ar hugain o Ragfyr	*the 31st of December*

When writing in a more formal style, the month is frequently placed first.

Hydref yr ugeinfed / yr ugeinfed o Hydref	*the 20th of October*

As noted above, **mis** can also be included, mutating softly after **o**. The month itself will then not mutate.

y chweched o fis Tachwedd	*the 6th of November*

Written abbreviations use the last letters of the ordinals after numbers. These are **–eg**, **–fed**, **–ed** or **–ain**.

16eg Ebrill	*the sixteenth of April*	yr unfed ar bymthe**g** o Ebrill
15fed Mai	*the fifteenth of May*	y pymtheg**fed** o Fai
5ed Awst	*the fifth of August*	y pum**ed** o Awst
23ain Chwefror	*the twenty-third of February*	y trydydd ar hug**ain** o Chwefror

In letters, abbreviations are frequently omitted.

14 Medi 2009	*14 September 2009*
7 Tachwedd 2010	*7 November 2010*

Number of years

Blwyddyn (*year*) is a feminine singular noun, the plural of which is **blynyddoedd**. **Blwyddyn** is used on its own, with the cardinal *one* and with all ordinals.

Buodd hi'n gweithio yn yr Adran am flwyddyn.	*She worked in the Department for a year.*
Mae hi yn y flwyddyn gyntaf yn y Brifysgol.	*She's in the first year at University.*
Dw i wedi byw yn yr ardal am flynyddoedd.	*I've lived in the area for years.*

Following a numeral apart from *one* **blwyddyn** changes to **blynedd**.

un flwyddyn	*one year*	un mlynedd ar ddeg	*eleven years*
dwy flynedd	*two years*	deuddeg mlynedd	*twelve*
tair blynedd	*three*	tair blynedd ar ddeg	*thirteen*
pedair blynedd	*four*	pedair blynedd ar ddeg	*fourteen*
pum mlynedd	*five*	pymtheg mlynedd	*fifteen*
chwe blynedd	*six*	un mlynedd ar bymtheg	*sixteen*
saith mlynedd	*seven*	dwy flynedd ar bymtheg	*seventeen*
wyth mlynedd	*eight*	deunaw mlynedd	*eighteen*
naw mlynedd	*nine*	pedair blynedd ar bymtheg	*nineteen*
deg mlynedd	*ten*	ugain mlynedd	*twenty*

Dw i wedi bod yn byw yn	*I have been living in*
Llansadwrn am ddeuddeg	*Llansadwrn for twelve years.*
mlynedd.	

As can be seen above, the traditional or '20' system (see Unit 12) tends to be used with *years*. In formal written Welsh **deng mlynedd, deuddeng mlynedd** and **pymtheng mlynedd** can also be used rather then **deg, deuddeg** and **pymtheg**.

If one chooses to use the decimal system in speech **blynedd** will still mutate after 10 according to the number it follows.

un deg dwy flynedd	*twelve years*
un deg pum mlynedd	*fifteen years*
un deg chwe blynedd	*sixteen years*

O flynyddoedd could also be used in such instances.

un deg tair o flynyddoedd	*thirteen years*
un deg pedair o flynyddoedd	*fourteen years*
dau ddeg o flynyddoedd	*twenty years*

When referring to age, **blwydd** is used rather than **blynedd**.

| Mae e'n ddwy flwydd oed. | *He is two years old.* |

··

Insight

Note that age is always feminine regardless of the gender of the subject. **Blwydd** can be omitted, but **oed** will remain.

| Mae'r efeilliaid yn bedair | *The twins are four (years old)* |
| oed erbyn hyn. | *by now.* |

··

On its own **blwydd** means *a year old*.

| Mae'r babi'n flwydd oed ym | *The baby is a year old in* |
| mis Ionawr. | *January.* |

Divisions of time

eiliad	*second*	dydd / diwrnod	*day*
munud	*minute*	hanner dydd	*midday*
awr	*hour*	hanner nos	*midnight*
chwarter awr	*quarter of an hour*	wythnos	*week*
hanner awr	*half an hour*	pythefnos	*fortnight*
bore	*morning*	mis	*month*
prynhawn	*afternoon*	blwyddyn	*year*
noswaith	*evening*	canrif	*century*
nos / noson	*night*	mileniwm	*millennium*

Eiliad can be masculine or feminine, so either the masculine or feminine forms of the numbers can be used in conjuction with it.

dau eiliad / dwy eiliad

Munud is feminine in South Wales and masculine in North Wales.

dwy funud (SW)   dau funud (NW)

While **dydd** refers to a particular day of the week or year, **diwrnod** is used when referring to the whole day's length. It is also used with adjectives and after numbers.

diwrnod o waith	*day of work*
diwrnod gwael	*a bad day*
tri diwrnod	*three days*

Nos and **noson** follow the same pattern as **dydd** and **diwrnod**.

nos Sul	*Sunday night*
noson o gwsg	*a night's sleep*
noson wael	*a bad night*
dwy noson	*two nights*

Expressions of time

y bore 'ma	*this morning*
y prynhawn 'ma	*this afternoon*
neithiwr	*last night*
echnos	*the night before last*
ddoe	*yesterday*
echddoe	*day before yesterday*
yfory	*tomorrow*
bore yfory	*tomorrow morning*
trannoeth	*day after tomorrow*
mewn tridiau	*in three days*
toriad y wawr	*daybreak*
yr wythnos diwethaf	*last week*
yr wythnos nesaf	*next week*
am wythnos	*for a week*
trwy'r dydd	*all day*
bob dydd	*every day*
amser maith yn ôl	*a long time ago*
ar hyn o bryd	*at the moment*
ar y pryd	*at the time*
maes o law	*in due course*
mewn pryd	*in time*
o'r blaen	*previously*
yn ddiweddar	*recently*
yn fisol	*monthly*
y tro nesaf	*next time*
am y tro	*for now*

Telling the time

The traditional system of counting in twenties, described in Unit 12, is the system used when telling the time in Welsh. Like the weather, the time is feminine. The Welsh word for *o'clock* is **o'r gloch.**

Faint o'r gloch yw / ydy hi?	*What time is it?*
Mae hi'n un ar ddeg o'r gloch.	*It's eleven o'clock.*

Mae hi is frequently contracted to **mae'n** in everyday speech.

Mae'n ddeuddeg o'r gloch.	*It's twelve o'clock.*
Mae'n dri o'r gloch.	*It's three o'clock.*

Note the mutation after **yn** and the fact that, while the concept of time is feminine, it is the masculine numbers that are used when telling the time – **tri o'r gloch** not **tair**.

> ### Insight
> As well as the phrase **Faint o'r gloch yw hi?** you may also hear **Beth yw'r amser?** This colloquial version is of course a literal translation from the English.

The Welsh word for *past* in relation to time is **wedi**.

Mae'n bum munud wedi dau.	*It's five past two.*
Mae'n ddeg munud wedi pedwar.	*It's ten past four.*
Mae'n chwarter wedi pump.	*It's a quarter past five.*

As can be seen above, **wedi** causes no mutation.

The traditional numbers are also used for saying *twenty past* and *twenty-five past*.

Mae'n ugain munud wedi saith.	*It's twenty past seven.*
Mae'n bum munud ar hugain wedi deg.	*It's twenty-five past ten.*
Mae'n hanner awr wedi un ar ddeg.	*It's half past eleven.*

The word **awr** (*hour*) must be included when referring to *half past*, but is omitted in *quarter past*.

The Welsh word for *to* in relation to time is **i**. Note that there is a soft mutation after **i**.

Mae'n bum munud ar hugain i ddau.	*It's twenty-five to two.*
Mae'n ugain munud i bedwar.	*It's twenty to four.*
Mae'n chwarter i ddeg.	*It's a quarter to ten.*
Mae'n naw munud ar hugain i dri.	*It's twenty-nine minutes to three.*

Am is used with expressions of time to mean *at*.

Am faint o'r gloch?	*At what time?*
Cyrhaeddodd e am ddwy funud ar bymtheg wedi chwech.	*He arrived at seventeen minutes past six.*

Munud has mutated following **dwy**. As explained in the previous unit, the noun follows the first part of the numeral in the '20' system.

Exercises

A Match up the English expressions of time 1–10 with their Welsh equivalents a–j.

1	the day after tomorrow	**a**	mewn pryd
2	at the time	**b**	trannoeth
3	a long time ago	**c**	am y tro
4	last week	**d**	mewn tridiau
5	daybreak	**e**	amser maith yn ôl
6	recently	**f**	ar y pryd
7	in three days	**g**	yn ddiweddar
8	for now	**h**	yr wythnos diwethaf
9	this afternoon	**i**	toriad y wawr
10	in time	**j**	y prynhawn 'ma

B What time is it? Write out in full the times shown on the clockfaces below.

C Put the appropriate form of the word **blynedd / blwydd** in the sentences below.
1 Roedd y teulu wedi byw yn y pentref am bum ....
2 Roedd e'n dair .... oed ar y pryd.
3 Mae'n ddwy .... ar hugain ers i fi fynd yno.
4 Doedden nhw ddim wedi bod yno am wyth ....
5 Dw i'n cofio fy mhenblwydd yn bedair .... oed.

D Place either **dydd** or **diwrnod** in the sentences below, remembering to mutate where necessary.
1 Roedd y tywydd yn hyfryd .... Llun.
2 Mae e wedi aros yn Llambed am .... arall.
3 Roedd heddiw yn .... arbennig.
4 Mae'n cysgu yn y .... ac yn gweithio yn y nos.
5 Bydd y dosbarth ar .... arall nawr.

Grammar in context

Write out the dates of Wales's international soccer matches in 2009, both in full and in abbreviation.

Wednesday 12th August	Montenegro	v	Wales
Wednesday 9th September	Wales	v	Russia
Saturday 10th October	Finland	v	Wales
Wednesday 14th October	Liechtenstein	v	Wales

Test yourself

Translate the following sentences into Welsh.

1 She's lived there for over six years.
2 My birthday is on St David's Day.
3 They have music lessons on Sunday afternoons
4 I worked with him for twenty years.
5 They are calling for me at quarter past ten.
6 Siân bought a house in Cilgerran two years ago.
7 The next train is at twenty seven minutes to three.
8 Gomer stayed with his friends in Llanwrda the night before last.
9 He will be fifty in August.
10 The trip to the pantomime is on the seventeenth of January.

14

Measures and dimensions

In this unit you will learn:
- **How to express arithmetical signs, decimals and fractions in Welsh**
- **Ways of talking about dimensions and units of measure**
- **Points of the compass**

Grammar in focus

Arithmetical signs

+ arwydd adio
1 + 3 = 4   mae un adio tri yn hafal i bedwar
− arwydd tynnu
7 − 5 = 2   mae saith tynnu pump yn hafal i ddau
× arwydd lluosi
2 × 2 = 4   mae dau wedi'i luosi â dau yn hafal i bedwar
÷ arwydd rhannu
12 ÷ 2 = 6   mae un deg dau wedi'i rannu gan ddau yn
                             hafal i chwech

arwydd	*sign / symbol*	lluosi	*to multiply*
adio	*to add*	rhannu	*to divide*
tynnu	*to subtract*	yn hafal i (SM)	*equals*
wedi'i luosi â (AM)	*multiplied by*		
wedi'i rannu gan (SM)	*divided by*		

Decimals

7.8	saith pwynt wyth
13.9	un deg tri pwynt naw
50.3	pum deg pwynt tri
pwynt	*point*

Fractions

The most common fractions are **hanner** (*a half*), **chwarter** (*a quarter*) and **traean** (*a third*). **O** follows **traean**, but not **hanner** or **chwarter**.

traean o'r gwaith	*a third of the work*
hanner y gacen	*half of the cake*
chwarter y bwyd	*a quarter of the food*

Other fractions can be expressed in one of two ways using the word **rhan** (*part*), using either cardinals or ordinals.

un rhan o chwech	*a sixth*
chweched ran	*a sixth*

Note the mutation of **rhan** if preceded by the ordinal.

When referring to more than one part of something, the first pattern above is used.

dwy ran o dair	lit. *two parts of three – two thirds*
chwe rhan o wyth	lit. *six parts of eight – sixth eighths*

The word *and* is represented between numbers and fractions by **a** or **ac** before a vowel. **A** causes an aspirate mutation.

tri a hanner	*three and a half*
pedwar a thraean	*four and a third*

Dimensions

Nouns

uchder	*height*	trwch	*thickness*
hyd	*length*	pwysau	*weight*
lled	*width*	mesuriad	*measurement*
dyfnder	*depth*		

Adjectives

uchel	*high*	dwfn	*deep*
isel	*low*	bas	*shallow*
hir	*long*	trwchus	*thick*
byr	*short*	tenau	*thin*
llydan	*wide*	trwm	*heavy*
cul	*narrow*	ysgafn	*light*

Verbs

mesuro	*to measure*	pwyso	*to weigh*

Units of measure

milimedr	*millimetre*	modfedd	*inch*
centimedr	*centimetre*	troedfedd	*foot*
medr	*metre*	llath	*yard*
cilomedr	*kilometre*	milltir	*mile*
gram	*gram*	peint	*pint*
cilogram	*kilogram*	galwn	*gallon*
litr	*litre*	pwys	*pound*
hectar	*hectare*	stôn	*stone*
acer / erw	*acre*	tunnell	*ton*

Expressions of quantity

faint?	*how much? / how many?*
sawl?	*how many?*

Faint is used to mean *how much* with singular nouns and *how many* with plural nouns. In both cases it needs to be followed by an **o**.

| Faint o fwyd dych chi ei eisiau? | *How much food do you want?* |
| Faint o blant oedd yn y dosbarth? | *How many children were in the class?* |

Sawl means *how many* and is used with a singular noun. No **o** is needed before the noun.

Sawl person oedd yn y dosbarth?	*How many people were in the class?*
gormod	*too much / too many*
digon	*enough*
rhagor	*more*
tipyn bach	*a little*
llawer	*a lot*
ychydig	*a little / a few*
Yfodd e ormod.	*He drank too much.*
Mae hi'n deall tipyn bach.	*She understands a little.*

When preceding a noun, the above are followed by an **o** which causes a soft mutation:

| Gaf i ragor o de? | *May I have more tea?* |
| Roedd gormod o sŵn yn y gwasanaeth. | *There was too much noise in the service.* |

Insight

A common error among learners is to precede **gormod** with the modifying adverb **rhy** (*too*) when translating the phrase *too much*.

Mae rhy gormod o blant yn y dosbarth.

This is unnecessary and therefore incorrect – **gormod** translates as *too much* and the sentence should read:

| Mae gormod o blant yn y dosbarth. | *There are too many children in the class.* |

Geometrical terms

llinell	*line*	hirsgwâr	*rectangle*
ongl	*angle*	cylch	*circle*
ongl sgwâr	*right angle*	triongl	*triangle*
ongl aflem	*obtuse angle*	radiws	*radius*
ongl lem	*acute angle*	diamedr	*diameter*
sgwâr	*square*	perimedr	*perimeter*

Solids

ciwb	*cube*	pyramid	*pyramid*
silindr	*cylinder*	côn	*cone*
sffêr	*sphere*		

Other measurement language

pren mesur	*ruler*	arwynebedd	*area*
dwbl	*double*	maint	*quantity*
gwerth	*value*	yn fwy na	*greater / bigger than*
gofod	*space*	yn llai na	*lesser / smaller than*
cyflymder	*speed*		

Points of the compass

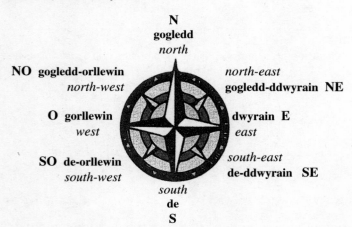

N
gogledd
north

NO gogledd-orllewin
north-west

north-east
gogledd-ddwyrain **NE**

O gorllewin
west

dwyrain **E**
east

SO de-orllewin
south-west

south-east
de-ddwyrain **SE**

south
de
S

Note the soft mutation of the second element: **gogledd-orllewin** *south-west*.

To the is expressed by **i'r**.

Aeth hi i'r Gogledd i fyw.   *She went to the North to live.*

Mid-Wales is known as **y Canolbarth** or **Canolbarth Cymru**.

Insight

All points of the compass are masculine and therefore **i'r De** is *to the South*, as opposed to **i'r dde** which is *to the right*.

Exercises

A Write out the numerical expressions below in Welsh

1	8 × 5 = 40	**6**	27 − 9 = 18
2	2 + 9 = 11	**7**	14 litres
3	100 metres	**8**	2/3
4	1/2 + 1/4 = 3/4	**9**	60 ÷ 3 = 20
5	7.97	**10**	4.31

B Match up the Welsh words and phrases 1–8 below with their English equivalents a–h.

1	gogledd-ddwyrain	**a**	depth
2	ongl lem	**b**	ruler
3	yn fwy na	**c**	speed
4	triongl	**d**	Mid-Wales
5	cyflymder	**e**	acute angle
6	pren mesur	**f**	north-east
7	y Canolbarth	**g**	more than
8	dyfnder	**h**	triangle

Grammar in context

Look at the map below and complete the chart, giving the location of the various towns along with their populations as shown in the example:

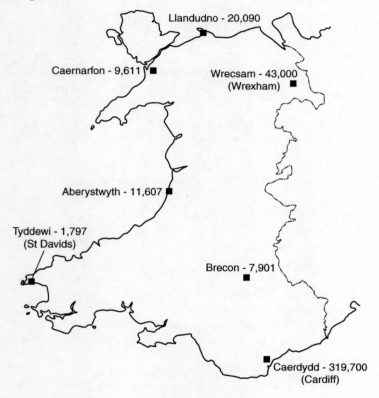

Llandudno - 20,090

Caernarfon - 9,611

Wrecsam - 43,000
(Wrexham)

Aberystwyth - 11,607

Tyddewi - 1,797
(St Davids)

Brecon - 7,901

Caerdydd - 319,700
(Cardiff)

Tref / Town	Lleoliad / Location	Poblogaeth / Population
Aberystwyth	gorllewin	un deg un mil, chwe chant a saith
Caernarfon		
Wrecsam		
Caerdydd		
Llandudno		
Aberhonddu		
Tyddewi		

Test yourself

Translate the following sentences into Welsh.

1 These wall are very thick.
2 What was the length of the lorry?
3 I had too much work to do.
4 How many tickets are left?
5 It weighed two tons.
6 The water is very shallow.
7 He has learnt a little bit of Welsh.
8 What is the value of the house?
9 Some of the roads in west Wales are very narrow.
10 They live less than half an hour from Cardiff.

15

Prepositions: simple and compound

In this unit you will learn:
- *The various simple prepositions in Welsh*
- *The various compound prepositions in Welsh*

Grammar in focus

A preposition is a word that is used to relate a noun or a pronoun to some other part of the sentence, e.g. *of*, *at*. There are two types of preposition in Welsh, namely **simple prepositions**, which consist of one word only and **compound prepositions**, which consist of two or more words. Compound prepositions are less common and operate in a different way to simple prepositions.

Simple prepositions

Most of the simple prepositions cause mutation.

Soft mutation: **am** (*for / at*) **ar** (*on*) **at** (*to / towards*)
dan (*under*) **dros** (*over*) **drwy** (*through*)
heb (*without*) **i** (*to*) **o** (*of / from*)
wrth (*by / near*) **gan** (*by*) **hyd** (*until / along*)

Nasal mutation: **yn** (*in – with definite nouns*)

Aspirate mutation: **â** (*with / with the help of*) **tua** (*towards / about*)
gyda (*with / in the company of*)

No mutation is caused by:

cyn (*before*)	**rhag** (*from*)
rhwng (*between*)	**ger** (*near*)
wedi (*after*)	**mewn** (*in – with indefinite nouns*)
nes (*until*)	**fel** (*like*)
erbyn (*by*)	**megis** (*as*)

ers (*since – when referring to an unspecific time in the past*)
er (*since – when referring to a specific time in the past*)

Conjugations
Simple prepositions can also be divided into those that conjugate
like verbs and those that don't conjugate.

Conjugating prepositions include **ar, at, o, am, dan, heb, yn, drwy,
rhag, rhwng, dros, gan, wrth.**

ar		**at**	
arna i	arnon ni	ata i	aton ni
arnat ti	arnoch chi	atat ti	atoch chi
arno fe / fo	arnyn nhw	ato fe / fo	atyn nhw
arni hi		ati hi	

o		**am**	
ohono i	ohonon ni	amdana i	amdanon ni
ohonot ti	ohonoch chi	amdanat ti	amdanoch chi
ohono fe / fo	ohonyn nhw	amdano fe / fo	amdanyn nhw
ohoni hi		amdani hi	

dan		**heb**	
dana i	danon ni	hebddo i	hebddon ni
danat ti	danoch chi	hebddot ti	hebddoch chi
dano fe / fo	danyn nhw	hebddo fe / fo	hebddyn nhw
dani hi		hebddi hi	

yn

yno i	ynon ni
ynot ti	ynoch chi
ynddo fe / fo	ynddyn nhw
ynddi hi	

drwy

drwyddo i	drwyddon ni
drwyddot ti	drwyddoch chi
drwyddo fe / fo	drwyddyn nhw
drwyddi hi	

rhag

rhagddo i	rhagddon ni
rhagddot ti	rhagddoch chi
rhagddo fe / fo	rhagddyn nhw
rhagddi hi	

rhwng

rhyngo i	rhyngon ni
rhyngot ti	rhyngoch chi
rhyngddo fe / fo	rhyngddyn nhw
rhyngddi hi	

dros

drosto i	droston ni
drostot ti	drostoch chi
drosto fe / fo	drostyn nhw
drosti hi	

gan

gen i	gennyn / gynnon ni
gen ti	gennych / gynnoch chi
ganddo fe / fo	
ganddi hi	ganddyn nhw

wrth

wrtho i	wrthon ni
wrthot ti	wrthoch chi
wrtho fe / fo	wrthyn nhw
wrthi hi	

Mae e wedi anfon y llyfrau atat ti.	*He's sent the books to you.*
Dw i ddim yn gwybod sut y bydda i'n gallu byw hebddyn nhw.	*I don't know how I will be able to live without them.*
Rhyngoch chi a fi, dw i'n credu ei bod hi'n gwastraffu ei hamser.	*Between you and me, I think that she's wasting her time.*

In the formal written language, prepositions are conjugated in one of three ways.

FIRST CONJUNCTION
ar, dan, am, at, o

arnaf	arnom
arnat	arnoch

arno   arnynt
arni

Although the preposition **o** ends with **–of** and **–ot** in the first and second person singular, the rest of it is regular.

SECOND CONJUNCTION
heb, yn, trwy, rhwng (rhyng–), rhag, dros

hebof   hebom
hebot   heboch
hebddo   hebddyn
hebddi

THIRD CONJUNCTION
gan, wrth

gennyf   gennym
gennyt   gennych
ganddo   ganddynt
ganddi

Note the third person singular and plural of **wrth**:

wrtho   wrthynt
wrthi

THE CONJUGATION OF *I*
The conjugation of the preposition **i** is irregular.

Spoken form		**Formal written form**	
i fi / mi	i ni	imi	inni
i ti	i chi	iti	ichwi
iddo fe / fo	iddyn nhw	iddo	iddynt
iddi hi		iddi	

Insight

As you can see, in the formal written language the personal pronoun is omitted except when required for emphasis. The personal pronoun is also sometimes omitted in colloquial speech, especially in the case of the third person singular.

NON-DECLINABLE PREPOSITIONS

The following prepositions do not conjugate:

gyda, â, tua, hyd, cyn, erbyn, fel, ger, mewn, wedi, nes, ers, er, megis.

Compound prepositions

As noted already, these consist of two elements and can be divided as follows:

▶ Those which are followed by a noun or verb-noun, but not a pronoun. For example:

ar fin	*about to*	trwy gydol	*throughout*
yn ystod	*during*	yn anad	*above all*

Dw i'n cofio gwersi Mrs Roberts yn anad dim.	*I remember Mrs Roberts' lessons above all.*
Roedd hi'n oer yn ei thŷ hi trwy gydol y flwyddyn.	*It was cold in her house throughout the year.*

▶ Those which are followed by a noun or pronoun. For example:

gyferbyn â	*opposite*	hyd at	*up to*
oddi ar	*from*	oddi mewn i	*within*
tuag at	*towards*	y tu allan i	*outside*
y tu mewn i	*inside*	ynglŷn â	*regarding*

Eisteddodd e gyferbyn â'r meddyg.	*He sat opposite the doctor.*
Parcion nhw'r car y tu allan i'r garej.	*They parked the car outside the garage.*

▶ Those which can be conjugated by placing a pronoun between the two parts. For example:

ar ben	*on top of*	ar ôl	*after*
ar draws	*across*	gerbron	*in front of*
uwchben	*above*	yn sgil	*in the light of*
ymhlith	*among*	er mwyn	*for (the sake of)*
ynghylch	*about*	yn lle	*in place of*
yn ymyl	*near*	ar gyfer	*for*
o gwmpas	*around*	o blaid	*in favour of*

Dododd hi'r llyfr ar y silff uwch ei phen hi.	*She put the book on the shelf above her head.*
Dw i'n fodlon dweud celwydd golau er dy fwyn di.	*I'm willing to say a white lie for your sake.*
Roedd Bob yno yn eu plith nhw.	*Bob was there among them.*
Doedd dim i'w weld o'n cwmpas ni.	*There was nothing to be seen around us.*

Insight

Note the difference between English and Welsh in the two commonly heard examples given below:

Where are you going to?

I ble wyt ti'n mynd?   NOT   Ble wyt ti'n mynd i?

Where does he come from?

O ble mae e'n dod?   NOT   Ble mae e'n dod o?

Exercises

A Translate the following:
1 without him
2 over them

3   in it (*fem.*)
4   by you
5   about me
6   on us
7   under them
8   of it
9   between us
10 through her

B Change the compound prepositions below according to the
guidance given and translate the new sentences into English.
For example:
>   Doedd dim lle ar gyfer y ferch. (nhw)
>   Doedd dim lle ar eu cyfer nhw.

1   Mae e'n byw ar ei ben ei hun. (fi)
2   Wyt ti'n mynd yn lle John? (hi)
3   Bues i'n byw yn ymyl Dewi am flynyddoedd. (nhw)
4   Ofynnaist ti ar ôl y teulu? (hi)
5   Mae llawer o ddysgwyr ymhlith y grŵp. (nhw)
6   Mae'n poeni ynghylch y sefyllfa. (ni)

Grammar in context

Certain prepositions are used with particular verbs, as is described
in greater detail in Unit 16. Can you find four such examples in this
letter from Mal the snail to his young Welsh readers?

Tudalen y Plant

Annwyl Ffrindiau,

Cwtshwch wrth y tân. Mae'r tywydd yn ddiflas – y gwynt, y
glaw a'r oerfel. Tywydd chware gemau bwrdd a gwylio teledu
yw hi.

Fyddwch chi yn dathlu Calan Gaeaf eleni? Fyddwch chi yn gosod lantern yn y ffenest ac yn towcio afalau yn y tŷ? Cofiwch mai hwyl a sbri yw Calan Gaeaf.

Mae hi bron yn adeg Guto Ffowc hefyd. Bydda i'n cysgodi o dan y sied. Cofiwch chi gadw eich anifeiliad anwes chi yn y tŷ rhag y tân gwyllt yn ystod y cyfnod hwn.

Anfonwch eich lluniau o'r tannau gwyllt ata i.

Hwyl am y tro,

Mal xxxx

cwtsho	*to snuggle* (colloquial usage – SW)
towcio afalau	*bobbing apples*

Test yourself

Correct the following sentences:

1 Ble mae'r plant yn dod o?
2 Mae e wedi rhoi llyfr i hi.
3 Roedd y car tu allan y tŷ.
4 Prynais ffrog newydd ar gyfer hi.
5 Dw i'n credu ei fod e wedi anfon y gwaith at nhw'n barod.
6 Roedd e'n arfer byw gyferbyn eu hathrawes Gymraeg.
7 Es i'r parti yn lle hi.
8 Doedd dim un o nhw'n medru canu.
9 Daeth e er mwyn chi wrth gwrs.
10 Ble bydd y teulu'n symud i?

16

Using prepositions

In this unit you will learn:
- **How to use prepositions in Welsh in certain constructions and idioms**

Grammar in focus

Welsh prepositions, as described in Unit 15, are different to English prepositions in that sometimes a preposition is used in Welsh, but not in English and vice-versa.

He is hoping to ask someone.   Mae e'n gobeithio gofyn i rywun.

Common prepositions and their usage

â, ag
- ▶ Before the name of an instrument:
  Torrais fy mys â chyllell.   *I cut my finger with a knife.*

- ▶ With a number of common verbs such as:

cwrdd â	*to meet*	cyffwrdd â	*to touch*
siarad â	*to speak*	cytuno â	*to agree*
dod â	*to bring*	mynd â	*to take*
ymweld â	*to visit*	peidio â	*to stop*

am

▶ With a selection of nouns such as:

hiraeth am	*longing for*	diolch am	*thanks for*
angen am	*need for*	rheswm am	*reason for*

▶ In expressions of time:

Galwaf am saith o'r gloch.   *I will call at 7.00 o'clock.*
Dw i wedi gwneud digon o   *I have done enough work*
  waith am y tro.   *for now.*

▶ After a wide range of verbs such as:

anghofio am	*to forget about*	edrych am	*to look for*
dweud am	*to tell about*	galw am	*to call for*
cofio am	*to remember about*	chwilio am	*to look for*
gwybod am	*to know about*	talu am	*to pay for*
clywed am	*to hear about*	aros am	*to wait for*
sôn am	*to speak of*	gofalu am	*to look after*

▶ In the idiom *to laugh at* – **chwerthin am ben.**

▶ With a verb-noun to denote intention:

Roedd e am fynd i'r parti   *He wanted to go to the party*
  nos yfory.   *tomorrow night.*

▶ With **dweud wrth** (*to tell*) and **gofyn i** (*to ask*):

Rhaid i ti ddweud wrtho fe   *You must tell him to go.*
  am fynd.   (not **i fynd**)
Gofynnwch iddi hi am wneud   *Ask her to do the work.*
  y gwaith.   (not **i wneud**)

ar

▶ With expressions of temporary physical or mental states:

Mae ofn arna i.   Mae annwyd arni hi.
I'm scared.   *She's got a cold.*

▶ In adverbial phrases such as:

ar goll	*lost*	ar gau	*closed*
ar werth	*for sale*	ar agor	*open*

▶ In the sense of *about to* when followed by a verb-noun:

Gwell i ni frysio, mae'r trên ar fynd.	*We'd better hurry, the train is about to go.*

▶ After a large selection of verbs such as:

achwyn ar	*to complain*	edrych ar	*to look at*
gweiddi ar	*to shout at*	syllu ar	*to stare at*
gwrando ar	*to listen to*	sylwi ar	*to notice*
blino ar	*to tire of*	ymosod ar	*to attack*

▶ With certain idioms:

cymryd ar	*to pretend*	lladd ar	*to condemn*

Faint sydd arna i i chi?	*How much do I owe you?*
Does dim dal arnyn nhw.	*One can not depend on them.*

Insight

The verb **eisiau** meaning *to want* follows the verb *to be* without the link word **yn**:

Mae e eisiau mwy o amser.	*He wants more time.*

It is followed by the preposition **ar** when referring to *need* as opposed to *want*.

Mae eisiau mwy o amser arno fe.	*He needs more time.*

at

▶ After certain nouns and adjectives:

agos at	*near to*	cariad at	*love for*
apêl at	*appeal to*		

▶ After some verbs such as:

anelu at	*to aim at*	synnu at	*to be surprised at*
apelio at	*to appeal to*	troi at	*to turn to*
nesáu at	*to approach*	rhoi at	*to give towards*
ychwanegu at	*to add to*		

at is also used when writing, sending or going to a person whereas **i** is used with places and institutions.

Dw i wedi ysgrifennu at John. Roedd e wedi ysgrifennu i'r Wasg.
I've written to John. *He had written to the Press.*
Mae e wedi anfon neges ati hi. Wyt ti wedi anfon llythyr i'r Cyngor?
He's sent her a message. *Have you sent a letter to the Council?*

Rhaid i fi fynd at y meddyg Rhaid iddo fe fynd i'r feddygfa.
I must go to the doctor. *He must go to the surgery.*

▶ In the sense of *for the purpose of*:
   At beth mae'r offer yna? *What are those tools for?*

▶ In a variety of phrases and idioms such as:

at ei gilydd	*on the whole*	at ddant	*to the taste of*
at hynny	*in addition to that*	ac ati	*and so forth*
dal ati	*to persevere*	mynd ati	*to set about*
dod at ei goed	*to come to his senses*	tynnu at ei gilydd	*to pull together*

Daliwch ati, dyw dysgu gramadeg *Keep at it, learning*
   ac ati ddim at ddant pawb! *grammar and so forth*
   isn't to everyone's liking!

dan

▶ When referring to a specific place **dan** is frequently preceded by **o**:
   o dan y ddesg *under the table*

▶ In the sense of *while* when used with a verb-noun:
   Bwytodd hi ei brecwast dan *She ate her breakfast while*
   wisgo. *dressing.*

▶ In expressions such as:

dan bwysau	*under pressure*	dan deimlad	*under emotion*
dan ei sang	*full to bursting (places)*	dan din	*underhand*
dan sylw	*in question*	dan y lach	*heavily criticized*

dros

▶ After a few nouns including:

esgus dros	*excuse for*	rheswm dros	*reason for*

▶ After certain verbs such as:

ateb dros	*to answer for*	chwarae dros	*to play for*
dadlau dros	*to argue for*	siarad dros	*to speak for*
gwylio dros	*to watch over*	edrych dros	*to look over*
wylo dros	*to cry over*	pleidleisio dros	*to vote for*

▶ In certain expressions:

dros ben llestri	*over the top*	dros ben	*exceedingly*
dros amser	*over time*	dros ei ben a'i glustiau	*head over heels*
drosodd a throsodd	*again and again*	dros dro	*temporarily*

er

▶ In the sense of *in order to*:

Es i i Gaerfyrddin er prynu siaced newydd.	*I went to Carmarthen in order to buy a new jacket.*

▶ With the meaning *despite* or *though*:

Er y tywydd garw, aeth y gêm yn ei blaen.	*Despite the rough weather, the game went on.*

▶ With the meaning *since* before a word or phrase denoting a specific point in time or a complete period of time:

Dyn nhw ddim wedi byw yno er 1996.	*They haven't lived there since 1996.*

Insight

As noted in Unit 15, **ers** is used in front of an unspecific time.

Maen nhw wedi byw yma ers blynyddoedd.	*They've lived here for years.*

Ers is frequently used incorrectly in place of **er**.

▶ In a range of expressions such as:

er cof	*in memory of*	er gwaethaf	*despite / in spite of*
er hynny	*despite that*	er mwyn	*for the sake of*
er lles	*for the benefit of*	er cyn cof	*since time immemorial*
ers talwm	*a long time ago*	ers tro	*for a long time*

gan

▶ To denote possession in North Wales (c/f **gyda** in South Wales):

Mae ganddi lawer o bres.   *She has a lot of money.*

▶ With the meaning of *by* in passive sentences:

Adeiladawyd y tŷ gan   *The house was built by*
Owen Burt.   *Owen Burt.*

▶ With an adjective to denote feeling (c/f **gyda**):

Mae'n dda gynnon ni glywed   *We're pleased to hear of your*
am eich apwyntiad chi.   *appointment.*
Roedd yn flin gen i glywed   *I was sorry to hear of your*
am dy ddamwain di.   *accident.*

▶ With the meaning of *from* or *off* when something has been given or handed over from one person to another (c/f **gyda**):

Ces i lawer o hen lyfrau   *I got a lot of old books from*
gynnon nhw.   *them.*

▶ Sometimes with verb-nouns **gan** can imply simultaneous action:

Rhedon nhw i lawr y stryd gan   *They ran down the street*
weiddi'n uchel.   *shouting loudly.*

▶ With a verb-noun it can also mean *because*:

Gan fod amser yn brin, dw i   *As time is short, I want to*
eisiau ceisio darllen yr erthygl   *try and read the article*
heno.   *tonight.*

▶ In a selection of expressions such as:

gan amlaf   *usually*   gan mwyaf   *mostly*
gan bwyll   *steadily*

▶ When referring to illnesses which refer to a particular part of the body (c/f **gyda**):

Mae gen i ben tost ofnadwy.   *I've got an awful headache.*

heb

▶ After the verb **bod** and in front of a verb-noun as an alternative negative construction equivalent to **ddim wedi**.

Mae e heb fynd eto. / Dyw e   *He hasn't gone yet.*
  ddim wedi mynd eto.

▶ In a variety of expressions such as:

heb amheuaeth   *without a doubt*
heb ei ail   *second to none*
heb flewyn ar ei dafod   *bluntly*
heb yn wybod   *without knowing*
yn amlach na heb   *more often than not*

hyd

▶ In many expressions, although it is not necessarily a preposition in all cases:

cael hyd i   *to find*
dod o hyd i   *to find*
o hyd   *still*
hyd y gwn i   *as far as I know*
ar hyd y lle   *all over the place*
hyd y gwela i   *as far as I can see*
hyd yn oed   *even*
hyd yn hyn   *up until now*
o hyd ac o hyd   *constantly*

i

▶ After a number of verbs-nouns to complete the meaning:

a In front of another verb-noun

llwyddo i   *to succeed*   tueddu i   *to tend to*
cytuno i   *to agree to*   dal i   *to continue to*

| Dw i wedi cytuno i wneud awr arall o waith cyn mynd. | *I've agreed to do another hour's work before going.* |

Insight

When learning the above verb-nouns, take particular note of the **i** needed to complete the meaning, as many verbs are followed immediately by another verb-noun without the intervening **i**. These include:

anghofio	*to forget*	bwriadu	*to intend*
casáu	*to hate*	gobeithio	*to hope*
dechrau	*to begin*	dysgu	*to teach*
hoffi	*to like*	gwrthod	*to refuse*

b In front of an object

addo i (rywun)	*to promise (someone)*
anfon i (rywle)	*to send to (somewhere)*
gadael i (rywun)	*to allow (someone)*
aros i (rywun)	*to wait for (someone)*
gofyn i (rywun)	*to ask (someone)*
ysgrifennu i (rywle)	*to write (somewhere)*
maddau i (rywun)	*to forgive (someone)*

| Ydy hi wedi gofyn iddo fe am y trip i Sir Benfro? | *Has she asked him about the trip to Pembrokeshire?* |
| Dyw hi ddim wedi maddau iddyn nhw eto. | *She hasn't forgiven them yet.* |

▶ To denote purpose:

| Aethon ni yno i weld yr adfeilion. | *We went there in order to see the ruins.* |

▶ In reason conjunctions (see Unit 11) after the prepositions **am** (*as*), **gan** (*as*), **oherwydd** (*because*), **achos** (*because*) with the verb-noun in the past tense:

| Ffoniodd e ei rieni fe oherwydd iddo fe golli'r bws adref. | *He phoned his parents because he missed the bus home.* |

▶ After an adjective to introduce a noun / pronoun and a verb:

Mae'n anodd iddyn nhw *It's difficult for them to*
anghofio beth ddigwyddodd. *forget what happened.*

▶ When an adjective is followed directly by a verb-noun however, no **i** is necessary:

Mae'n hawdd bwyta gormod *It's easy to eat too much in*
mewn lle fel hwn. *a place like this.*

▶ In front of a noun or pronoun after some other prepositions in time conjunctions (see Unit 11):

Dylet ti lofnodi hwn cyn i ti *You should sign this before*
fynd. *you go.*
Ar ôl i'r saer orffen hwn bydd *After the carpenter has*
e'n mynd ar ei wyliau. *finished this he will be*
going on his holidays.

▶ In front of a noun or pronoun in some phrases such as:

angen i	*need to*	rhaid i	*must*
eisiau i	*need to*	pryd i	*time to*
gwell i	*better*	cystal i	*might as well*

Rhaid i ti weithio'n galetach! *You must work harder!*

In the present tense affirmative, **mae / mae'n** can be placed in front of the above. **Yn** is never placed before **eisiau** or **angen**. **Eisiau, angen** and **rhaid** are indefinite and **oes** is used in questions and **does dim** in the negative in the present tense.

Mae eisiau iddo fe wrando *He needs to listen to them*
arnyn nhw eto. *again.*
Does dim angen i ni alw yna *We don't need to call there*
eleni. *this year.*

Ydy and **dyw** are used with the other phrases cited above:

Dyw hi ddim yn bryd iddo fe *It's not time for him to*
alw eto. *call yet.*

Note that the verb-noun always mutates in such constructions even if a noun, which is itself mutated, is placed before it.

Ydy hi'n well i bobl wybod?   *Is it better for people to know?*

▶ To introduce a noun-clause (*that*) in the past tense (see Unit 10):

Dywedodd hi iddi holi ei thad yn   *She said that she asked her father first.*
  gyntaf.

▶ In certain expressions:

i ffwrdd	*away*	i fyny	*up*
i mewn i	*into*	i lawr	*down*
i'r dim	*perfectly*	i'r gad	*into battle*

i'r carn	*through and through*
mynd i'r afael â	*to get to grips with*
Mae'n Gymro i'r carn.	*He's a true Welshman.*

mewn

▶ In front of indefinite nouns and **rhyw** (*some*), **rhai** (*some / a few*), **peth** (*some*), **sawl** (*several*), **ambell** (*a few*). If the last element of the expression is definite then **yn** is used:

Doedd dim llawer o wybodaeth   *There wasn't much information in some of them.*
  yn rhai ohonyn nhw.

▶ In expressions such as:

mewn gobaith	*in hope*	mewn brys	*in a hurry*
mewn cariad	*in love*	mewn pryd	*on time*
mewn gair	*briefly*	mewn cawl	*in a mess*
mewn gwirionedd	*in fact*	mewn golwg	*planned*

o

▶ Between a word denoting number, size or quality and a noun:

deg o blant   *ten children*   llawer o waith   *a lot of work*

▶ To denote a division or part of something bigger:

y rhan gyntaf o'r traethawd	*the first part of the essay*
y gorau ohonyn nhw	*the best of them*

▶ One exception however is the word **gweddill** (*rest / remainder*).

Mae gweddill y plant yn cysgu.	*The rest of the children are sleeping.*

▶ With verb-nouns occasionally:

O ystyried y tywydd garw roedd nifer dda yno.	*Considering the bad weather there was a good number there.*
Mae prisiau tai'n uchel yma o'u cymharu â rhannau eraill o Gymru.	*House prices are high here compared to other parts of Wales.*

(**o'u** as referring to a plural noun).

▶ After some words to complete the meaning:

cyhuddo o	*to accuse of*	balch o	*to be proud of / to*
euog o	*guilty of*	teilwng o	*to be worthy of*
tueddol o	*tending to*	siŵr o	*sure of*
dod o	*to come from*	hoff o	*to be fond of*

▶ Between two nouns or between an adjective and a noun where the descriptive element comes first:

tipyn o ganwr	*quite a singer*
cawr o ddyn	*a giant of a man*

▶ Between two nouns when the second describes the first:

dysgwr o oedolyn	*an adult learner*

▶ In a wide range of expressions such as:

diolch o galon	*many thanks*	o bryd i'w gilydd	*from time to time*
o dipyn i beth	*gradually*	o ganlyniad	*as a result of*

o bell ffordd	*by a long way*	o ddifrif	*seriously*
o fwriad	*intentionally*	o leiaf	*at least*
o blaid	*in favour of*	o raid	*out of necessity*
o'i le	*out of place*	o ran	*with regards to*
o'i wirfodd	*voluntarily*	o'r diwedd	*at last*
pleser o'r mwyaf	*great pleasure*	o'r gorau	*all right*
y byd sydd ohoni	*the world as it is*		

Insight

Note particularly the idiomatic expression **o ganlyniad**.
A common error is to translate *as a result of* literally as **fel canlyniad.**

---

rhag

▶ After certain verbs to express defence or escape from something:

achub rhag	*to save from*	amddiffyn rhag	*to defend against*
cuddio rhag	*to hide from*	gwared rhag	*to save from*
cadw rhag	*to keep from*	dianc rhag	*to escape from*
diogelu rhag	*to safeguard from*	ffoi rhag	*to flee from*

▶ As part of the conditional conjunction **rhag ofn** (see Unit 11):

Ffoniwch heno rhag ofn i mi anghofio. *Telephone tonight in case I forget.*

▶ In a small number of expressions such as:

Rhag dy gywilydd di! *Shame on you!*

wrth

▶ After a variety of verbs such as:

dweud wrth	*to tell*	adrodd wrth	*to relate to*
glynu wrth	*to stick to*	cenfigennu wrth	*to be jealous of*
digio wrth	*to be angry with*	cyfaddef wrth	*to admit to*

▶ After a selection of adjectives such as:

caredig wrth	*kind to*	cas wrth	*nasty to*
creulon wrth	*cruel to*	tyner wrth	*gentle to*

▶ **Wrth** and **wrth + i** together with a verb-noun are used in time conjunctions to mean *as* or *while* (see Unit 11).

Clywodd hi am y ddamwain ar y radio wrth yrru i'r ysgol.	*She heard about the accident on the radio while driving to school.*
Wrth iddo fe ysgrifennu'r nodyn dechreuodd ei law e grynu.	*As he wrote the letter his hand began to shake.*

▶ With **oddi** to mean from a person as opposed to **o** which is from a place.

Gest ti'r neges oddi wrth Tom?	*Did you get the message from Tom?*

▶ In a selection of expressions such as:

mae e wrthi (+ **yn** + verb-noun)   *he's busy (doing something)*

mae rhaid wrth	*there is need for*	wrth reswm	*obviously*
wrth fy modd	*in my element*	wrth y llyw	*at the helm*
wrth gefn	*in reserve*	wrth law	*to hand*

yn

▶ Before definite nouns and pronouns:

yn y dosbarth	*in the classroom*
yng Nghaerdydd	*in Cardiff*
yn ein barn ni	*in our opinion*

Definite nouns include **angau** (*death*), **paradwys** (*paradise*), **uffern** (*hell*) and **tragwyddoldeb** (*eternity*). **Yng ngharchar** means *in jail* whereas **mewn carchar** is *in a jail*.

▶ With a small number of verbs such as:

arbenigo yn	*to specialize in*
cydio yn	*to grasp*
gafael yn	*to grasp*
credu yn	*to believe in*
ymddiddori yn	*to be interested in*
ymddiried yn	*to trust*

▶ In combination with a small number of adjectives to make one word:

ymhell   *distant*   ynghynt   *quicker*   ynghlwm   *tied*

▶ In a variety of expressions:

yn y bôn	*basically*
yn llawn dop	*full to the brim*
yn fy myw	*for the life of me*
yn sgil	*as a result of*
yn y pen draw	*ultimately*
yn llygaid ei le	*spot on*

▶ Note that the preposition **yn** meaning *in*, unlike the particle **yn**, can not be shortened to **'n** after a vowel.

Mae Sara'n byw yn y dref.   *Sara lives in town.*

NOT

Mae Sara'n byw'n y dref.

Exercises

A Match the English and Welsh verbs and decide which preposition follows each one in Welsh.

1	to believe in	**a**	cuddio + ?
2	to tell	**b**	anelu + ?
3	to play for	**c**	balch + ?
4	to shout at	**d**	pleidleisio + ?
5	to be angry with	**e**	credu + ?
6	to agree to	**f**	chwarae + ?
7	to vote for	**g**	dweud + ?
8	to aim at	**h**	gweiddi + ?
9	to be proud of	**i**	cytuno + ?
10	to hide from	**j**	digio + ?

B Fill the gaps in the sentences below with the correct idiomatic expressions:

wrth y llyw, o ganlyniad, heb yn wybod, i'r dim, wrth eu bodd, o'i wirfodd, yn llygaid ei lle, cael hyd iddo

1 Gadawodd e'r swydd ....
2 .... i'r ddamwain aeth hi fyth yn ôl.
3 Roedd hi'n deall fy mhroblemau ....
4 Mae llwyddiant yr ysgol yn dibynnu pwy fydd ....
5 Penderfynais i fynd i Lundain i geisio ....
6 Roedd y plant .... yn cael diwrnod arall o wyliau.
7 Yn fy marn i, roedd Elen .... yn yr hyn a ddywedodd.
8 .... i'w fam aeth i lawr i'r siop i brynu losin.

Grammar in context

Two adverts, two mistakes – one in each. Can you correct them?

Test yourself

Translate the following paragraph.

> In the supermarket in town last night I met a girl called Carys who was in my class in school. She started talking to me by the fruit stall and I couldn't get away from her. She went on and on! I told her that I had to go, but she wasn't willing to listen to me. She was visiting her mother for the weekend. Carys lives in Cardiff now and she asked me to send her an email if I decide to go shopping there sometime. I agreed in order to get rid of her. I don't want to be nasty to her, but it's possible that I will have to lose her address... I hope that she'll forgive me!

17

The verb *to be* – present and perfect tenses

In this unit you will learn:

- *How to form and use the present tense of* bod, *the verb to be in Welsh*
- *How to form and use the perfect tense of* bod
- *How to use the adjective* newydd *to mean* just *in the sense of* just happened.

Grammar in focus

Present tense (is / are)

The present tense is used to state what is happening and what is going to happen.

Dw i'n gwylio'r teledu.　　　*I am watching television.*
Mae e'n mynd i Landeilo yfory.　*He's going to Llandeilo*
　　　　　　　　　　　　　　tomorrow.

In English there are three ways of expressing the present tense, i.e. *I watch, I am watching, I do watch*. In Welsh all three can be expressed as **dw i'n gwylio**. This is known as the periphrastic or long form in which various forms of **bod**, the verb *to be*, are combined with verb-nouns or adjectives by means of the link-word **yn**. A verb-noun describes an action, but does not tell you who is doing the action or when it occurred. **Yn** sometimes corresponds to **ing** in English and after a vowel is reduced to **'n**.

Dyn ni'n deall.	*We understand.*
Mae hi'n gweithio.	*She is working.*
Maen nhw'n hapus.	*They are happy.*

Notice the word order of a basic Welsh sentence – the verb generally comes first in Welsh.

verb	subject	yn	verb-noun / adjective	meaning
Mae	John	yn	araf	*John is slow*
Rwyt	ti	'n	gwybod	*You know*

The subject is the person who does the action. The object is the target of the action.

Mae'r ferch yn darllen y llyfr.   *The girl is reading the book.*
The girl is the subject. The book is the object.

Perfect tense (has / have)

The perfect tense is used to note that an action has happened or finished. **Yn**, which links the present tense form of **bod** and the verb-noun, is replaced by **wedi**.

Mae'r ferch **wedi** darllen y llyfr.	*The girl <u>has</u> read the book.*
Ydy'r ferch **wedi** darllen y llyfr?	*<u>Has</u> the girl read the book?*
Dyw'r ferch **ddim wedi** darllen y llyfr.	*The girl <u>has not</u> read the book.*

Wedi bod yn can be used with the present tense and a verb-noun or adjective to convey the meaning *has been*.

Ydy'r babi wedi bod yn crio?   *Has the baby been crying?*

Just

To say that something has just happened the adjective **newydd** is used in place of **wedi**.

| Mae'r ferch newydd ddarllen y llyfr. | *The girl has just read the book.* |

Do note also that **newydd** causes the word it describes to mutate softly.

| Dw i newydd orffen y gwaith. | *I have just finished the work.* |

Newydd fod translates as *just been*.

| Ydy'r plant newydd fod i'r sinema? | *Have the children just been to the cinema?* |

Present tense affirmative forms

dw i'n dysgu Cymraeg	*I am learning / I learn Welsh*
rwyt ti'n dysgu Cymraeg	*you are learning / you learn Welsh*
mae e / o'n dysgu Cymraeg	*he is learning / he learns Welsh*
mae hi'n dysgu Cymraeg	*she is learning / she learns Welsh*
mae Sioned yn dysgu Cymraeg	*Sioned is learning / Sioned learns Welsh*
mae'r teulu yn dysgu Cymraeg	*the family are learning / the family learn Welsh*
dyn ni'n dysgu Cymraeg	*we are learning / we learn Welsh*
dych chi'n dysgu Cymraeg	*you are learning / you learn Welsh*
maen nhw'n dysgu Cymraeg	*they are learning / they learn Welsh*

FORMAL WRITTEN AFFIRMATIVE

While there are many spoken variations of the verbal forms, there are also standardized literary forms which can be traced back to 1588, to the translation of the Bible by William Morgan. These forms are used when writing a formal essay or letter and will be given alongside their more informal equivalents in the following units on Welsh verbs.

yr ydwyf	*I am*	yr ydym	*we are*
yr wyt	*you are*	yr ydych	*you are*
y mae	*he / she is*	y maent	*they are*

The formal auxiliary pronouns (see Unit 8) are not generally included with the literary written forms of the verb in any tense except when required for emphasis.

Y maent **hwy** yn yfed gormod.   *They are drinking too much.*

Interrogative forms

ydw i'n dod?	*am I coming?*
wyt ti'n dod?	*are you coming?*
ydy e / o'n dod?	*is he coming?*
ydy hi'n dod?	*is she coming?*
ydy Gareth yn dod?	*is Gareth coming?*
ydy'r plant yn dod?	*are the children coming?*
dyn ni'n dod?	*are we coming?*
dych chi'n dod?	*are you coming?*
dyn nhw'n dod?	*are they coming?*

a ydwyf?	*am I?*	a ydym?	*are we?*
a wyt?	*are you?*	a ydych?	*are you?*
a yw / a ydyw?	*is he / she?*	a ydynt?	*are they?*

Note the inclusion of **a** before the verb at the start of a normal question in all tenses.

| A ydym yn rhydd i fynd? | *Are we free to go?* |

Negative forms

dw i ddim yn ysmygu	*I am not smoking / do not smoke*
dwyt ti ddim yn ysmygu	*you are not smoking / do not smoke*
dyw e / o ddim yn ysmygu	*he is not smoking / does not smoke*
dyw hi ddim yn ysmygu	*she is not smoking / does not smoke*
dyw'r ferch ddim yn ysmygu	*the girl is not smoking / does not smoke*
dyw'r bechgyn ddim yn ysmygu	*the boys are not smoking / do not smoke*
dyn ni ddim yn ysmygu	*we are not smoking / do not smoke*
dych chi ddim yn ysmygu	*you are not smoking / do not smoke*
dyn nhw ddim yn ysmygu	*they are not smoking / do not smoke*

Insight

A common mistake among early stage learners is to use **mae +
ddim** in the negative:

| Mae hi ddim yn y parti heno. | *She isn't at the party tonight.* |

rather than:

Dyw hi ddim yn y parti heno.

Note that **yn** is not needed before **ddim**.

FORMAL WRITTEN NEGATIVE

nid wyf	*I am not / do not*	nid ydym	*we are not / do not*
nid wyt	*you are not / do not*	nid ydych	*you are not / do not*
nid yw /	*he / she is not / does*	nid ydynt	*they are not / do not*
nid ydyw	*not*		

Answer forms

There is no one word for *yes* or *no* in Welsh. A question is
answered by mirroring the verb form used to ask the question.
Affirmative replies are sometimes repeated for emphasis.

Affirmative

ydw	*yes, I am / do*	ydyn	*yes, we are / do*
wyt	*yes, you are / do*	ydych	*yes, you are / do*
ydy	*yes, he / she / it is / does*	ydyn	*yes, they are / do*

Negative

nac ydw	*no, I am not / do not*	nac ydyn	*no, we are not / do not*
nac wyt	*no, you are not / do not*	nac ydych	*no, you are not / do not*
nac ydy	*no, he / she / it is not / does not*	nac ydyn	*no, they are not / do not*

Ydy e'n iawn?	Ydy, mae e'n iawn.
Is he all right?	*Yes, he's all right.*
Ydyn nhw'n fodlon aros amdanon ni?	Nac ydyn, dyn nhw ddim yn fodlon.
Are they willing to wait for us?	*No, they aren't willing.*
Ydy'r merched yn barod?	Nac ydyn, dyn nhw ddim yn barod.
Are the girls ready?	*No, they aren't ready.*
Ydy'r cwpan gyda chi?	Ydy, mae'r cwpan gyda fi.
Have you got the cup?	*Yes, I've got the cup.*

The same rules apply when giving a perfect meaning (*has / have*) to
a verb in the present tense, by replacing **yn** with **wedi**.

Ydy Frances wedi clywed?	Ydy, ydy, mae hi wedi clywed.
Has Frances heard?	*Yes, yes, she's heard.*

While **ydy** is used with definite nouns or pronouns, **oes** is placed in front of questions containing indefinite nouns.

Note the negative form **does dim** (*there is not / there are not*) which in spoken Welsh is often shortened to **'sdim**. Both are an abbreviation of the formal written form **nid oes**.

Oes arian gyda dy frawd?	Nac oes, does dim arian gyda fe.
Has your brother got money?	*No, he's got no money.*
Oes car gyda nhw?	Nac oes, 'sdim car gyda nhw.
Have they got a car?	*No, they haven't got a car.*

No-one can be translated as **does neb**.

Oes rhywun yn byw yn y tŷ?	Nac oes, does neb yn byw yn y tŷ.
Is there someone living in the house?	*No, there is no-one living in the house.*

Identification sentences

When identifying someone or something, the natural word order of the sentence in Welsh is changed – that which is being emphasized or identified is always placed first.

Pwy dych chi?	<u>Tomos</u> dw i.
Who are you?	*I am <u>Thomas</u>.*
Beth ydy e?	<u>Eliffant</u> ydy e.
What is it?	*It's an <u>elephant</u>.*

Affirmative forms
Christine dw i	*I am Christine*
Marged wyt ti	*you are Margaret*
Dylan yw / ydy e / o	*he is Dylan*
Rhian yw / ydy hi	*she is Rhian*
Cymry dyn ni	*we are Welsh people*
athrawon dych chi	*you are teachers*
myfyrwyr dyn nhw	*they are students*

FORMAL WRITTEN FORMS
Christine ydwyf i	Cymry ydym ni
Marged wyt ti	athrawon ydych chwi
Dylan yw / ydyw ef	myfyrwyr ydynt hwy
Rhian yw / ydyw hi	

Interrogative forms
In speech, these are the same as the affirmative – the only change being in the tone of your voice. Sometimes in South Wales **ife** is placed in front of the noun. In the formal written language this is replaced by **ai**.

Athro dych chi?	*Are you a teacher?*
Hi yw'r orau?	*Is she the best?*
Ife Ifan ydy e?	*Is it Ifan?*
Ai Martin yw'r beirniad?	*Is it Martin who is the judge?*

Negative forms

In such identification sentences *not* is expressed by placing **nid** at the beginning of the sentence.

nid Elin dw i	*I am not Elin*
nid meddyg wyt ti	*you are not a doctor*
nid fe yw / ydy'r cyntaf	*he's not the first*
nid hi yw / ydy'r olaf	*she's not the last*
nid dysgwyr dyn ni	*we are not learners*
nid artistiaid dych chi	*you are not artists*
nid plant Mr a Mrs Jones dyn nhw	*they are not Mr and Mrs Jones's children*

The formal written negative is expressed in a similar manner.

Nid plentyn ydwyf.	*I'm not a child.*
Nid dysgwyr ydynt.	*They're not learners.*

Answer forms

The answer forms to questions which do not begin with a verb are **ie** (*yes*) and **nage** (*no*).

Owen dych chi?	Ie, Owen dw i.
Are you Owen?	*Yes, I'm Owen.*
Mam Rhys dych chi?	Nage, nid mam Rhys dw i.
Are you Rhys's mum?	*No, I'm not Rhys's mum.*

Exercises

A Change the following sentences from the affirmative or interrogative to the negative.

1 Ydy'r plant yn gallu cofio?
2 Mae llawer o arian gyda fi.
3 Maen nhw eisiau symud.
4 Dw i'n darllen llyfr bob wythnos.

5 Oes lluniau o'r ysgol gyda ni?

6 Ie, postmon ydy tad Sue.

B Choose the correct present tense form of the verb **bod** to place in the following sentences.

1 .... nhw yn aros yn y Castell?

2 .... ni ddim yn hapus iawn.

3 .... dim gobaith gyda ni.

4 .... hi ddim yn hoffi darllen.

5 .... ti'n gwybod yr ateb?

6 Athrawes .... i.

7 .... amlen gyda dy fam?

8 ....'r plant yn chwarae pêl-droed heno?

9 Ffermwyr .... nhw?

10 .... chi'n gallu bwyta yn yr ardd?

C Change the following sentences from the present to the perfect tense and translate the new sentences into English.

1 Mae fy mam yn golchi'r dillad y bore 'ma.

2 Maen nhw'n mynd i'r coleg yn Llambed.

3 Wyt ti'n deall y neges?

4 Dych chi ddim yn gwneud digon o arian yn anffodus.

5 Dw i'n rhoi'r lluniau ar y wal.

6 Dyn nhw'n cael brecwast?

_____

Grammar in context

Having studied the family tree below answer the following questions in Welsh. Obviously, in the case of questions 1 and 2, more than one answer is possible – try to think of as many as you can!

1 Pwy yw Elin?

2 Pwy yw Gruff?

3 Pwy yw brawd Angharad?

4 Pwy yw cyfnither Olivia?

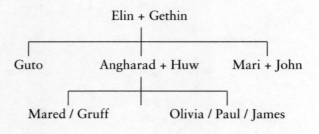

Elin + Gethin

Guto   Angharad + Huw   Mari + John

Mared / Gruff   Olivia / Paul / James

Test yourself

Translate the following sentences into Welsh

1 Have the teachers been to see the new school?
2 She isn't feeling very well.
3 The children are learning Spanish for the first time this term.
4 Have you got time to go to the supermarket?
5 I've just finished painting the living room.
6 They are singing in the concert next week.
7 No, we haven't heard from him yet.
8 Yes, I'm Teleri, Lowri's mother.
9 No-one wants to go on holiday there.
10 I am not the only one who hopes to retire soon.

18

The verb *to be* – future and past tenses

In this unit you will learn:
- *The formation and usage of the future tense of* bod
- *The formation and usage of the past tense of* bod

Grammar in focus

Future tense (will)

The rules regarding the usage of the future tense of the verb *to be* are similar to those for the present tense (see Unit 17). The future tense is used to describe something that is going to happen. It can also be used in place of the present tense to convey the fact that something occurs regularly.

Bydd e yn y gwaith yfory.
He will be at work tomorrow.

Byddan nhw'n cael tost i frecwast bob bore.
They have toast for breakfast every morning.

Once again **wedi** can be used to convey the English meaning *will have* and **wedi bod** *will have been*.

Bydda i wedi paratoi popeth cyn i chi ddod.	*I will have prepared everything before you come.*
Fyddan nhw ddim wedi bod yno yn ddigon hir.	*They won't have been there long enough.*

Past tense (was / has / have been)

The past tense is used to refer to an action that occurred once in the past, but has now been completed. For example, being in or visiting a particular place, becoming ill or behaving in a particular way.

Bues i yn Llanymddyfri ddoe.	*I was in Llandovery yesterday.* (but I'm not there today)
Buon ni'n dost yn y cwch.	*We were ill in the boat.* (but we are fine now)
Buodd e'n siomedig.	*He was disappointed.* (but he has got over it now)

It also occurs in certain idioms such as **bu farw** (*died*). Notice that the verb-noun **marw** is not preceded by **yn** and is always mutated.

Insight

Notice that the verb-noun **marw** is itself never conjugated. **Marwodd hi,** etc. is incorrect.

Pryd bu farw dy fam?	*When did your mother die?*
Bu farw yn dri deg naw oed.	*She died aged thirty-nine.*

Future tense affirmative forms

bydda i'n canu	*I will be singing*
byddi di'n canu	*you will be singing*
bydd e / o'n canu	*he will be singing*
bydd hi'n canu	*she will be singing*
bydd yr actor yn canu	*the actor will be singing*
bydd y côr yn canu	*the choir will be singing*
byddwn ni'n canu	*we will be singing*
byddwch chi'n canu	*you will be singing*
byddan nhw'n canu	*they will be singing*

Formal written affirmative

byddaf	*I will*	byddwn	*we will*
byddi	*you will*	byddwch	*you will*
bydd	*he / she will*	byddant	*they will*

Interrogative forms

fydda i'n gallu mynd?	*will I be able to go?*
fyddi di'n gallu mynd?	*will you be able to go?*
fydd e / o'n gallu mynd?	*will he be able to go?*
fydd hi'n gallu mynd?	*will she be able to go?*
fydd yr athro'n gallu mynd?	*will the teacher be able to go?*
fydd yr aelodau'n gallu mynd?	*will the members be able to go?*
fyddwn ni'n gallu mynd?	*will we be able to go?*
fyddwch chi'n gallu mynd?	*will you be able to go?*
fyddan nhw'n gallu mynd?	*will they be able to go?*

Note the soft mutation at the start of the interrogative form every time.

The verb forms are also mutated when following the interrogative pronouns **pwy?** (*who?*) and **beth?** (*what?*).

Pwy **fydd** yn ennill y Cwpan?	*Who will win the Cup?*
Beth **fydd** y wobr?	*What will the prize be?*

Formal written interrogative

a fyddaf?	*will I?*	a fyddwn?	*will we?*
a fyddi?	*will you?*	a fyddwch?	*will you?*
a fydd?	*will he / she?*	a fyddant?	*will they?*

Negative forms

fydda i ddim yn dawnsio	*I will not be dancing*
fyddi di ddim yn dawnsio	*you will not be dancing*
fydd e / o ddim yn dawnsio	*he will not be dancing*
fydd hi ddim yn dawnsio	*she will not be dancing*
fydd y plentyn ddim yn dawnsio	*the child will not be dancing*
fydd y plant ddim yn dawnsio	*the children will not be dancing*

fyddwn ni ddim yn dawnsio	*we will not be dancing*
fyddwch chi ddim yn dawnsio	*you will not be dancing*
fyddan nhw ddim yn dawnsio	*they will not be dancing*

> ## Insight
> Never forget the link word **yn**! If in doubt, include it. A
> common mistake is to forget to include it with a verb in the
> negative following **ddim** as in the examples above.

As in the interrogative, there is a soft mutation at the start of the
negative form every time. **Dim** is placed in front of indefinite nouns
as in the present tense negative.

| Fydd dim seddau ar ôl. | *There will be no seats left.* |
| Fydd dim amser gyda fi i alw. | *I will not have time to call.* |

Formal written negative

ni fyddaf	*I will not*	ni fyddwn	*we will not*
ni fyddi	*you will not*	ni fyddwch	*you will not*
ni fydd	*he / she will not*	ni fyddant	*they will not*

Answer forms

A question is generally answered by mirroring the form used to ask
the question, without soft mutation.

Affirmative

byddaf	*I will*	byddwn	*we will*
byddi	*you will*	byddwch	*you will*
bydd	*he / she / it will*	byddant	*they will*

Negative
Na is placed before the verb, followed by soft mutation.

na fyddaf	*I will not*	na fyddwn	*we will not*
na fyddi	*you will not*	na fyddwch	*you will not*
na fydd	*he / she / it will not*	na fyddant	*they will not*

Fyddan nhw yn y cyngerdd heno?   Byddan.
Will they be in the concert tonight?   *Yes (they will).*
Fydd e'n gallu galw amdana i?   Na fydd.
Will he be able to call for me?   *No (he will not).*

Past tense affirmative forms

bues i'n gweithio trwy'r bore   *I was working all morning*
buest ti'n gweithio trwy'r bore   *you were working all morning*
buodd e / o'n gweithio trwy'r bore   *he was working all morning*
buodd hi'n gweithio trwy'r bore   *she was working all morning*
buodd y dyn yn gweithio trwy'r bore   *the man was working all morning*
buodd y ffermwyr yn gweithio trwy'r bore   *the farmers were working all morning*
buon ni'n gweithio trwy'r bore   *we were working all morning*
buon chi'n gweithio trwy'r bore   *you were working all morning*
buon nhw'n gweithio trwy'r bore   *they were working all morning*

Formal written affirmative

bûm	*I was / have been*	buom	*we were / have been*
buest	*you were / have been*	buoch	*you were / have been*
bu	*he / she was / has been*	buont	*they were / have been*

Interrogative forms

Once again the forms are the same as the affirmative except that the initial consonant is mutated softly.

Fuest ti yn y disgo neithiwr?   *Were you at the disco last night?*
Fuodd y teulu'n byw yn Aberystwyth am gyfnod?   *Did the family live in Aberystwyth for a while?*

Formal written interrogative

a fûm?	*was I? / did I?*	a fuom?	*were we? / did we?*
a fuest?	*were you? / did you?*	a fuoch?	*were you? / did you?*
a fu?	*was he / she? did he / she?*	a fuont?	*were they? / did they?*

Negative forms

fues i ddim yn y parti ddoe	*I was not at the party yesterday*
fuest ti ddim yn y parti ddoe	*you were not at the party yesterday*
fuodd e / o ddim yn y parti ddoe	*he was not at the party yesterday*
fuodd hi ddim yn y parti ddoe	*she was not at the party yesterday*
fuodd Aled ddim yn y parti ddoe	*Aled was not at the party yesterday*
fuodd y lleill ddim yn y parti ddoe	*the others were not at the party yesterday*
fuon ni ddim yn y parti ddoe	*we were not at the party yesterday*
fuoch chi ddim yn y parti ddoe	*you were not at the party yesterday*
fuon nhw ddim yn y parti ddoe	*they were not at the party yesterday*

As in the interrogative, the first consonant is mutated softly. **Dim** is again placed in front of indefinite nouns as in the present and future tense negative.

Fuodd dim gobaith gyda ni o ennill.	*We had no hope of winning.*
Fuodd dim cyfle iddyn nhw holi.	*They had no chance to ask.*

Formal written negative

ni fûm	*I was not / have not been*	ni fuom	*we were not / have not been*
ni fuest	*you were not / have not been*	ni fuoch	*you were not / have not been*
ni fu	*he / she was not / had not been*	ni fuont	*they were not / have not been*

Answer forms

Answer forms in the past tense are straightforward – **do** (*yes*) and **naddo** (*no*) regardless of who is asking the question.

Fuodd e yn yr ysgol gyda chi?
Do, buodd e yn yr un
   dosbarth â fi.
Naddo, fuodd e ddim yr ysgol
   yn Llansadwrn.

Was he in school with you?
Yes, he was in the same
   class as me.
No, he wasn't in school in
   Llansadwrn,

Exercises

A Change the following sentences from the past tense to the future tense.
1 Bues i yn y gwaith ddoe.
2 Buon ni yn Llandudno dros yr haf.
3 Buodd e'n canu yn y côr ddydd Sul diwethaf.
4 Fuest ti yn y cyfarfod neithiwr?
5 Fuodd hi ddim yn aros yn y gwesty.
6 Fuon nhw ym mhriodas Elin y llynedd?

B Change the following sentences from the future to the past tense.
1 Bydda i'n unig iawn am ychydig hebddo fe.
2 Bydd y dosbarth yn ymweld â'r Llyfrgell Genedlaethol yr wythnos nesaf.
3 Fyddan nhw'n siomedig?
4 Fydd y Blaid Lafur ddim yno chwaith.
5 Byddwn ni'n siarad â'r heddlu eto yfory.
6 Byddi di'n dwp i wrando arno fe.

Grammar in context

Many festivals are held in Wales during the summer, including the Small Nations Festival, which is a new and growing festival that celebrates the music of small nations around the world. The following piece describes what will be happening in the activities tent.

Gorwelion Newydd

Yw enw'n pabell weithdai, ac yn unol â'r enw, byddwn yn cynnig nifer o ddigwyddiadau i ddysgwyr – manylion i ddilyn. Hefyd bydd dau ddigwyddiad dysgu gyda siaradwyr Cymraeg. Bydd faint byddan nhw'n defnyddio'r iaith yn dibynnu ar y rhai sy'n cymryd rhan – hint!

1 Why should Welsh learners visit this tent?
2 What is suggested or implied in the final sentence?

gorwelion	*horizons*
yn unol â	*in accordance with*

Test yourself

Translate the following sentences into Welsh using the future or past tense of **bod**.

1 I was very ill for two weeks.
2 He wasn't at all happy when he heard the news.
3 We will be calling for the present around ten o'clock.
4 She walks the dog every night after supper.

5 They were very kind to him when he was in hospital.

6 Will you be performing the drama again before the end of term? (*fam.*)

7 You will not have any money left before long.

8 We were not angry about it, just disappointed.

9 I learn about ten new Welsh words every night.

10 Was he in the army during the Second World War?

19

The verb *to be* – imperfect and pluperfect tenses

In this unit you will learn:
- *How to form and use the imperfect tense of* bod
- *How to form and use the pluperfect tense of* bod
- *How to use* ar *to mean* about to

Grammar in focus

Imperfect tense (was / were)

The imperfect tense is used to express a continuous or repeated action in the past. Unlike the past tense, completion is not specified. If the repetitive or continuous nature of the action needs to be emphasized then the verb-noun **arfer** (*to use*) occurs together with the imperfect forms. The imperfect is frequently used as description, especially for the background to a story or event that is being narrated.

Roeddwn i'n gwylio'r teledu.	*I was watching television.* (i.e. a continuous, relatively lengthy action)
Roedd y Ficer yno bob dydd Sul.	*The Vicar was there every Sunday.* (i.e a repeated action – not just one Sunday)
Roedden nhw'n arfer byw yn Ffrainc.	*They used to live in France.*

The imperfect, rather than the past tense, is also used with the following verb-nouns.

poeni	*to worry*	meddwl	*to think*
gwybod	*to know (a fact)*	deall	*to understand*
adnabod	*to know (a person)*	credu	*to believe*
hoffi	*to like*	perthyn	*to belong*
gobeithio	*to hope*		

Oeddech chi'n deall?   *Did you understand?*
Doedden nhw ddim yn hoffi cig.   *They didn't like meat.*

Pluperfect tense (had)

The pluperfect tense is used to convey that something happened before something else did. **Yn** which links the imperfect tense form of the verb *to be* and the verb-noun is replaced by **wedi**.

Roedden nhw wedi dysgu Cymraeg   *They had learnt Welsh before*
  cyn mynd i fyw yng Nghymru.   *going to live in Wales.*

As in the present and future, *just* can be conveyed by means of the adjective **newydd**.

Oeddech chi newydd gofio?   *Had you just remembered?*

Ar on the other hand can be used in place of **wedi** to say that something is or was going to happen.

Dw i ar fynd i'r gwaith.   *I am about to go to work.*
Roedd e ar fynd i'r coleg pan   *He was about to go to college*
  ganodd y ffôn.   *when the phone rang.*

Wedi bod yn can be used with the imperfect + a verb-noun to convey the meaning *had been*.

Roedden nhw wedi bod yn aros yn yr oriel am oriau.	*They had been waiting in the gallery for hours.*

Imperfect affirmative forms

roeddwn i'n gobeithio dod	*I was hoping to come*
roeddet ti'n gobeithio dod	*you were hoping to come*
roedd e / o'n gobeithio dod	*he was hoping to come*
roedd hi'n gobeithio dod	*she was hoping to come*
roedd Ann yn gobeithio dod	*Ann was hoping to come*
roedd y teulu'n gobeithio dod	*the family was hoping to come*
roedden ni'n gobeithio dod	*we were hoping to come*
roeddech chi'n gobeithio dod	*you were hoping to come*
roedden nhw'n gobeithio dod	*they were hoping to come*

In spoken Welsh, particularly in South Wales, the affirmative imperfect forms are sometimes shortened to:

ro'n i	*I was*		ro'n ni	*we were*
ro't ti	*you were*		ro'ch chi	*you were*
roedd e / o	*he was*		ro'n nhw	*they were*
roedd hi	*she was*			

Formal written affirmative

yr oeddwn	yr oeddem
yr oeddet	yr oeddech
yr oedd	yr oeddynt

Interrogative forms

The only difference between the interrogative and the affirmative forms is that **r** is dropped in the interrogative.

Oeddech chi'n gwybod yr ateb?	*Did you know the answer?*
Beth oedd e'n ei astudio?	*What was he studying?*

Once again in the spoken language the forms can be shortened.

O't ti yn y gwaith pan alwodd Rob? — *Were you at work when Rob called?*

Formal written interrogative

a oeddwn?	*was I?*	a oeddem?	*were we?*
a oeddet?	*were you?*	a oeddech?	*were you?*
a oedd?	*was he / she?*	a oeddynt?	*were they?*

Negative forms

doeddwn i ddim yno	*I was not there*
doeddet ti ddim yno	*you were not there*
doedd e / o ddim yno	*he was not there*
doedd hi ddim yno	*she was not there*
doedd y gath ddim yno	*the cat was not there*
doedd y myfyrwyr ddim yno	*the students were not there*
doedden ni ddim yno	*we were not there*
doeddech chi ddim yno	*you were not there*
doedden nhw ddim yno	*they were not there*

In spoken Welsh, the imperfect negative forms are sometimes shortened to:

do'n i ddim	*I was not*	do'n ni	*we were not*
do't ti ddim	*you were not*	do'ch chi	*you were not*
doedd e / o ddim	*he was not*	do'n nhw	*they were not*
doedd hi ddim	*she was not*		

Insight

Don't be put off by the fact that you will come across different forms of the verb *to be* in different courses and books. Frequently books for children will use the longer forms like **doeddwn i ddim** or **rydw i**, while courses for adults will choose **do'n i ddim** and **dw i**. Use what you feel comfortable with, focus on what you know. No single form is more acceptable than another in speech.

Formal written negative

nid oeddwn	nid oeddem
nid oeddet	nid oeddech
nid oedd	nid oeddynt

Answer forms

Affirmative

A question is once again generally answered by mirroring the form used to ask the question.

oeddwn	*yes, I was*	oedden	*yes, we were*
oeddet	*yes, you were*	oeddech	*yes, you were*
oedd	*yes, he / she / it was*	oedden	*yes, they were*

Negative

Nac is placed before the appropriate form of the verb.

nac oeddwn	*no, I was not*	nac oedden	*no, we were not*
nac oeddet	*no, you were not*	nac oeddech	*no, you were not*
nac oedd	*no, he / she / it was not*	nac oedden	*no, they were not*

Oedd y gwesty yn ddrud?   Oedd.
Was the hotel expensive?   *Yes (it was).*
Oeddech chi'n synnu?   Nac oeddwn.
Were you surprised?   *No (I was not).*

Exercises

A Match up the following questions with the appropriate answers.
1 Oedd John wedi bod yn dysgu? (✓)
2 Oedden nhw yn cysgu lan llofft? (✗)
3 Oeddech chi'n gwrando ar y radio? (✗)

4 Oedden ni'n iawn? (✓)

5 Oedd y plentyn wedi mynd? (✗)

6 Oeddwn i gartref pan ddigwyddodd hynny? (✓)

   a oedden

   b oedd

   c oeddech

   d nac oeddwn

   e nac oedd

   f nac oedden

B Fill in the gaps in the sentences below with either the past tense or imperfect tense of **bod**.

   1 .... hi'n stormus iawn dros y penwythnos.

   2 .... Sam yn helpu ei dad y bore 'ma?

   3 Beth .... chi'n gobeithio ei wneud?

   4 .... nhw .... yn arfer bod mor ddrwg.

   5 .... hi .... yn gofyn llawer o gwestiynau ar ôl y wers.

   6 .... chi'n arfer helpu yn y stablau yn Llangrannog?

   7 Pwy .... yn cynrychioli'r ysgol yn y mabolgampau ddydd Sadwrn?

   8 .... i'n byw yn Llambed am dair blynedd.

   9 .... nhw'n poeni am y canlyniadau?

  10 .... ti'n grac pan glywaist ti?

Grammar in context

The interview below with Welsh actress Siwan Morris has been adapted from the learners' magazine *Lingo Newydd*. Note the use of the informal forms of the imperfect tense in Siwan's replies.

Pryd roedd eich diwrnod gorau chi?
Y diwrnod pasiais i fy mhrawf gyrru! Ro'n i wedi trio ddwywaith o'r blaen. Pan basiais i, dechreuais i grio! Dywedais i, 'O diolch ... 'a dechreuodd fy llygaid i lenwi. Ro'n i'n reit emosiynol!

Dych chi wedi prynu car eto?
Ydw! Fiesta Gear ydy e ac mae e'n sionc iawn.

Sut bydd e'n newid eich bywyd chi?
Dw i wedi bod yn defnyddio trafnidiaeth cyhoeddus tan nawr. Mae trenau yn ffordd ddrud o fynd i Fanceinion neu Lundain i weld ffrindiau neu i weithio. Ac maen nhw'n gallu bod yn hwyr. Bydd mwy o ryddid gyda fi nawr.

Sut roeddech chi'n teimlo cyn y prawf?
Roedd hi wedi bod yn wythnos fawr yn y gwaith ac ro'n i wedi blino. Y diwrnod cyn y prawf dywedais i wrth fy hun, 'Dw i byth yn mynd i basio!' Ond erbyn y bore wedyn ro'n i'n meddwl yn bositif. Ro'n i'n poeni rhag ofn i fi wneud rhywbeth ffôl fel rhoi'r car yn y gêr anghywir.

1 Why did Siwan feel emotional?
2 Give two disadvantages of travelling by train.
3 Why was Siwan worried?

Test yourself

Translate the following sentences into Welsh.

1 They didn't like the food in the hotel.
2 Aled was the only one in the audience to complain.
3 It was very sunny last week.
4 The children weren't able to go.
5 Had they been there before?

6 I didn't know her when she was a child.
7 We were about to go when my mother's friend called.
8 Was her father hoping to get a job in the college?
9 I had just got home when I received your message.
10 They believed that Gordon Brown would win the election.

20

Regular verbs – present and future tenses

In this unit you will learn:
- **The formation and use of regular verbs in the short form present and future tenses**
- **The use of gwneud** *(to do / to make)* **as an auxiliary verb**

Grammar in focus

The short form is generally used when describing something that will happen in the near future.

Gofynna i iddo fe nawr.   *I will ask him now.*

The more distant future is generally expressed by means of the future tense of **bod** together with the appropriate verb-noun.

Byddaf i'n gofyn iddo fe eto   *I will ask him again before the*
  cyn y penwythnos.   *weekend.*

In the formal literary language the short forms are used to express the present as well as the future tense.

Darllenant am awr cyn swper.   *They read / will read for an hour*
    before supper.

Affirmative forms

dysga i	*I will learn*	dysgwn ni	*we will learn*
dysgi di	*you will learn*	dysgwch chi	*you will learn*
dysgith e / o / hi	*he / she will learn*	dysgan nhw	*they will learn*

The ending **–iff** rather than **–ith** in the 3rd person singular is also common in certain areas in South Wales.

Insight

Don't forget that as with **bod** all plural and collective nouns take the third person singular ending.

Dysgiff y plant y caneuon y prynhawn 'ma.   *The children will learn the songs this afternoon.*

Remember also the direct object of a short form or concise verb takes the soft mutation (see Unit 2).

Dysgiff y plant ganeuon y prynhawn 'ma.   *The children will learn songs this afternoon.*

(as opposed to <u>the</u> songs.)

Formal written affirmative

dysgaf	*I learn / will learn*	dysgwn	*we learn / will learn*
dysgi	*you learn / will learn*	dysgwch	*you learn / will learn*
dysg	*he / she learns / will learn*	dysgant	*they learn / will learn*

Many verbs in the written language have irregular endings in the 3rd person singular (*he / she*) which involve vowel changes to the stem of the verb, as indicated in the following list.

Infinitive	Meaning	3rd person sing.
agor	*to open*	egyr
aros	*to stay*	erys

Infinitive	Meaning	3rd person sing.
ateb	*to answer*	etyb
bwyta	*to eat*	bwyty
cadw	*to keep*	ceidw
ceisio	*to try*	cais
codi	*to get up*	cwyd
cysgu	*to sleep*	cwsg
chwerthin	*to laugh*	chwardd
dal	*to hold*	deil
dangos	*to show*	dengys
deffro	*to wake up*	deffry
galw	*to call*	geilw
parhau	*to continue*	pery
peidio	*to stop*	paid
peri	*to cause*	pair
rhoddi	*to give*	rhydd
sefyll	*to stand*	saif

Many verbs in the literary language add **–a** to the stem of the 3rd person singular. Once again here is a selection of the most common ones:

Infinitive	Meaning	3rd person sing.
anghofio	*to forget*	anghofia
brysio	*to hurry*	brysia
caniatáu	*to allow*	caniatâ
cefnogi	*to support*	cefnoga
cerdded	*to walk*	cerdda
croesawu	*to welcome*	croesawa
cuddio	*to hide*	cuddia
cystadlu	*to compete*	cystadla
chwilio	*to look for*	chwilia
deall	*to understand*	dealla
dibynnu	*to depend*	dibynna
dihuno	*to wake up*	dihuna
gofalu	*to look after*	gofala
gwario	*to spend*	gwaria
gwerthu	*to sell*	gwertha
gwisgo	*to wear*	gwisga

Infinitive	Meaning	3rd person sing.
llwyddo	*to succeed*	llwydda
meddwl	*to think*	meddylia
mwynhau	*to enjoy*	mwynha
newid	*to change*	newidia
paratoi	*to prepare*	paratoa
sicrhau	*to ensure*	sicrha
sylwi	*to notice*	sylwa
symud	*to move*	symuda
teimlo	*to feel*	teimla
trefnu	*to arrange*	trefna

In the case of other verbs, such as **dysgu** already cited, the stem of the verb without any ending is the form of the third person in the literary language.

Infinitive	Meaning	3rd person sing.
canu	*to sing*	cân
clywed	*to hear*	clyw
credu	*to believe*	cred
cwympo	*to fall*	cwymp
cymryd	*to take*	cymer
digwydd	*to happen*	digwydd
dweud	*to say*	dywed
dysgu	*to learn*	dysg
eistedd	*to sit*	eistedd
gallu	*to be able*	gall
gorffen	*to finish*	gorffen
gorwedd	*to lie down*	gorwedd
gweld	*to see*	gwêl
lladd	*to kill*	lladd
mynnu	*to insist*	myn
rhedeg	*to run*	rhed
sychu	*to dry*	sych
talu	*to pay*	tâl
tynnu	*to pull*	tyn
yfed	*to drink*	yf

Interrogative forms

Initial consonants (if possible) take the soft mutation in questions:

Ganwch chi'r gân nesaf?	*Will you sing the next song?*
Werthi di'r car?	*Will you sell the car?*

In spoken Welsh there is often a tendency to use the periphrastic or long form, i.e. **bod**, with the interrogative rather than the shortened form of the relevant verb (see Unit 18).

Fyddan nhw'n galw cyn y gêm?	*Will they (be) call(ing) before the game?*

Formal written interrogative

a welaf?	*will I see?*	a welwn?	*will we see?*
a weli?	*will you see?*	a welwch?	*will you see?*
a wêl?	*will he / she see?*	a welant?	*will they see?*

Negative forms

Verbs at the start of negative sentences take the aspirate mutation or the soft mutation if appropriate.

Chofi di ddim yn y bore.	*You will not remember in the morning.*
Ddysga i ddim rhagor heno.	*I will not learn any more tonight.*
Nofian nhw ddim yn y gystadleuaeth.	*They will not swim in the competition.*

....

Insight

Ddim o, which is sometimes contracted to **mo**, is a construction that some learners find difficult to grasp. It is used with a definite object as the following examples indicate. The preposition **o** conjugates with pronouns (see Unit 15).

Ddysgiff e ddim o'r gân.	*He will not learn the song.*
Ddarllenith Claire ddim ohoni fe.	*Claire will not read it.*
Olcha i mo'r car yn y bore.	*I will not wash the car in the morning.*
Symudwn ni mohonyn nhw.	*We won't move them.*

Formal written negative

ni chanaf	*I will not sing*	ni chanwn	*we will not sing*
ni cheni	*you will not sing*	ni chanwch	*you will not sing*
ni chân	*he / she will not sing*	ni chanant	*they will not sing*

Mo is not used in the literary language.

Ni chanaf y gân.	*I will not sing the song.*

Answer forms

Affirmative
These consist of the appropriate short form of the verb without the soft mutation.

Allan nhw ddod?	Gallan.
Can they come?	*Yes (they can).*

Negative
Na is placed before the short form of the verb, followed by either the soft mutation or, in the case of those verbs beginning with **c**, **t** or **p**, the aspirate mutation.

Welwn ni'r ddrama?	Na welwn.
Will we see the drama?	*No (we will not see it).*
Bryni di'r llun?	Na phryna.
Will you buy the picture?	*No (I will not buy it).*

Gwneud *as an auxiliary verb*

In informal speech, **gwneud** (*to do / to make*) is often used as an auxiliary verb in the future tense particularly with interrogatives and negatives.

Wnei di ofyn iddo fe?

Rather than:

Ofynni di iddo fe?
Will you ask him?

Wnawn ni ddim holi rhagor o gwestiynau.

Rather than:

Holwn ni ddim rhagor o gwestiynau.
We will not ask any more questions.

For a complete list of the short forms of the verb **gwneud** see Appendix 2.

Insight

Mo is not needed with auxiliary or periphrastic futures.

Chofiwch chi mo'r geiriau i gyd.
Wnewch chi ddim cofio'r geiriau i gyd.
You will not remember all the words.

Exercises

A Give the short form third person singular of the following verbs.
eistedd, dibynnu, ateb, aros, parhau, bwyta, codi, yfed, gwisgo, meddwl

B Translate the following sentences using **mo**.

  1 Dylan has learnt his words, he won't forget them now.
  2 They won't change the lesson tomorrow morning.
  3 Catrin loves the house, she won't sell it if possible.
  4 We won't support your suggestion unfortunately.

C Translate the following sentences using **gwneud** as an auxiliary verb.

  1 Will you explain the situation to him?
  2 He will not listen to me.
  3 She will call tonight before supper.
  4 They will not argue now that he's agreed to go.
  5 Will we allow them to compete next year?
  6 You will sleep well after a long journey like that.

Grammar in context

> Un wennol ni wna wanwyn

  1 The third person of which verb can be found in this familiar saying?
  2 What is the English equivalent?

> Gwyn y gwêl y frân ei chyw

  1 Which verb is used in the above proverb?
  2 How would you interpret this proverb?

Test yourself

Change the following sentences from the periphrastic to the short form.

1 Bydd e'n dysgu Ffrangeg i flwyddyn 7 yfory.
2 Fydda i ddim yn canu'r ddeuawd gyda Carol.
3 Fyddan nhw'n rhedeg yn Ras yr Wyddfa?
4 Fyddwn ni ddim yn clywed am ychydig eto.
5 Byddi di'n gweld y gwahaniaeth yn syth.
6 Byddwch chi'n gwerthfawrogi yr amser gyda'ch gilydd.
7 Fyddi di'n dysgu Astudiaethau Cymraeg yn y coleg?
8 Fydd hi ddim yn codi'r post cyn 10.00.
9 Fyddwn ni'n gallu mynd i gael pryd o fwyd yn y bwyty
   newydd yng Nghaerfyrddin?
10 Bydda i'n talu am y bwyd os bydd Adrian yn gofalu am
   y plant.

21

Regular verbs – imperfect and past tenses

In this unit you will learn:
- *How to form and use regular verbs in the short form imperfect and past tenses*

Grammar in focus

Imperfect tense (was / used to / would)

As explained under **bod** (Unit 17), the imperfect is used to express an incomplete, unfinished action or state in the past, often happening at a time a finished action took place and interrupted it. It can be used to say that something happened repeatedly or many times in the past. The imperfect is also frequently used to express an intention or wish (*would* in English) and to express the future from the point of view of the past.

> Edrychai'r plant ar eu mam mewn syndod pan agorodd hi'r drws. Roedd y plant yn edrych…
> *The children looked at their mother in surprise when she opened the door.*

(i.e. were looking – no completion is specified unlike with the verb **agor**)

Gweithiai fy nhad ar fferm ger Llandeilo.
Roedd fy nhad yn gweithio…
My father worked on a farm near Llandeilo.
(i.e. was working/used to work)

Gofynnodd hi a orffennen ni'r gwaith mewn pryd.
She asked whether we would finish the work in time.
(i.e. were intending to)

Note that **a** meaning *whether* is used before an indirect question, not **os** which is discussed under Unit 27.

Dywedodd Ellie y cerddai hi i'r ysgol ddydd Llun.	*Ellie said she would walk to school on Monday.*

Past tense

This tense is used to denote a completed action in the past. The past tense of regular verbs is formed by adding the past endings to the stem of the verb. For a selection of regular and irregular verb stems see Appendix 1.

Anfonais i ebost ato fe cyn gadael y gwaith.	*I sent him an email before leaving work.*

Imperfect tense affirmative forms

helpwn	*I would help*	helpen ni	*we would help*
helpet	*you would help*	helpech chi	*you would help*
helpai fe / fo / hi	*he / she would help*	helpen nhw	*they would help*

Helpen nhw lanhau'r stabl bob bore cyn yr ysgol.	*They would help / helped clean the stable every morning before school.*
Helpai'r plant o gwmpas y tŷ yn ystod y penwythnosau.	*The children would help / helped around the house during the weekends.*

Formal written affirmative

helpwn	helpem
helpit	helpech
helpai	helpent

Interrogative forms

Initial consonants (if possible) take the soft mutation in questions.

Gerddech chi i'r ysgol bob dydd pan oeddech chi'n ifanc?	*Did you used to walk to school every day when you were young?*
Dyfai lawer o goed wrth yr afon?	*Were there a lot of trees growing by the river?*

Formal written interrogative

a redwn?	*would I run?*	a redem?	*would we run?*
a redit?	*would you run?*	a redech?	*would you run?*
a redai?	*would he / she run?*	a redent?	*would they run?*

Negative forms

Verbs at the start of negative sentences take the aspirate mutation (if possible) or the soft mutation. Note once again the use of **ddim + o** or **mo** with definite objects.

Chysgen ni ddim yn yr ystafell honno am flynyddoedd.	*We wouldn't / didn't sleep in that room for years.*
Arhosai e ddim yno yn hir.	*He wouldn't / didn't stay there long.*

Formal written negative

ni ddywedwn	*I would not say*	ni ddywedem	*we would not say*
ni ddywedit	*you would not say*	ni ddywedech	*you would not say*
ni ddywedai	*he / she would not say*	ni ddywedent	*they would not say*

Answer forms

Affirmative
The appropriate form of the relevant verb is used in the answer or the appropriate form of **gwneud**. For the imperfect forms of **gwneud** see Unit 22.

Wisgai hi yr un dillad bob dydd?	Gwisgai / Gwnâi
Did she wear the same clothes every day?	*Yes (she did).*

Negative
Na is used with the appropriate form of the relevant verb or **gwneud**. Where possible **na** once again causes either the soft mutation or the aspirate mutation in the case of **t, c** and **p**.

Holent lawer o gwestiynau?	*Did they used to ask a lot of questions?*
Na holent.	*No (they did not).*
Na wnânt.	

Past tense affirmative forms

bwytais i	*I ate*	bwyton ni	*we ate*
bwytaist ti	*you ate*	bwytoch chi	*you ate*
bwytodd e / o / hi	*he / she ate*	bwyton nhw	*they ate*

Bwytais i ormod o bwdin amser cinio.	*I ate too much pudding at lunch time.*

Insight

Here again, as mentioned in the previous unit, you see the soft mutation to the direct object of a short form verb. **Gormod** has become **ormod**. **Bwytais i** is a short form verb, whereas **dw i'n bwyta** or **roedd hi'n bwyta** are long form verbs as no stem has been added.

Formal written forms

bwyteais	bwytasom
bwyteaist	bwytasoch
bwytaodd	bwytasant

Interrogative forms

Initial consonants take the soft mutation where possible.

Goginioch chi swper i'r teulu neithiwr?	*Did you cook supper for the family last night?*

Formal written interrogative

a yfais?	*did I drink?*	a yfasom?	*did we drink?*
a yfaist?	*did you drink?*	a yfasoch?	*did you drink?*
a yfodd?	*did he / she drink?*	a yfasant?	*did they drink?*

Negative forms

Verbs at the start of negative sentences take the aspirate or soft mutation where possible.

Phrynais i mo'r tocynnau.	*I didn't buy the tickets.*
Lwyddon nhw ddim i orffen y cwrs.	*They didn't succeed in finishing the course.*

For a discussion on **mo** see Unit 20.

Formal written negative

ni orffennais	*I did not finish*	ni orffenasom	*we did not finish*
ni orffennaist	*you did not finish*	ni orffenasoch	*you did not finish*
ni orffennodd	*he / she did not finish*	ni orffenasant	*they did not finish*

Answer forms

Answer forms in the past are straightforward – **do** (*yes*) and **naddo** (*no*) regardless of person.

Olchodd e'r llestri?	*Did he wash the dishes?*
Do, golchodd e'r llestri.	*Yes, he washed the dishes.*
Naddo, olchodd e ddim o'r llestri.	*No, he didn't wash the dishes.*
Dynnon nhw luniau?	*Did they take pictures?*
Do, tynnon nhw luniau.	*Yes, they took pictures.*
Naddo, thynnon nhw ddim lluniau.	*No, they didn't take pictures.*

Exercises

A Look at Siôn's diary below. State what occurred every day, using the third person past tense ending for 'he'.

e.e. Dydd Sadwrn – cerdded o gwmpas y dref
Dydd Sadwrn cerddodd e o gwmpas y dref.

Sadwrn – prynu crys newydd
Sul – ymweld â Nigel
Llun – teithio i Fiwmaris
Mawrth – cerdded yr arfordir
Mercher – gyrru i Gaerdydd
Iau – gweithio gartref
Gwener – darllen llyfr John Davies, *Hanes Cymru*

Now repeat with the first person ending 'i'.
e.e. Dydd Sadwrn cerddais i o gwmpas y dref.

B Complete the sentences below by choosing the correct form of the verb given in brackets. Beware of any mutation!

1 .... ni losin o'r siop ar y gornel bob dydd ar ôl yr ysgol. (prynu)
2 .... ti'r llyfr i waith cartref neithiwr? (darllen)
3 .... hi'r ras am y tro cyntaf erioed. (ennill)
4 .... e mo'r tabledi neithiwr wedi'r cyfan. (cymryd)
5 .... i'n drist iawn yn gwrando ar ei straeon e bob nos. (teimlo)
6 .... y plant eu cinio nhw i gyd? (bwyta)

Grammar in context

Until recently the registered national charity CYD brought learners and native speakers together through a variety of social events. The organisation of such social events is now the responsibility of the regional Welsh for Adults Centres (see the **Taking it Further** section). Many CYD groups have continued however as independent bodies, and they are a useful way of practising your Welsh in an informal atmosphere. The following extract is from the magazine *Cadwyn Cyd* and describes a ramble undertaken by CYD members.

How many past tense forms can you find? Give their infinitives.

Cychwynnodd deg ohonon ni o Hen Orsaf Erwyd ar fore braf. Ar ôl dringfa eitha serth, cyrhaeddon ni'r rhostir efo golygfeydd bendigedig o Fannau Brycheiniog a'r Mynydd Du. Cyn i ni gyrraedd Aberbedw gwelon ni ogof Llywelyn. Wedyn mwynhaodd pawb ginio ardderchog yn y Seven Stars, Aberbedw. Dychwelon ni i Erwyd heibio i Greigiau Aberbedw (anhygoel!) ac ar lan Afon Gwy.

serth	*steep*	**anhygoel**	*amazing*
rhostir	*moor, plain*	**Afon Gwy**	*the Wye*

Test yourself

This piece contains a range of verbal forms discussed in Units 17–21.
In it, Elan is describing her childhood to her grandchildren.
Can you translate what she says into Welsh?

Our house was a small house near the station. My father
drove a lorry and my mother used to teach music. Marged
and I would help 'Mamgu' prepare supper for everyone after
school. I used to walk to school every day in the summer and
winter. I was never late. I remember we had just arrived in
school one day when Mrs Watkins, the head teacher, called
me into her office – my father had had a bad accident. We
never saw him again. He died the next morning. It was a very
sad and difficult time.

22

Irregular verbs

In this unit you will learn:
- **The forms of the irregular verbs in Welsh, apart from bod**

Grammar in focus

Apart from the verb **bod,** the four main irregular verbs are:

mynd	*to go*	gwneud	*to do / to make*
dod	*to come*	cael	*to get / to obtain*

Present / future tense affirmative forms – *mynd, cael and gwneud*

Mynd

af i	*I shall go*	awn ni	*we shall go*
ei di	*you will go*	ewch chi	*you will go*
aiff / eith e / o	*he will go*	ân nhw	*they will go*
aiff / eith hi	*she will go*		

Awn ni i'r sinema am dy benblwydd.	*We will go to the cinema for your birthday.*

FORMAL WRITTEN FORMS

af	awn
ei	ewch
â	ânt

Cael and **gwneud** follow the same pattern as **mynd**:

Cei di gyfle i ymlacio ar dy wyliau.	*You will get a chance to relax on your holiday.*
Cawn ni lyfrau newydd yr wythnos nesaf.	*We will get new books next week.*
Gwnân nhw lawer o bethau yn ystod y penwythnos.	*They will do a lot of things during the weekend.*

Interrogative forms
Mynd

Ei di i'r cyngerdd gan Bryn Terfel eleni?	*Will you go to the concert by Bryn Terfel this year?*

Insight

You will see that as with the regular verbs, **a** is included at the start of the formal interrogative, and the personal pronoun generally omitted unless required for emphasis.

A ânt i'r Eidal ar wyliau eto?	*Will they go to Italy on holiday again?*

Cael and **gwneud** once again follow the same pattern as **mynd**, but the initial consonants mutate softly.

Gaf fi ofyn iddo fe eto?	*Can I ask him again?*
Wneith e'r gwaith?	*Will he do the work?*
A gawn losgi'r sbwriel yn y cae?	*Can we burn the rubbish in the field?*

Negative forms
Mynd

Af i ddim i'r dref yfory wedi'r cyfan.	*I won't go to town tomorrow after all.*

FORMAL WRITTEN FORMS

nid af	nid awn
nid ei	nid ewch
nid â	nid ânt

Cael takes the aspirate mutation in the negative and **gwneud** the soft mutation.

Chaiff e mo'r amser i orffen y gwaith.	*He will not get the time to finish the work.*
Ni chaiff ddiwrnod rhydd cyn y Pasg.	*He / she will not get a free day before Easter.*
Wnawn ni ddim treulio gormod o amser arno fe.	*We will not spend too much time on it.*

Present / future tense affirmative forms – dod

Dod in the present / future tense is slightly different to the other three verbs.

dof i	*I shall come*	down ni	*we shall come*
doi di	*you will come*	dewch chi	*you will come*
daw e / o	*he will come*	dôn nhw	*they will come*
daw hi	*she will come*		

Daw hi am gyfweliad yfory.	*She will come for an interview tomorrow.*

FORMAL WRITTEN FORMS

deuaf / dof	deuwn / down
deui / doi	deuwch / dowch
daw	deuant / dônt

Interrogative (soft mutation)

Ddôn nhw i'n gweld ni cyn mynd?	*Will they come and see us before going?*
A ddeuant ynghyd yfory?	*Will they come together tomorrow?*

Negative (soft mutation)

Ddof i ddim i'r Cwrdd Diolchgarwch nos Iau.	*I shall not come to the Harvest Festival on Thursday night.*

ni ddeuaf / ni ddof ni ddeuwn / ni ddown
ni ddeui / ni ddoi ni ddeuwch / ni ddowch
ni ddaw ni ddeuant / ni ddônt

Past tense affirmative forms – *mynd, dod and gwneud*

Mynd

es i	*I went*	aethon ni	*we went*
est ti	*you went*	aethoch chi	*you went*
aeth e / o	*he went*	aethon nhw	*they went*
aeth hi	*she went*		

FORMAL WRITTEN FORMS

euthum	aethom
aethost	aethoch
aeth	aethant

In the past tense **dod** and **gwneud** follow the same pattern as **mynd**.

Des i gyda'r teulu rywbryd y llynedd.	*I came with the family sometime last year.*
Daethon nhw i'w weld e cyn iddo fe symud i Awstralia.	*They came to see him before he moved to Australia.*
Gwnaethoch chi elw da ar y tŷ.	*You made a good profit on the house.*

Interrogative forms

Mynd, dod and **gwneud** follow the same pattern, mutating appropriately.

Aeth hi i'r pwll nofio ddydd Sul?	*Did she go to the swimming pool on Sunday?*
A aethoch i'r gwaith ddydd Llun?	*Did you go to work on Monday?*
Ddaethon nhw adref cyn swper?	*Did they come home before supper?*
A ddeuthum yn ôl mewn pryd?	*Did I come back in time?*

Wnaethon ni ddigon o waith ddoe?	*Did we do enough work yesterday?*
A wnaethost yr hyn a ofynnais?	*Did you do what I asked?*

Negative forms
Mynd

Es i ddim i weld sioe Peter Kay.	*I didn't go to see Peter Kay's show.*

FORMAL WRITTEN FORMS

nid euthum	nid aethom
nid aethost	nid aethoch
nid aeth	nid aethant

Dod and **gwneud** take the soft mutation.

Ddaeth e ddim i'r ysgol am wythnos.	*He didn't come to school for a week.*
Ni ddaethant i'r eglwys y bore 'ma.	*They didn't come to church this morning.*
Wnes i mo'r gwaith i'r gystadleuaeth.	*I didn't do the work for the competition.*
Ni wnaethom bopeth.	*We didn't do everything.*

Past tense affirmative forms – cael

Cael in the past tense is slightly different to the other three verbs.

ces i	*I had / got*	cawson ni	*we had / got*
cest ti	*you had / got*	cawsoch chi	*you had / got*
cafodd e / o	*he had / got*	cawson nhw	*they had / got*
cafodd hi	*she had / got*		

Cafodd e amser bendigedig yng Nghaerdydd.	*He had a wonderful time in Cardiff.*

FORMAL WRITTEN FORMS

cefais	cawsom
cefaist	cawsoch
cafodd	cawsant

Interrogative (soft mutation)

Gawsoch chi ddigon o fwyd?	*Did you have enough food?*
A gawsant amser i astudio'r gwaith yn fanwl?	*Did they have time to study the work in detail?*

Negative (aspirate mutation)

Ches i ddim llawer o wybodaeth oddi wrtho fe.	*I didn't get much information from him.*

FORMAL WRITTEN FORMS

ni chefais	ni chawsom
ni chest	ni chawsoch
ni chafodd	ni chawsant

Insight

Don't be concerned by the fact that there are sometimes a variety of possible forms you could use, especially in the imperfect. Stick to one set and be consistent. Generally the more standardized form is placed first in the text. What is important is that you are aware of the existence of different forms, in case you come across them in speech or in writing.

Imperfect forms

Mynd

awn / elwn i	*I would go*
aet / elet ti	*you would go*
âi / e / o / elai fe / fo	*he would go*
âi / elai hi	*she would go*
aen / elen ni	*we would go*
aech / elech chi	*you would go*
aen / elen nhw	*they would go*
Awn ni i'r archfarchnad unwaith yr wythnos.	*We would go / went to the supermarket once a week.*

awn   aem
ait   aech
âi   aent

Cael and **gwneud** once again follow the same pattern as **mynd** and mutate appropriately in the interrogative and negative forms.

Caen ni hwyl yn chwarae gyda'n gilydd ar y traeth.	*We would have fun playing with each other on the beach.*
Gwnâi bopeth y gallai ei wneud.	*He'd do everything that he could.*

Interrogative

Elen nhw eto?	*Would they go again?*
A wnait weithio tan oriau mân y bore?	*Would you work until the early hours of the morning?*

Negative

Elai fe ddim i'r ysgol Sul gyda'i frodyr.	*He wouldn't go to Sunday school with his brothers.*

FORMAL WRITTEN FORMS
nid awn   nid aem
nid ait   nid aech
nid âi   nid aent

Cael takes the aspirate mutation and **gwneud** the soft mutation.

Chawn i mo'r siawns i'w wneud e ar ôl iddo fe fynd.	*I wouldn't get the chance to do it after he went.*
Wnelen nhw mo'r gwaith.	*They wouldn't do the work.*

Dod in the imperfect is slightly different to the other three verbs.

deuwn / down / delwn i	*I would come*
deuet / doet / delet ti	*you would come*
deuai / dôi / delai fe / fo	*he would come*

deuai / dôi / delai hi	*she would come*
deuen / doen / delen ni	*we would come*
deuech / doech / delech chi	*you would come*
deuen / doen / delen nhw	*they would come*

Delen nhw i'r tŷ ar ôl yr ysgol bob nos Wener.	*They would come / came to the house after school every Friday night.*

FORMAL WRITTEN FORMS

deuwn / down	deuem / doem
deuit / doit	deuech / doech
deuai / dôi	deuent / doent

Interrogative (soft mutation)

Ddeuen nhw i chwarae rygbi yn erbyn tîm y dref?	*Did they used to come to play rugby against the town team?*
A ddeuai ei thad i'r cyfarfodydd wythnosol?	*Did her father come to the weekly meetings?*

Negative (soft mutation)

Ddeuai fe ddim yn aml iawn.	*He didn't come very often.*

Formal written forms

ni ddeuwn / ddown	ni ddeuem / ddoem
ni ddeuit / ddoit	ni ddeuech / ddoech
ni ddeuai / ddôi	ni ddeuent / ddoent

Gwybod

Another less common irregular verb which does not follow the pattern of **mynd** is **gwybod** (*to know a fact*).

Present tense

gwn i	*I know*	gwyddon ni	*we know*
gwyddost ti	*you know*	gwyddoch chi	*you know*
gŵyr e / o	*he knows*	gwyddan nhw	*they know*
gŵyr hi	*she knows*		

Unlike most other verbs, these forms convey the present rather than the future tense. The soft mutation occurs in the interrogative and the negative and the formal written forms are formed in a similar manner to those verbs already listed.

Wyddost ti pwy sy'n pregethu nos Sul?	*Do you know who is preaching on Sunday night?*
Wn i ddim.	*I don't know.*
A wyddoch pam fod rhaid iddo ymddiswyddo?	*Do you know why he has to resign?*
Ni wyddant arwyddocâd ei benderfyniad.	*They do not know the significance of his decision.*

Imperfect tense

gwyddwn i	*I would know / I knew*
gwyddet ti	*you would know / you knew*
gwyddai fe / fo	*he would know / he knew*
gwyddai hi	*she would know / she knew*
gwydden ni	*we would know / we knew*
gwyddech chi	*you would know / you knew*
gwydden nhw	*they would know / they knew*
Gwydden ni mai fe oedd yn gyfrifol am y ddamwain.	*We knew that it was he who was responsible for the accident.*
Wyddwn i ddim fod y ddau'n briod.	*I didn't know that the two were married.*

The past tense of **gwybod** is rarely used in speech.

For a quick reference summary of the affirmative forms of the four prime irregular verbs see Appendix 2.

Exercises

A Put the correct form of the verb given in brackets in the sentences below. Remember to mutate if necessary!

1 .... hi ei fod e wedi ceisio ei thwyllo. (gwybod)
2 Pan .... nhw yn ôl o'u gwyliau roedd llawer o waith i'w wneud. (dod)
3 Dw i o'r farn na .... ni ein harian yn ôl yn anffodus. (cael)
4 .... chi fwynhau'r ffilm? (gwneud)
5 .... i mo'r amser i fynd ar gwrs Cymraeg eleni. (cael)
6 Wyt ti'n gallu esbonio pam .... ti ddim i'r cyfarfod? (mynd)
7 .... nhw ddim bod rhaid cadw'n dawel. (gwybod)
8 .... di draw am gwpanaid o de nes ymlaen? (dod)

B Change the irregular verbs in the sentences below from the singular to the plural.
1 Est ti i Abertawe i brynu beic dros y Sul?
2 Chaiff e ddim caniatâd y brifathrawes.
3 Down i i'w weld e yn aml pan fuodd e'n byw yn y pentref.
4 Af i ddim i ofyn iddyn nhw nawr.
5 Gwneith hi'r trefniadau i gyd.
6 Wn i ddim beth ddigwyddodd iddo fe wedyn.

Grammar in context

What does Radio 1 DJ Huw Stephens think of the music of Jen Jenerio?

'Ces i'r pleser o ddarlledu sesiwn newydd gwych gan Jen Jenerio yn ddiweddar ar C2 – gwerth gwrando arni eto ar y we os gwnaethoch chi ei cholli...'

Test yourself

Translate the following sentences into Welsh using the short forms of the irregular verbs.

1 We would go to see them every afternoon at about four o'clock.
2 She first came here in 1973 to visit relatives in Pembrokeshire.
3 Did they have a lovely time at the party?
4 He knows that I am hoping to move house soon.
5 Their parents didn't come to come to see them in the show every year.
6 We had awful weather over the Bank holiday.
7 They knew that it was he who was to blame for everything.
8 I didn't have the opportunity to speak to them after the service.
9 A lot of people will come here in August for the Eisteddfod.
10 They didn't do anything to help with the arrangements.

23

Commands (imperatives)

In this unit you will learn:
* **How to tell people to do or not to do things**

Grammar in focus

Commands, although the word suggests something rather dominating, are really the way you tell people to do, or not to do things. This can be as everyday as saying, 'go and shut the door'. You can command a single person or many people. There are five different types of commands or imperatives in Welsh:

1 second person singular
2 second person plural
3 third person singular
4 first person plural
5 third person plural

Insight

The third person singular is only heard occasionally, while the third person plural is purely a literary form.

Second person singular command

The second person singular or **ti** (*you*) command is used with friends, family, young children and people of similar social rank.

The second person singular command usually corresponds to the stem of the verb-noun.

verb-noun	stem	ti command	meaning
darllen	darllen–	darllen!	*read!*
edrych	edrych–	edrych!	*look!*
sefyll	saf–	saf!	*stand!*
clywed	clyw–	clyw!	*listen!*

Verbs whose stems end in **–i** and verbs formed from adjectives or nouns add **–a** to the stem to form the second person singular command.

verb-noun	stem	ti command	meaning
ysgrifennu	ysgrifenn–	ysgrifenna!	*write!*
meddwl	meddyli–	meddylia!	*think!*
stopio	stopi–	stopia!	*stop!*
taflu	tafl–	tafla!	*throw!*
ffonio	ffoni–	ffonia!	*phone!*
nofio	nofi–	nofia!	*swim!*
yfed	yf–	yfa!	*drink!*

A small number of verbs have different **ti** commands in formal written Welsh.

verb-noun	informal	formal	meaning
codi	coda!	cwyd!	*get up!*
cysgu	cysga!	cwsg!	*sleep!*

The **ti** command of the irregular verbs are:

mynd	cer! (SW)	dos! (NW)	*go!*
dod	dere! (SW)	tyrd! (NW)	*come!*
gwneud	gwna!		*make! do!*
bod	bydd!		*be!*

Cael (*to get / to obtain*) has no **ti** form in the imperative.

Second person plural command

The second person plural or **chi** (*you*) command is used with strangers, older people and groups and is formed by adding –**wch** to the stem of the verb.

verb-noun	stem	chi command	meaning
eistedd	eistedd–	eisteddwch!	*sit!*
rhoi	rho–	rhowch!	*give! put!*
cau	cae–	caewch!	*shut!*
prynu	pryn–	prynwch!	*buy!*
golchi	golch–	golchwch!	*wash!*

The **chi** command of the irregular verbs are:

mynd	cerwch! (SW)	ewch! (NW)
dod	dewch! (SW)	dowch! (NW)
gwneud	gwnewch!	
bod	byddwch!	

Cael has no **chi** form in the imperative.

Third person singular command

The third person singular or **fe / fo / hi** (*he / she*) command is a command given to a third person who isn't in earshot of the speaker. It is formed by adding –**ed** to the stem of the verb.

Caned y gân!	*Let him / her sing the song!*
Edryched ar y llyfr!	*Let him / her look at the book!*

The **fe / fo / hi** command of the irregular verbs are:

mynd	aed! / eled!
dod	deued! / doed! / deled!
gwneud	gwnaed! / gwneled!
bod	bydded! / boed!

Cael has no **fe / fo / hi** form in the imperative.

First person plural command

The first person plural or **ni** (*we*) command is a command given to a group of people of which the speaker is a member. It is formed by adding **–wn** to the stem of the verb.

Sibrydwn!   *Let's whisper!*
Arhoswn!   *Let's wait!*

The **ni** commands of the irregular verbs are:

mynd	*awn! / elwn!*
dod	*deuwn! / down! / delwn!*
gwneud	*gwnawn! / gwnelwn!*
bod	*byddwn!*

Cael has no **ni** form in the imperative.

Third person plural command

The third person plural or **nhw** (*they*) command is a command given to two or more people who aren't in earshot of the speaker. It is formed by adding **–ent** to the stem of the verb.

Canent y gân!   *Let them sing the song!*
Edrychent ar y llyfr!   *Let them look at the book!*

The **nhw** commands of the irregular verbs are:

mynd	*aent! / elent!*
dod	*deuent! / doent! / delent!*
gwneud	*gwnaent! / gwnelent!*
bod	*byddent!*

Cael has no **nhw** form in the imperative.

Negative

To tell someone not to do something, the various forms of **peidio** (*to cease / to stop*) are used, e.g. **paid â / ag** is used in the **ti** form, **peidied â / ag** with **fe / fo / hi** and **peidiwch â / ag** in the **chi** form, together with the relevant verb-noun. **Â** causes the aspirate mutation.

Paid â bwyta'r bisgedi i gyd!	*Don't eat all the biscuits!*
Peidiwch â gwneud gormod o sŵn!	*Don't make too much noise!*

> ## Insight
>
> If you want to emphasize your point, the pronoun can be included before the verb-noun.
>
> Paid ti ag anghofio y ffordd! *Don't <u>you</u> forget the way!*

In formal written Welsh **na / nac** is placed in front of the imperative verb. **Na** causes the aspirate mutation. **Nac** occurs before a vowel.

Na chwsg!	*Don't sleep!*
Nac edrychwch!	*Don't look!*

Polite commands

Requesting or asking someone to do something, rather than ordering them, can be achieved through the following verbs:

▶ **Gwneud** – wnei di? / wnewch chi?
   Wnei di agor y drws i mi? *Will you open the door for me?*

▶ **Gallu** – alli / elli di? / allwch / ellwch chi?
   Allwch chi ffonio fy nhad? *Can you telephone my father?*

▶ **Medru** – fedri di? / fedrwch chi?
   Fedri di gofyn i dy frawd? *Can you ask your brother?*

In the case of **gallu** and **medru**, the conditional subjunctive (*could*) is also possible (see Unit 27).

Allet ti sicrhau fod lle i fi yn y neuadd?	*Could you make sure that there is a place for me in the hall?*

Popular idioms using command forms

Cer o 'ma!	*Get away!*
Ewch amdani!	*Go for it!*
Gad lonydd iddo fe!	*Leave him alone!*
Gad iddo fe fod!	*Let it be!*
Daliwch ati!	*Keep at it!*
Gwna fel y mynnoch.	*Do as you wish.*

_____

Exercises

A Give an appropriate command response to the following sentences:
e.g. Dw i eisiau torth wen. .... i'r siop fara!
(mynd – chi)
Ewch i'r siop fara!

1 Mae hi'n rhy dwym yn yr ystafell. .... y ffenestr!
(agor – chi)

2 Dw i wedi blino. .... i'r gwely!
(mynd – ti)

3 Mae chwant bwyd arna i. .... ychydig o spaghetti!
(coginio – ni)

4 Mae syched arna i. .... botel o ddŵr!
(prynu – chi)

5 Mae pen tost 'da fi. .... at y meddyg!
(mynd – chi)

6 Mae rhywun wedi cael damwain. .... yr heddlu!
(ffonio – ti)

7 Mae rhywbeth yn bod ar y car. .... i fy mrawd!
(gofyn – ni)

8 Mae llawer o waith 'da fi. .... nawr cyn ei bod hi'n rhy hwyr!
(dechrau – chi)

B Translate the following popular idioms into Welsh.
   1 Leave them alone! (*plural*)
   2 Do as you wish. (*plural*)

3 Let her be! (*singular*)
4 Go for it! (NW – *singular*)

Grammar in context

Mr Hughes is being questioned over a burglary that occurred at his house some months previously. Fill in the gaps in the conversation between Mr Hughes and the policeman.

Heddwas:	Helo Mr Hughes ……… i mewn.
Mr Hughes:	Diolch.
Heddwas:	……… eich cot ac ……… i lawr. Te ynteu coffi?
Mr Hughes:	Coffi os ……… yn dda. ……… ddigon o siwgr ynddo fe.
Heddwas:	Iawn. ……… eich hunan i fisgedi.
Mr Hughes:	Dim diolch.
Heddwas:	……… chi esbonio i mi beth ddigwyddodd ar y noson dan gwestiwn?
Mr Hughes:	Medraf, ond ………â disgwyl i mi gofio popeth. Mae'n amser hir yn ôl.
Heddwas:	Wrth gwrs, ……… eich amser.

Test yourself

Translate the following using the verbs given in brackets.

1 Think about it! (*meddwl – ti*)
2 Quiet! (*tawel – chi*)
3 Shut the door! (*cau – chi*)
4 Do your best! (*gwneud – ti*)
5 Let's go for it! (*mynd – ni*)
6 Let her stand up! (*sefyll – hi*)
7 Don't listen to him! (*peidio – chi*)
8 Let's keep at it! (*dal – ni*)
9 Let them take care! (*cymryd – nhw*)
10 Write to the Prime Minister! (*ysgrifennu – ti*)

24

Relative clauses

In this unit you will learn:
- *How to join clauses (parts of sentences) together with the relative particle*

Grammar in focus

The relative particle, which corresponds to *who*, *that* and *which* in English, is used to join or relate a dependent clause to the main clause of a sentence. A dependent clause refers to something or someone previously mentioned known as the 'antecedent'.

Relative forms of bod (to be)

Present tense
In the present tense **sy'n** (*who is / are, which is / are*) is used with long forms of the verb.

Dw i wedi gweld y dyn sy'n cynnig am y swydd.	*I have seen the man who is applying for the job.*

Sy is used in front of prepositions and adverbs.

Wyt ti'n adnabod y ferch sy wrth y drws?	*Do you know the girl who is by the door?*

Sy wedi is used when referring to something that has happened.

Dyn ni eisiau gwybod beth sy
  wedi digwydd iddyn nhw.

*We want to know what's
  happened to them.*

In the formal written language **sydd** is used in place of **sy** and **sydd yn** rather than **sy'n**.

Gobeithiaf siarad â'r dyn
  sydd yn gyfrifol.

*I hope to speak to the man who
  is responsible.*

Negative
To make the sub-clause negative in spoken Welsh **ddim** is placed after **sy / sydd**.

Dw i'n credu dy fod ti'n hoffi'r
  bachgen gwallt golau sy ddim
  yn y tîm.

*I think that you like the blond-
  haired boy who isn't in the
  team.*

....

Insight

Unlike in the positive, in the formal negative in all tenses, the verb in the relative clause always agrees in number with the antecedent.

Pwy yw'r ferch nad yw'n
  fodlon dweud gair?
A ydych yn gwybod enwau'r
  myfyrwyr nad ydynt yn dod?

*Who is the girl who isn't
  willing to say a word?*
*Do you know the names of the
  students who aren't coming?*

....

Imperfect and pluperfect tenses
(A) oedd is used in place of **sy** in clauses in the imperfect and pluperfect.

Oeddech chi'n adnabod y fenyw a
  oedd yn athrawes ysgol gynradd?
Roeddwn i'n arfer byw ger y fenyw
  a oedd wedi cynnig am y swydd.

*Did you know the woman who
  was a primary school teacher?*
*I used to live near the woman
  who had tried for the job.*

A is frequently omitted in casual speech, but is always included in writing.

Negative
In speech the negative is represented by **oedd ddim,** while in formal written Welsh **nad oedd** and **nad oeddynt** are used.

Roedden nhw'n adnabod perchennog y ci oedd ddim wedi ennill.

They knew the owner of the dog that hadn't won.

Yr oedd wedi clywed am y llyfrau nad oeddynt ar gael yn y llyfrgell leol.

He had heard of the books which weren't available in the local library.

Imperfect habitual / conditional
(A) fyddai is used to convey a conditional meaning or when referring to a regular action in the past. **Ddim** once again is used in the informal negative and **na fyddai / na fyddent** in the formal written negative.

Roedd y Ficer yn gwybod fyddai ddim llawer o bobl yn cytuno.

The Vicar knew that not many people would agree.

Future tense
(A) fydd is used in place of **sy** in the future tense with **ddim** in the negative once again and **na fydd / na fyddant** in the formal written language.

Maen nhw wedi darllen llawer am y cantorion fydd yn perfformio heno.

They have read a lot about the singers who will be performing tonight.

Dw i'n weddol siŵr fydd ein cymdogion ddim yno.

I'm pretty certain that our neighbours won't be there.

Past tense
(A) fuodd is used in place of **sy** in the past tense with **ddim** in the negative and **na fu / na fuont** in the formal written negative.

Nid oes neb yn medru deal acen y dyn na fu yn y wers neithiwr.

No one can understand the accent of the man who wasn't in the lesson last night.

Regular verbs and the relative clause

In the case of regular verbs, the relative clause is formed as follows:

antecedent	relative particle	relative clause
y ferch	a	gollodd
the girl	*who*	*lost*

The antecedent of the relative clause can be the subject or the direct object of the verb.

SUBJECT
Gwaeddodd y plentyn a dorrodd y ffenestr.

The child who broke the window shouted.

OBJECT
Gwelais i'r plentyn a dorrodd y ffenestr.

I saw the child who broke the window.

Insight

Remember if the antecedent is plural, the verb following the relative particle in the affirmative is always in the singular.

Dyma aelodau'r côr **a ganodd** y gân.

Here are the choir members who sang the song.

When emphasizing the subject or object, the noun or a pronoun is placed at the beginning of the sentence.

Aelodau'r côr a ganodd y gân.

It was the choir members who sang the song.

Dau lyfr a brynodd Wendy.

It was two books that Wendy bought.

The subject or object in such emphatic sentences is negated by means of **nid**.

Nid Owen ofynnodd iddo fe.   *It wasn't Owen who asked him.*

In all sentences **a** is frequently omitted in the spoken language.

A is also the form of the relative particle with all conjugated forms of the verb-noun **cael** in the passive (see Unit 25).

Es i i'r ddarlith a gafodd ei
  chynnal yn y coleg neithiwr.
Dw i wedi derbyn manylion
  rhaglenni a gaiff eu darlledu
  yfory.

*I went to the lecture which was
  held in the college last night.*
*I've received the details of the
  programmes which will be
  broadcast tomorrow.*

Negative

The negative written form of the relative particle **a** is **na** before verbs beginning with consonants and **nad** before verbs beginning with vowels. **Na** causes an aspirate mutation when the verb begins with **t**, **c** or **p** and soft mutation when the verb begins with **b**, **g**, **d**, **ll**, **m**, **rh**.

Hi oedd y fenyw na thalodd am
  ei siopa.
Yr oeddwn yn gwybod nad
  anghofiwn y stori fyth.

*She was the woman who didn't
  pay for her shopping.*
*I knew that I would never forget
  the story.*

In speech **na** is often omitted and **ddim** added after the verb.

Angharad oedd y ferch wisgodd
  ddim cot.

*Angharad was the girl who didn't
  wear a coat.*

Unlike in the affirmative, in the negative, the plural of the verb is used if **na / nad** refers to a plural noun or pronoun.

Dyma'r myfyrwyr **na wnaethant**
  y traethawd.

*Here are the students who didn't
  do the essay.*

Nas is used in the written language when the relative clause is the object of the verb. You may not need to use it, but it is important that you can recognize what it means if you come across it in articles, books, etc.

Dysgodd wers galed nas anghofiodd.	*He learnt a hard lesson that he didn't forget.*

Y *and the relative clause*

In certain other cases the relative clause is represented by **y**:

► When the sub-clause is in the genitive case, that is when it refers to someone or something already mentioned. **Y** in such instances corresponds to the English pronoun *whose* and is followed by the verb and the pronoun **ei** (*his*), **ei** (*her*) or **eu** (*their*) in agreement with the antecedent.

Fe yw'r dyn y lladdwyd ei wraig mewn damwain car.	*He's the man whose wife was killed in a car accident.*
Dyma'r plant y cafodd eu mam ei harestio.	*Here are the children whose mother was arrested.*

Yr is used in front of a vowel and **h**.

Oeddet ti'n adnabod y bachgen yr oedd ei fam yn yr ysgol gyda dy dad?	*Did you know the boy whose mother was in school with your father?*
Fe oedd y dyn yr atebais ei lythyr.	*He was the man whose letter I answered.*

The same rules apply in the negative as already outlined under **a**, with **ddim** following the verb in informal contexts and **na / nad** used to introduce a negative clause in more formal contexts.

Nid wyf yn hoffi'r dyn na phrynais ei gwch.	*I don't like the man whose boat I didn't buy.*

Gwelais i'r darlithydd	*I saw the lecturer whose*
ddarllenais i mo'i lyfr.	*book I didn't read.*

▶ When the relative particle is dependent on the preposition that follows a verb e.g. **sôn am** (*to mention*), **dweud wrth** (*to tell*), etc. For a full list of such prepositions see Units 15 / 16. **Y / yr** is followed by the verb and then the preposition and, in spoken Welsh, the relevant pronoun. The preposition is always in the third person and corresponds in number and gender to the antecedent. If the preposition is one which does not decline, then the appropriate pronoun must be included in written as well as spoken Welsh.

Dych chi'n adnabod yr actor y	*Do you know the actor*
soniais i amdano fe?	*I mentioned?*
Es i i weld y swyddfa y	*I went to see the office in*
bwriadaf weithio ynddi hi.	*which I intend working.*
A oeddech yn adnabod y	*Did you know the woman*
fenyw y cwrddais â hi?	*I met?*

The same rules apply for the negative as already outlined, with **ddim** following the verb in informal contexts and **na / nad** used to introduce a negative clause in more formal contexts.

Dyma'r rhestr chyfeiriais i	*Here's the list which I didn't*
ddim ati hi yn fy neges.	*refer to in my message.*
Luned oedd y ferch nad	*Luned was the girl with*
oeddwn wedi siarad â hi.	*whom I hadn't spoken.*

▶ When the antecedent is a word denoting time, place or reason and takes the place of an adverb.

Ffoniodd e'r diwrnod y	*He phoned on the day the*
cyrhaeddodd y lluniau.	*pictures arrived.*
Dw i'n cofio enw'r stryd lle y	*I remember the name of the*
gwelais y bechgyn yn ymladd.	*street where I saw the boys*
	fighting.
Dyna'r wythnos na alwodd y	*That's the week the fishman*
dyn pysgod.	*didn't call.*

Emphatic sentences follow a similar pattern.

Ddoe y clywon ni fod yr ysgol   *It was yesterday that we*
yn mynd i gau.   *heard that the school is*
                                 going to shut.

▶ To introduce clauses with the long form of the verb in written Welsh.

A hoffet weld y llun y mae   *Would you like to see*
Siôn yn ei beintio?   *the picture that Siôn is*
                                 painting?

Beth oedd enw'r ddrama yr   *What was the name of the*
oedd dy fam eisiau ei gweld?   *play that your mother*
                                 wanted to see?

Insight

Note in the examples above that the prefixed pronoun refers back to the antecedent and agrees with it according to gender and number causing a soft mutation if appropriate. **Llun** is a masculine singular noun so the pronoun is also masculine causing a soft mutation. **Drama** is feminine therefore **gweld** doesn't mutate. In speech the relative particle y and the prefixed pronoun are not usually pronounced, but the mutation remains.

Piau

Piau is another relative form which means *to whom belongs, who / which owns*. The mutated form **biau** is generally used, with **sy(dd)** sometimes being omitted.

Hi yw'r ferch sydd biau'r beic   *She's the girl who owns the*
hyfryd.   *lovely bike.*

In other tenses, the third person singular of **bod** is used in front of **piau**.

Pwy fydd biau'r bwthyn   *Who will own the cottage after*
ar ôl i'w dad farw?   *his father dies?*

The negative is as already described under **a** and **y**.

Nhw oedd yr unig rai nad
oeddynt biau car.

*They were the only ones who
didn't own a car.*

Oes unrhyw un yma sydd ddim
biau ei gartref ei hunan?

*Is there anyone here who doesn't
own his own home?*

Exercises

A Link the two sentences in each of the following pairs in
accordance with the example. In the case of negative sentences
use **na / nad** rather than **ddim**.

Dyma'r gadair. Eisteddodd y meddyg ar y gadair.

Dyma'r gadair yr eisteddodd y meddyg arni hi.

1 Beth oedd lliw y llenni?
Cafodd y llenni eu gwerthu gan Tesco.

2 Eleri yw enw'r ferch.
Mae Eleri'n byw ar waelod y stryd.

3 Cyrhaeddodd y trên yn hwyr.
Daeth y trên o Lundain.

4 Dw i'n credu mai fe yw'r dyn.
Phrynodd y dyn mo'r tŷ.

5 Ble mae'r bachgen?
Rhoiais i'r arian i'r bachgen.

6 Hi yw'r ferch.
Chanodd y ferch ddim yn y cyngerdd.

7 Dw i'n poeni am y plant.
Cafodd eu cartref ei losgi neithiwr.

8 Mae pentrefi hyfryd yng Ngogledd Sir Benfro.
Does neb bron yn byw yn y pentrefi yn ystod y gaeaf.

9 Dyma'r merched o Ysgol Llansadwrn.
Roedd y merched yn cynrychioli'r ysgol yng
nghystadleuaeth nofio yr Urdd.

10 Stephen Jones yw capten newydd tîm rygbi Cymru.
Mae tîm rygbi Cymru'n chwarae Awstralia ddydd
Sadwrn.

B Fill the gaps in the sentences below, remembering to mutate
if necessary!
   1 Yfory ……. cawn ni gyfle i'w holi ymhellach.
   2 Dych chi'n credu ……… enillan nhw eu gêm nesaf?
   3 Dyna'r fenyw ………. collodd y bws.
   4 Nid Gomer ……. gwnaeth e.
   5 Wyt ti'n cofio'r ffilm ….. cyfeiriais ati hi?

Grammar in context

October 2006 was the 40th anniversary of the Aberfan disaster,
when 144 people in the small village of Aberfan in South Wales
were killed following the collapse of one of the coal tips. 116 of
those killed were children. An advert for one of the several TV
programmes broadcast in 2006 to commemorate the anniversary
consists of a picture of the memorial garden together with one line
in Welsh, containing the following stark message.

Y trychineb na allwn fyth ei anghofio.

1 How would you translate this sentence into English?
2 Explain the relative clause used here along with the prefixed
pronoun ei.

Test yourself

Translate the following questions into Welsh.

1 Who does the book on Welsh grammar belong to?
2 Did you know the woman I was talking to?

3 What novels are you going to read next?
4 Does he remember the day he first saw her?
5 Who are the people that complained?
6 What were the names of the children who didn't do their homework?
7 Who was the MP who lost his seat in Cardiff?
8 Have you heard that she will be visiting us before long?
9 Did you see the students that didn't attend the memorial lecture?
10 Where are the boxes in which the chairs came?

25

The passive

In this unit you will learn:
- *How to use the passive in Welsh and how to convert sentences from the active to the passive voice*

Grammar in focus

As already shown in Unit 17, an ordinary sentence is made up of a verb, a subject and an object, together with whatever adjectives, adverbs or other types of words are necessary to give any further appropriate information.

Ysgrifennodd y darlithydd y llyfr.   *The lecturer wrote the book.*

Such a sentence is said to be in the active voice. In the active voice, the subject performs the action of the verb. However the word order can be changed without altering the meaning of the sentence. If the subject then receives the action of the verb, or is acted upon by the object, the sentence is said to belong to the passive voice.

Cafodd y llyfr ei ysgrifennu gan y darlithydd.
Ysgrifennwyd y llyfr gan y darlithydd.
The book was written by the lecturer.

The actual sense of the sentence doesn't change, but there is a shift in emphasis. The passive is particularly useful when the 'agent' is not known.

Cafodd y llyfr ei ysgrifennu y llynedd.
Ysgrifennwyd y llyfr y llynedd.
The book was written last year.

As can be seen from the above examples, there are two ways in which the passive can be conveyed in Welsh:

1 using **cael** in a periphrastic construction.
2 using special impersonal forms in a non-periphrastic construction.

Cael

The verb-noun **cael** has several meanings, such as *to obtain*, *to get* and *to allow*.

Wyt ti wedi cael y neges?	*Have you received the message?*
Dyw e ddim yn cael mynd.	*He's not allowed to go.*

It also means *to have*.

Dw i wedi cael digon o'r lle 'ma!   *I've had enough of this place!*

It should not be confused with **gyda** which is used to express possession.

Mae dwy gath gyda fi.   *I've got two cats.*

The passive is generally conveyed in speech by using the following formula:

cael + personal pronoun (**fy, dy,** etc) + verb-noun.

It is possible to convey all tenses of the verb with this construction by using the appropriate tense of **cael**.

Mae dawns yn cael ei chynnal yn neuadd y dref heno.	*There's a dance being held in the town hall tonight.*

Roedd y car wedi cael ei ddinistrio yn y ddamwain.	*The car had been destroyed in the accident.*
Bydd e'n cael ei wahodd i ymuno â ni.	*He will be invited to join us.*
Gafodd hi ei magu yng Ngogledd Cymru?	*Was she brought up in North Wales?*

The preposition **gan** (*by*) is used to denote the agent or doer of the deed.

Ydy rhan Falstaff yn cael ei chymryd gan Bryn Terfel?	*Is the part of Falstaff being taken by Bryn Terfel?*

After **wedi** (*has / had*), **cael** can be omitted, especially in writing – formal or otherwise.

Roedd y llyfr wedi'i ysgrifennu gan fenyw o'r Alban.	*The book had been written by a woman from Scotland.* (= wedi cael ei ysgrifennu)
A oedd y traethawd wedi'i gwblhau?	*Had the essay been completed?* (= wedi cael ei gwblhau)

Cael can also be removed from passive constructions where **newydd** (*just*) is used in place of **wedi**:

Mae ei gyfrol o gerddi newydd (gael) ei chyhoeddi.	*His volume of poems has just been published.*

Impersonal forms

These forms are not used very often in everyday speech, but are heard frequently on the radio and television and are used when writing formally in the language.

Present tense

In order to convey what is happening now or what will happen in the future **ir** is added to the stem of the verb. Verb-stems ending in **–i** drop this before adding **ir**.

If the vowel before the last consonant of the stem is –a–, this is changed to –e– before **ir** is added e.g. **cynnal** (*to hold*) > **cynhali–** > **cynhelir.**

Cynhelir y cyngerdd nos Sul.
The concert will be held on Sunday night.
(= Bydd y cyngerdd yn cael ei gynnal nos Sul.)

Gwahoddir sylwadau gan aelodau'r cyngor.

Comments are invited from members of the council.

Past tense

In order to convey an action in the past **wyd** is added to the stem of the verb.

Noddwyd y noson gan S4C.
The evening was sponsored by S4C.
(= Cafodd y noson ei noddi gan S4C.)

Darllenwyd y newyddion neithiwr gan Huw Edwards.

The news was read last night by Huw Edwards.

Imperfect

In order to denote a number of events or a state or condition **id** is added to the stem of the verb-noun.

Addysgid llawer o blant yr ardal yn yr ysgol honno yn ystod y ganrif ddiwethaf.
Many of the children of the area were taught in that school during the last century.
(= Roedd llawer o blant yr ardal wedi cael eu haddysgu...)

Cosbid y ddau fachgen yn gyson gan y prifathro.

The two boys were frequently punished by the headmaster.

Impersonal interrogative

In the case of the interrogative **a** is placed in front of the impersonal form as it is essentially a written form.

A gyhoeddwyd enillydd y gystadleuaeth ar y teledu?	*Was the winner of the competition announced on the television?*

Impersonal negative

The negative particle **ni** (**nid** in front of a vowel) is placed before the impersonal form to create the negative. **Ni** causes verbs beginning with **t, c** and **p** to take the aspirate mutation and verbs beginning with **b, d, g, m, ll** and **rh** to mutate softly.

Ni chaniateir bwyta nac yfed yn y neuadd.	*Eating and drinking are not allowed in the hall.*
Nid anfonwyd yr wybodaeth at y person cywir.	*The information was not sent to the correct person.*

Impersonal imperative

The imperative form is used to note a command or wish (see Unit 23). **Er** is added to the stem of the verb-noun. In the negative the impersonal form is preceded by **na** or **nac**. **Na** causes the same mutations as **ni**.

Am fanylion pellach gweler isod.	*For further details see below.*
Nac ysmyger.	*Do not smoke.*
Na nofier.	*Do not swim.*

Such negative formal commands can also be expressed more informally by the use of **dim** (*no*) and the verb-noun.

dim ysmygu   *no smoking*
dim nofio   *no swimming*

Insight

As the above examples indicate, the impersonal imperative is used primarily in public notices and formal documents as a polite request.

Impersonal forms of the irregular verbs

infinitive	present	past	imperfect	imperative
mynd	eir	aethpwyd / aed	eid	eler
dod	deuir	daethpwyd	deuid / doid	deler
cael	ceir	cafwyd / caed	ceid	caffer
gwneud	gwneir	gwnaethpwyd / gwnaed	gwneid	gwneler
bod	ydys	buwyd	byddid	bydder
gwybod	gwyddys	gwybuwyd	gwyddid	gwybydder

Ceir llawer o wybodaeth am ei deulu yn y Llyfrgell Genedlaethol.

Much information on his family is to be had in the National Library.

Gwnaethpwyd arolwg manwl o'u defnydd o'r Gymraeg yn y gweithle.

A detailed survey was made of their use of Welsh in the workplace.

Exercises

A Re-write the sentences below using the traditional written impersonal forms.

   1 Cafodd fy mam ei geni yn Aberystwyth.
   2 Bydd y cae 'n cael ei werthu.

3 Byddai'r tŷ 'n yn cael ei arddurno bob Nadolig.
4 Chafodd y dyn mo'i arestio.
5 Bydd llawer o sŵn yn cael ei wneud.
6 Dyw nifer o hen eiriau amaethyddol ddim yn cael eu defnyddio erbyn hyn.
7 Mae'r llyfr yn cael ei ysgrifennu yn ddwyieithog.
8 Chafodd y parti mo'i gynnal wedi'r cyfan.
9 Ydy'r plant yn mynd i gael eu cosbi am dorri'r ffenestr?
10 Cafodd y Beibl ei ysgrifennu gan William Morgan.

B Translate the following impersonal commands.
1 See page seven.
2 Do not write on the wall.
3 Do not fish in the river.
4 Do not worry.
5 Write in ink.
6 Do not pull.

Grammar in context

Impersonal forms are particularly common in news bulletins on
S4C and Radio Cymru. Having read the bulletin below, answer the
questions about it.

Cynhaliwyd streic undydd heddiw ledled Cymru gan
ddarlithwyr mewn Colegau Addysg Bellach. O ganlyniad
gohiriwyd nifer o arholiadau tan yr wythnos nesaf.

Daethpwyd o hyd i gorff dyn ifanc mewn coedwig ger Abertawe
yn gynnar y bore yma. Darganfuwyd y corff gan fenyw tra'n
cerdded ei chi. Nid yw'r heddlu wedi rhyddhau enw'r dyn eto.

Codwyd dros bedair mil o bunnau at uned gofal dwys Ysbyty
Singleton neithiwr mewn cyngerdd yn Neuadd y Brangwyn.
Trefnwyd y cyngerdd gan David Jones, dyn o Lansamlet,

a dreuliodd gyfnod hir yn yr ysbyty y llynedd yn dilyn damwain car.

1 What has been postponed until next week?
2 Who found what and where?
3 How much money was raised in the concert and for what cause?
4 How many examples of the impersonal can you find in the complete bulletin and what are the infinitives of the forms in question?

_____

Test yourself

Translate the following sentences using the impersonal.

1 Heavy rain is expected tonight.
2 The meeting was held in spite of the opposition.
3 Was the film shown in black and white?
4 It is said that Pembrokeshire is the prettiest county.
5 Do not write below this line.
6 The subjects are not taught through the medium of Welsh.
7 The soldiers were taken to hospital in a taxi.
8 Not enough work was done in order to ensure success.
9 You are kindly asked not to take pictures during the performance.
10 Many more books for children were published last year.

26

Defective verbs

In this unit you will learn:
- *The formation of verbs with limited forms*

Grammar in focus

Defective verbs, which are also known as incomplete verbs, are those which do not possess the full range of tenses and / or personal forms.

Dylwn (should / ought)

This verb occurs in the imperfect and pluperfect tenses with a conditional meaning (see Unit 27).

Imperfect affirmative forms

dylwn i	*I should*
dylet ti	*you should*
dylai fe / fo / hi	*he / she should*
dylai'r plentyn	*the child should*
dylai'r dynion	*the men should*
dylen ni	*we should*
dylech chi	*you should*
dylen nhw	*they should*

Dylech chi wneud ymdrech
  i ddod i'r cyfarfod.

*You should make an effort to come
  to the meeting.*

Dylai myfyrwyr fynychu
  darlithoedd yn gyson.

*Students should attend lectures
  regularly.*

Formal written affirmative

dylwn	dylem
dylet	dylech
dylai	dylent

INTERROGATIVE FORMS

The verb takes the soft mutation in questions.

Ddylwn i ddweud wrtho fe?   *Should I tell him?*

In the formal written interrogative **a** precedes the verb causing it to mutate softly.

A ddylem fynd i'w weld?   *Should we go to see him?*

NEGATIVE FORMS

The negative forms of the verb also take the soft mutation.

Ddylen ni ddim newid y cynllun
  gwreiddiol.

*We shouldn't change the original
  plan.*

In the formal written negative **ni** precedes the verb causing it to mutate softly.

Ni ddylem newid amser y
  cyfarfod.

*We shouldn't change the time of
  the meeting.*

ANSWER FORMS

Affirmative

These consist of the appropriate form of the verb without the soft mutation.

Ddylen ni alw yfory?   Dylen.
Should we call tomorrow?   *Yes (we should).*

Negative

Na is placed before the short form of the verb causing it to mutate softly.

Ddylen nhw ofyn iddo fe?   Na ddylen.
Should they ask him?   *No (they should not).*

IMPERSONAL FORM

The impersonal form is **dylid** (*should be*). Remember that the direct object of an impersonal form doesn't mutate.

Dylid bwyta digon o lysiau a
ffrwythau bob dydd.

*Plenty of fruit and vegetables
should be eaten every day.*

Pluperfect affirmative forms

dylwn i fod wedi	*I should have*
dylet ti fod wedi	*you should have*
dylai fe / fo / hi fod wedi	*he / she should have*
dylai'r dosbarth fod wedi	*the class should have*
dylai'r aelodau fod wedi	*the members should have*
dylen ni fod wedi	*we should have*
dylech chi fod wedi	*you should have*
dylen nhw fod wedi	*they should have*
Dylen nhw fod wedi gwrando ar eu mam.	*They should have listened to their mother.*

Formal written affirmative

dylaswn	dylasem
dylaset	dylasech
dylasai	dylasent

Euthum yn ffôl ond chwi a'm
gyrrodd i hyn.

*I went foolishly, but it was you
who drove me to this.*

Oherwydd dylaswn i gael fy
nghanmol gennych.

*Because I should have been
commended by you.*
(II Corinthians. xii. II)

INTERROGATIVE FORMS

Once again the verb takes the soft mutation in questions and in the formal written interrogative **a** precedes the verb causing it to mutate softly.

Ddylech chi fod wedi holi ei fam?
A ddylasech holi ei fam?
Should you have asked his mother?

NEGATIVE FORMS

The negative forms of the pluperfect also take the soft mutation and in the formal written negative **ni** precedes the verb causing it to mutate softly.

Ddylwn i ddim bod wedi anfon y llythyr.
Ni ddylaswn anfon y llythyr.
I shouldn't have sent the letter.

ANSWER FORMS

Affirmative

These consist of the appropriate form of the verb without the soft mutation.

Dylwn i fod wedi gweithio'n galetach.	Dylech.
Dylaswn weithio'n galetach.	Dylasech.
I should have worked harder.	*Yes (you should have).*

Negative

Na is placed before the short form of the verb causing it to mutate softly.

Ddylen nhw fod wedi derbyn ei gyngor? Na ddylen.
A ddylasent dderbyn ei gyngor? Na ddylasent.
Should they have accepted his advice? No (they should not have).

IMPERSONAL FORM

The formal written impersonal form is **dylasid** (*should have been*).
Dylid bod wedi is also acceptable. Remember that the direct object
of an impersonal form doesn't mutate.

Dylasid cwblhau'r ymchwil mewn mis.
Dylid bod wedi cwblhau'r ymchwil mewn mis.
The research should have been completed in a month.

Meddaf (to say)

Meddaf has a present and an imperfect tense. Both are used in
quotative speech, while the present tense can also be used to
express someone's idea or opinion.

Present tense

meddaf i	*I say*	meddwn ni	*we say*
meddi di	*you say*	meddwch chi	*you say*
medd e / o / hi	*he / she says*	meddan nhw	*they say*

medd yr athro	*the teacher says*
medd y gweithwyr	*the workers say*
Cymraeg yw iaith y nefoedd, meddan nhw.	*Welsh is the language of heaven, so they say.*

Imperfect tense

meddwn i	*I said*	medden ni	*we said*
meddet ti	*you said*	meddech chi	*you said*
meddai fe / fo / hi	*he / she said*	medden nhw	*they said*

'Bydda i 'nôl cyn cinio,' meddai fe.	*'I'll be back before lunch,' he said.*
'Dw i'n hoffi gwylio'r rygbi,' meddwn i.	*'I like watching the rugby,' I said.*

Other incomplete verbs

Byw (*to live*)
The personal forms of **bod** are always used with **byw** as **byw** has
no personal forms itself.

Oeddet ti'n byw gyda dy fam?   *Were you living / did you live*
                                                      with your mother?

Marw (*to die*)
Marw likewise has no personal forms (see Unit 18). It too is used
with the forms of **bod**.

Bu farw fy nhad flynyddoedd yn ôl.   *My father died years ago.*

Gorfod (*to have to*)
Gorfod is used after the forms of **bod**.

Mae e'n gorfod mynd.   *He has to go.*

The form in the past tense is **gorfu i**.

Gorfu iddyn nhw weithio yn y   *They had to work in the coal*
    pyllau glo.   *mines.*
Gorfu i fi fwyta'r cig.   *I had to eat the meat.*

Gweddu (*to suit*)
Gweddu only has two forms, namely **gwedda** in the present and
gweddai in the imperfect.

| Gwedda'r celfi i blasdy o'r fath. | *The furniture suits such a mansion.* |
| Gweddai ei hesgidiau i liw ei gwisg. | *Her shoes suited the colour of her outfit.* |

Geni (*to be born*)

Geni only has impersonal forms, **genir** in the present and **ganwyd** and **ganed** in the past.

| Genir un neu ddau o ebolion bob gwanwyn. | *One or two foals are born every spring.* |
| Ganwyd fy mam yn ystod yr Ail Ryfel Byd. | *My mother was born during the Second World War.* |

The verb-noun **geni** can be used after the personal forms of **cael** in the passive construction (see Unit 25).

| Cafodd Owen ei eni yn Lloegr. | *Owen was born in England.* |

Exercises

A Complete the sentences below with the correct verbal form of the defective verb given in brackets.

1 .... chi gymryd mwy o amser dros y gwaith. (dylwn)
2 'Paid â phoeni am hynny', ... fe. (meddaf).
3 Bu .... fy nhad dros ugain mlynedd yn ôl. (marw)
4 Ni .... gwastraffu adnoddau prin. (dylwn)
5 .... hi dreulio ei phrynhawnau'n glanhau'r tŷ. (gorfod)
6 .... un bob munud .... nhw. (geni + meddaf)

B Change the following sentences from informal Welsh into formal literary Welsh. Remember that the personal pronoun is not normally included in the literary language.

1 Dylai fe fod wedi cyrraedd erbyn hyn.
2 Ddylwn i ddim chwerthin am ei ben e.
3 Dylen ni geisio codi'n gynharach.
4 Ddylet ti fod wedi dod â'r gwaith adref?
5 Ddylen nhw ddim cael eu beirniadu am ddweud hynny.

Grammar in context

The following extract from the short story *Y Gath Ddu* by Richard Hughes, written in 1923, (*Goreuon y Ganrif*, ed. Christine Jones, Gomer Press, 2004), contains several examples of the incomplete verb **meddaf** and North Walian dialect. The author has lost his tailless cat and gets some local children to help him look for her.

Fodd bynnag, yr oedd un o'r bechgyn wedi gweld cath gynffon gwta.

'Ym mha le?' gofynnais iddo.

'Ar ben cloc mawr,' atebodd.

'Wel, dos yno i'w nôl hi,' meddwn wrtho.

'Fedra i ddim,' atebodd.

'Wel does dim chwech i'w gael am ei gweld. Rhaid i ti ddod â hi yma.'

Tynnodd y bachgen ei law trwy ei wallt, nes ei wneud yn fwy dyryslyd nag oedd cyn hynny.

'Fedra i ddim hedag,' meddai yn y man.

'Leicwn i ddim dy weld ti yn ceisio,' meddwn wrtho.

'Ond sut y ca' i hi i lawr?'

Dyro dipyn o bupur ar ei chynffon hi.'

'Ond roeddach chi yn deud nad oedd gyni hi ddim cynffon, syr.'

'Wel, dyro bupur ar y fan y dylai ei chynffon hi fod, ynte,' meddwn wrtho.

'Ond does gin i ddim pupur.'

'Aros am funud, ac fe af i chwilio am dipyn i ti.'

dos (NW) **cer** (SW)	*go*
dyryslyd	*tangled*
hedag *i.e.* **ehedeg**	*to fly*
dyro *i.e.* **rho**	*put*
gyni hi (NW)	*i.e.* ganddi hi, gyda hi

1 Where has the boy seen a tailless cat?
2 What does the author suggest the boy should do to get the cat down?

Test yourself

Translate the following sentences.

1 He shouldn't drink and drive.
2 I should have realised that she had a problem.
3 His brother died of cancer.
4 Many children were born in very sad circumstances.
5 A higher level of service should be provided.
6 Did they have to go?
7 It's easier to learn French than Welsh, so they say.
8 They shouldn't have listened to him.
9 The flowery wallpaper suits this old house.
10 You *(plural)* shouldn't have gone without her permission.

27

The subjunctive

In this unit you will learn:
* **The formation and use of the subjunctive in Welsh**

_____

Grammar in focus

Up until now we have concentrated on verb formations in the **indicative mood**. This final unit looks at the **subjunctive mood**, which is another set of structures used to express desire, hope and uncertainity.

There are two forms of the subjunctive in Welsh:

1 the formulaic subjunctive
2 the conditional subjunctive

The formulaic subjunctive

The formulaic subjunctive only occurs in a limited number of set phrases in spoken Welsh. These include:

da boch chi	*goodbye*
gorau po gyntaf	*the quicker the better*
lle bo angen	*where there is a need*
cyn bo hir	*before long*

Regular verbs

The endings for regular verbs are:

–wyf	–om
–ych	–och
–o	–ont
y nefoedd a'n helpo!	*heaven help us!*

Irregular verbs

Bod		Mynd		Dod	
bwyf	bôm	elwyf	elom	delwyf	delom
bych	bôch	elych	eloch	delych	deloch
bo / po	bônt	elo	elont	dêl / delo	delont

Gwneud		Cael	
gwnelwyf	gwnelom	caffwyf	caffom
gwnelych	gwneloch	ceffych	caffoch
gwnêl / gwnelo	gwnelont	caffo	caffont

Pawb at y peth a bo.	*Each to his own.*
Gwnaf fy ngorau doed a ddêl.	*I will do my best come what may.*

In speech and in writing the subjunctive can be used in adverbial clauses where some sense of the indefinite future is implied.

Bydd yr ysgol yn cynnig dosbarthiadau nos tra bo galw ar eu cyfer.	*The school will offer night classes while there is a demand for them.*
Awn ni yno rywbryd pan fo'r tywydd yn braf.	*We will go there sometime when the weather is fine.*

The indicative mood is used when there is reference to a specific time.

Awn ni yno yn yr haf pan fydd y tywydd yn well.	*We will go there in the summer when the weather will be better.*

The conditional subjunctive

The conditional subjunctive endings are the same as the imperfect indicative endings (see Unit 21).

Spoken Welsh		**Written Welsh**	
–wn i	–en ni	–wn	–em
–et ti	–ech chi	–it	–ech
–ai fe / fo / hi	–en nhw	–ai	–ent

In the spoken language five verbs choose these endings, namely **gallu** (*to be able*), **medru** (*to be able*), **hoffi** (*to like*), **licio** (*to like*) and **caru** (*to love / like*) while other verbs choose the periphrastic construction with **bod**.

Gallech chi holi dy frawd di am yr achos.	*You could ask your brother about the case.*
Hoffai dy fam di ddod gyda ni?	*Would your mother like to come with us?*

Liciwn i ddim ceisio cerdded yr holl ffordd.	*I wouldn't like to try and walk the whole way.*
Garech chi ysgrifennu atyn nhw ar ein rhan?	*Would you like to write to them on our behalf?*

The mutational rules governing the interrogative and the negative are the same as in the indicative mood (see Unit 21) and the appropriate personal form is used in replying to a question.

Garen nhw symud i Gaerdydd?	*Would they like to move to Cardiff?*
Caren.	*Yes (they would).*
Na charen.	*No (they would not).*

Bod wedi is inserted between the personal form of the verb and the infinitive to express impossibility.

Hoffai e fod wedi gofyn cwestiwn ond roedd e'n rhy hwyr.	*He would have liked to have asked a question but he was too late.*

i.e. as he was too late, it was impossible for him to ask a question.

Caren ni fod wedi gweld Rhufain ond doedd dim amser gyda ni.	*We would have liked to have seen Rome but we didn't have time.*

i.e. lack of time made seeing Rome an impossibility.

Note the soft mutation of **bod** as it is the direct object of the verb.

The defective verb **dylwn** (*ought / should*) (see Unit 26) is formed by adding the subjunctive personal endings to the verb stem **dyl–**.

Dylwn i werthu'r car.	*I should sell the car.*
Dylen ni fod wedi prynu car newydd.	*We should have bought a new car.*

The conditional subjunctive of bod

Affirmative forms
In spoken Welsh there are two sets of forms in the affirmative
which are interchangeable. **Baswn i** etc. is also frequently
abbreviated to **'swn i, 'set ti** and so forth.

byddwn i	baswn i	*I would be*
byddet ti	baset ti	*you would be*
byddai fe / fo / hi	basai fe / fo / hi	*he / she would be*
byddai Sioned	basai Sioned	*Sioned would be*
byddai'r rhieni	basai'r rhieni	*the parents would be*
bydden ni	basen ni	*we would be*
byddech chi	basech chi	*you would be*
bydden nhw	basen nhw	*they would be*

Byddai Sioned yn ddewis da.	*Sioned would be a good choice.*
'Sen nhw'n ddiolchgar iawn am unrhyw gymorth.	*They would be very grateful for any help.*

Wedi is used to convey impossibility.

Byddech chi wedi mwynhau'r noson.	*You would have enjoyed the evening.*

i.e. if you had been able to come.

FORMAL WRITTEN FORMS

byddwn / buaswn	byddem / buasem
byddit / buasit	byddech / buasech
byddai / buasai	byddent / buasent

Interrogative forms
The verb mutates softly in the interrogative. In the written language
a precedes the verb.

Fyddwn i'n cael dod gyda
   chi?

Would I be allowed to come with
   you?

A fyddai'n fodlon cadeirio'r
   noson?

Would he / she be willing to chair
   the evening?

Negative

The verb mutates softly in the negative and is preceded by **ni** in the
formal written language.

Fyddwn i ddim yn ystyried
   symud nawr.

I wouldn't consider moving now.

Ni fyddit yn gyfrifol am dalu
   am y noson.

*You wouldn't be responsible for
   paying for the evening.*

Answer Forms

AFFIRMATIVE

Questions are answered by using the appropriate form of the verb.

Fydden nhw'n fodlon dod?
Would they be willing to come?

Bydden.
Yes (they would).

NEGATIVE

Na is placed before the appropriate form of the verb, causing it to
mutate softly.

Fyddai hi'n hapus yno?
Would she be happy there?

Na fyddai.
No (she would not).

Conditional clauses

There are two words in Welsh which mean *if*, namely **os** and **pe**.
Os is used in the indicative mood in the present, future, past and
imperfect tenses.

Awn ni i'r parti yfory os bydd
   amser gyda ni.

*We will go to the party
   tomorrow if we've got time.*

Os oedden nhw allan o brint, pam nad oedd neb wedi sylweddoli hynny?	*If they were out of print, why hadn't anyone realised that?*	

Insight

A common error, as noted in Unit 21, is to translate *whether* as **os**, rather than **a**.

Dw i ddim yn gwybod os bydd Mared yn dod.

This should read:

Dw i ddim yn gwybod a fydd Mared yn dod.	*I don't know if / whether Mared will be coming.*

The subjunctive form **pe** is used to express doubt or uncertainty. It is used in front of the conditional subjunctive forms of **bod** already listed.

Pe byddwn i'n gallu byddwn i'n mynd.
Pe baswn i'n gallu baswn i'n mynd.
If I were able I would go.

Pe byddai'r plant yn hapus bydden ni'n ei ystyried e.
Pe basai'r plant yn hapus basen ni'n ei ystyried e.
If the children were happy we would consider it.

Other variants when **pe** is connected with the forms of the verb **bod** include:

pe bawn i	petawn i	(pe)taswn i	*if I were*
pe baet ti	petaet ti	(pe)taset ti	*if you were*
pe bai e / o	petai fe	(pe)tasai fo	*if he were*
pe bai hi	petai hi	(pe)tasai hi	*if she were*
pe bai Bronwen	petai Bronwen	(pe)tasai Bronwen	*if Bronwen were*
pe bai ceffylau	petai ceffylau	(pe)tasai ceffylau	*if horses were*

pe bawn ni	petaen ni	(pe)tasen ni	*if we were*
pe baech chi	petaech chi	(pe)tasech chi	*if you were*
pe baen nhw	petaen nhw	(pe)tasen nhw	*if they were*

Petawn i etc. is heard primarily in South Wales, whereas **petaswn i** etc. is more of a North Walian form. **Pe bawn i** etc. also has a formal written alternative.

pe bawn	pe baem
pe bait	pe baech
pe bai	pe baent

Petai disgyblion yn cael mwy o amser bydden nhw'n gwneud yn well.	*If pupils were to have more time they would do better.*
Beth fasech chi'n ei wneud tasai hynny'n digwydd i chi?	*What would you do if that happened to you?*
Petawn i yn dy le di faswn i ddim yn ateb y ffôn.	*If I were you I wouldn't answer the phone.*
Pe baent wedi gofyn buasem wedi ceisio eu helpu.	*If they had asked we would have tried to help them.*

In formal written Welsh **pe** can also be used with other verbs.

Pe cawn gyfle symudwn i Batagonia i ddysgu Cymraeg.	*If I had a chance I would move to Patagonia to teach Welsh.*

Negative

The negative in spoken Welsh is created by placing **ddim** after the verb form.

Basen nhw'n ffôl tasen nhw ddim yn gwrando arni hi.	*They would be foolish if they didn't listen to her.*

A more formal written alternative would be to place **na** between **pe** and the verb form.

Byddent yn ffôl pe na buasent yn gwrando arni.

Insight

As you can see from the previous example, although **na** normally causes an apirate or soft mutation, forms of **bod** do not mutate after **pe na**.

In the written language **oni bai** (*unless*) is also used to convey the negative in place of **pe** (see Unit 11).

▶ oni bai + bod
Oni bai fy mod yn gweithio, byddwn wedi dod gyda chi.
If I wasn't working, I would have come with you.
Petaswn i ddim yn gweithio, baswn i wedi dod gyda chi.

▶ oni bai + i
Oni bai iddi ddweud, buasai'r athrawes wedi anghofio.
If she hadn't said, the teacher would have forgotten.
Pe basai hi ddim wedi dweud, basai'r athrawes wedi anghofio.

▶ oni bai + am

Oni bai am gefnogaeth fy nheulu, byddwn i wedi colli diddordeb ynddo fe.	*Were it not for the support of my family, I would have lost interest in it.*
Byddai'r tîm wedi chwalu oni bai amdani hi.	*The team would have collapsed were it not for her.*

Note also the idiom **heb os nac oni bai** – *without a doubt.*

Mae ysgrifennu'r llyfr hwn wedi bod yn brofiad pleserus iawn heb os nac oni bai!	*Writing this book has been a very pleasurable experience without a doubt!*

Exercises

A Answer the following questions in accordance with the example.

Beth fyddech chi'n ei wneud pe byddech chi'n ennill y loteri?
(*buy a house in Italy*)

Pe byddwn i'n ennill y loteri byddwn i'n prynu tŷ yn yr Eidal.

1 Beth fyddai dy fam di'n ei wneud pe byddai hi ddim yn gallu gyrru?
(*move to Swansea*)

2 Beth fyddai'r plant yn ei wneud pe byddai'r tocynnau i gyd wedi'u gwerthu?
(*watch the concert on television*)

3 Beth fyddech chi'n ei wneud pe bydden nhw ddim yn gallu dod nos yfory?
(*postpone the meeting*)

4 Beth fydden nhw'n ei wneud pe byddai hi'n bwrw eira?
(*stay at home in front of the fire*)

5 Beth fyddet ti'n ei wneud pe byddet ti ddim yn deall?
(*look for the answer in my grammar book*)

6 Beth fyddech chi a Sara'n ei wneud pe byddech chi'n gallu ymddeol y flwyddyn nesaf?
(*go to Australia for six months*)

B Place **os** or **pe** together with the relevant form of **bod** in the sentences below.

1 Af i i'r traeth yfory .... hi'n braf.

2 .... chi'n cofio, ysgrifennwch y manylion i lawr.

3 .... i'n cytuno byddwn i'n ffôl iawn.

4 Pam mae Ifor yn dod i'r dosbarth .... e'n teimlo mor sâl?

5 Ble byddai hi'n mynd .... ei swyddfa hi'n cau?

6 Pwy fyddai'n eu credu nhw .... nhw'n rhyddhau eu stori?

Grammar in context

The following paragraph comes from a leaflet published by NHS Wales (*GIG Cymru*) which discusses organ donation.

Gall un rhoddwr roi bywyd i nifer o bobl ac adfer golwg dau berson arall. Po fwyaf o bobl sy'n ymrwymo i gyfrannu eu horganau ar ôl iddynt farw, y mwyaf o bobl fydd yn elwa. Drwy ymuno â Chofrestr Cyfrannu Organau'r GIG gallech helpu i wneud yn siŵr fod bywyd yn mynd yn ei flaen.

rhoddwr   *donor*
adfer   *restore*
ymrwymo   *pledge*

1 What is the infinitive of the present subjunctive verb form found here?
2 The conditional subjunctive of which verb is also found in this paragraph?

Test yourself

Translate the following sentences into Welsh.

1 I'll buy the tickets now while I've got the chance.
2 We would like to go there again in the New Year.
3 They'd better wait there until the rain stops.
4 You could have come to see us in the play.
5 Would she like to visit us again before long?
6 He shouldn't have reacted like that.
7 If they had been informed what to do, they would have done it at once.
8 Could the older children join us for supper?
9 The mother asked if the swimming pool would be open after school.
10 There are more resources available for Welsh learners today, without a doubt!

Appendix 1

Stems of a selection of common Welsh verb-nouns

verb	noun	stem
addo	addaw–	*to promise*
aros	arhos–	*to wait*
arwain	arweini–	*to lead*
bwrw	bwri–	*to hit*
bwyta	bwyt–	*to eat*
cadw	cadw–	*to keep*
canu	can–	*to sing*
cau	cae–	*to shut*
cerdded	cerdd–	*to walk*
codi	cod–	*to get up*
cyffwrdd	cyffyrdd–	*to touch*
cymryd	cymer–	*to take*
cynnal	cynhali–	*to hold / to support*
cynnig	cynigi–	*to offer*
cyrraedd	cyrhaedd–	*to arrive*
chwerthin	chwerthin–	*to laugh*
dadlau	dadleu–	*to argue*
dal	dali–	*to hold / to catch*
dangos	dangos–	*to show*
darllen	darllen–	*to read*
deall	deall–	*to understand*
dechrau	dechreu–	*to start*
derbyn	derbyni–	*to accept*
dianc	dihang–	*to escape*
disgwyl	disgwyli–	*to expect*
disgyn	disgynn–	*to fall*
dweud	d(y)wed–	*to say*

dwyn	dyg–	*to steal*
edrych	edrych–	*to look*
eistedd	eistedd–	*to sit*
ennill	enill–	*to win*
ffonio	ffoni–	*to phone*
gadael	gadaw–	*to leave*
gallu	gall–	*to be able*
glanhau	glanha–	*to clean*
gofyn	gofynn–	*to ask*
gorffen	gorffenn–	*to finish*
gweiddi	gwaedd–	*to shout*
gweithio	gweithi–	*to work*
gweld	gwel–	*to see*
gwrando	gwrandaw–	*to listen*
gyrru	gyrr–	*to drive*
helpu	help–	*to help*
hoffi	hoff–	*to like*
llenwi	llanw–	*to fill*
meddwl	meddyli–	*to think*
mwynhau	mwynha–	*to enjoy*
newid	newidi–	*to change*
osgoi	osgo–	*to avoid*
paratoi	parato–	*to prepare*
prynu	pryn–	*to buy*
rhedeg	rhed–	*to run*
sefyll	saf–	*to stand*
siarad	siarad–	*to talk*
sibrwd	sibryd–	*to whisper*
symud	symud–	*to move*
taflu	tafl–	*to throw*
taro	traw–	*to strike*
trefnu	trefn–	*to arrange*
treulio	treuli–	*to spend (time)*
tynnu	tynn–	*to pull*
yfed	yf–	*to drink*
ymadael	ymadaw–	*to depart*
ysgrifennu	ysgrifenn–	*to write*

Appendix 2

Full conjugations of *mynd, cael, gwneud* and *dod*

Mynd

Informal

Present / Future		Past	
af i	awn ni	es i	aethon ni
ei di	ewch chi	est ti	aethoch chi
aiff / eith e / o	ân nhw	aeth e / o	aethon nhw
aiff / eith hi		aeth hi	

Imperfect

awn / elwn i	aen / elen ni
aet / elet ti	aech / elech chi
âi e / o / hi	aen / elen nhw
elai fe / fo / hi	

Formal

Present / Future		Past	
af	awn	euthum	aethom
ei	ewch	aethost	aethoch
â	ânt	aeth	aethant

Imperfect

awn	aem
ait	aech
âi	aent

Cael

Informal
Present / Future

		Past	
caf i	cawn ni	ces i	cawson ni
cei di	cewch chi	cest ti	cawsoch chi
caiff / ceith	cân nhw	cafodd e / o	cawson nhw
e / o / hi		cafodd hi	

Imperfect

cawn / celwn i	caen / celen ni
caet / celet ti	caech / celech chi
câi e / o / hi	caen / celen nhw
celai fe / fo / hi	

Formal
Present / Future

		Past	
caf	cawn	cefais	cawsom
cei	cewch	cefaist	cawsoch
caiff	cânt	cafodd	cawsant

Imperfect

cawn	caem
cait	caech
câi	caent

Gwneud

Informal
Present / Future

		Past	
gwnaf i	gwnawn ni	gwnes i	gwnaethon ni
gwnei di	gwnewch chi	gwnest ti	gwnaethoch chi
gwnaiff e / o / hi	gwnân nhw	gwnaeth	gwnaethon nhw
gwneith e / o / hi		e / o / hi	

Imperfect

gwnawn / gwnelwn i
gwnaet / gwnelet ti
gwnâi e / o / hi
gwnelai fe / fo / hi

gwnaen / gwnelen ni
gwnaech / gwnelech chi
gwnaen / gwnelen nhw

Formal
Present / Future

		Past	
gwnaf	gwnawn	gwneuthum	gwnaethom
gwnei	gwnewch	gwnaethost	gwnaethoch
gwna	gwnânt	gwnaeth	gwnaethant

Imperfect

gwnawn	gwnaem
gwnait	gwnaech
gwnâi	gwnaent

Dod

Informal
Present / Future

		Past	
dof i	down ni	des i	daethon ni
doi di	dewch chi	dest ti	daethoch chi
daw e / o	dôn nhw	daeth e / o	daethon nhw
daw hi		daeth hi	

Imperfect

deuwn / down / delwn i
deuet / doet / delet ti
deuai / dôi e /o / hi
delai fe / fo / hi

deuen / doen / delen ni
deuech / doech / delech chi
deuen / doen / delen nhw

Formal
Present / Future

		Past	
deuaf / dof	deuwn / down	deuthum	daethom
deui / doi	deuwch / dewch	daethost	daethoch
daw	deuant / dônt	daeth	daethant

Imperfect

deuwn / down	deuem / doem
deuit / doit	deuech / doech
deuai / dôi	deuent / doent

For the complete conjugations of **bod** and the regular verbs see the relevant units, namely Units 17–23. For a more comprehensive description of the Welsh verbal system and examples of all irregular stems and verbal forms see *Y Llyfr Berfau: A Check-list of Welsh Verbs* by D. Geraint Lewis, Gomer Press (2000).

Taking it further

There is a wealth of resources available to help you become fluent in Welsh. Here is a selection of them:

Courses

If you live in Wales, classes can be found for all levels including Saturday schools and residential courses through the six **Teaching Welsh to Adults Centres.** For their contact details see: http://cymraegioedolion.org

Nant Gwrtheyrn, the Welsh Language and Heritage Centre in North Wales offers residential courses for all standards throughout the year. Website: http://www.nantgwrtheyrn.org

An accredited web-based Welsh course for beginners co-authored by Christine Jones is available via the **School of Welsh and Bilingual Studies, University of Wales, Trinity Saint David.** The school also offers week and week end-long residential language courses. Website: http://www.trinitysaintdavid.ac.uk

The **Open University** offers an internet language course for beginners, along with a course on Welsh history. Descriptions can be found at http://www.open.ac.uk/wales

A free **online introductory course** together with other Welsh-related information can be found at http://www.siaradcymraeg.com

The **Madog Center for Welsh Studies** at the University of Rio Grande, Ohio offers Welsh courses including online courses, and **Cymdeithas Madog,** the Welsh Studies Institute in North America, Inc., holds an annual week-long course. See http://madog.rio.edu and http://www.madog.org

Learning materials and resources

Acen produces a wide range of learning materials and resources for tutors as well as learners, including an online beginners' course and downloadable reading resources such as a magazine for beginners and intermediate learners together with files for iPods and mobile phones via the Acen online Language Centre. Website: http://www.acen.co.uk

The **BBC Wales Learn Welsh** site is another excellent site for Welsh learners containing an online dictionary, spellchecker, lessons, activities, audio and video clips and regularly updated links to a variety of other useful sites such as online courses, online language tools and Welsh interest sites. This can be accessed on http://www.bbc.co.uk. *Radio Cymru*, which broadcasts over 20 hours a day, can also be accessed via this site.

Golwg 360 is a news site for intermediate and advanced learners which can be accessed on http://www.golwg360.com. A weekly paper-based arts magazine entitled *Golwg* is also produced, together with *Lingo Newydd,* a bi-monthly magazine for beginners and intermediate learners, obtainable by subscription from ymholiadau@golwg.com

The **Welsh Books Council** offers an online ordering service through their site http://www.gwales.com where you can find information and reviews about Welsh-language books including books for Welsh learners and books of Welsh interest.

S4C broadcasts a wide range of Welsh-language television programmes. The majority of programmes carry English subtitles. Website: http://www.s4c.co.uk

There are several free online Welsh dictionaries, including http://www.geiriadur.net and http://www.geiriadur.bangor.ac.uk/termiadur

Key to the exercises

Unit 1

Test yourself
1 tŷ **2** diflannu **3** cyrhaeddoch **4** casáu **5** gwên **6** synnu **7** carreg
8 apêl **9** gweddïo **10** cynyddu.

Unit 2

A 1 fy mherthnasau **2** nefoedd ac uffern **3** ym Mangor **4** dau gi
5 tad neu fab **6** y bedwaredd ganrif **7** ei chrib hi **8** cathod a
chwningod **9** i'w hysgol nhw **10** lyfrau.

B 1 fy tad. Nasal mutation after **fy**. This should read **fy nhad**. **2** dw
i'n weithio. Verbs don't mutate after **yn**. This should read **dw i'n
gweithio**. **3** a cerdded. Aspirate mutation after **a**. This should read
a cherdded.

Grammar in context
Advert **1 am roi** – soft mutation following **am**, **o gestyll** – soft
mutation following **o**, **am ddim** – soft mutation following **am**, **o
fewn** – soft mutation following **o**. Advert **2 o lyfrau** – soft mutation
following **o**, **a chardiau** – aspirate mutation following **a**, **y farchnad** –
mutation of a feminine singular noun following **y**.

Test yourself
1 Dw i'n dod o Fangor yn wreiddiol, ond dw i'n byw yng
Nghaerdydd nawr. **2** Daloch chi lawer o arian am y fodrwy?
3 Bwytodd e ddwy gacen siocled amser cinio. **4** Doedd y ferch
fach ddim yn gwrando ar ei hathrawes. **5** Cofiwch fynd â darn o
bapur a phensil gyda chi. **6** Byddwn ni ym Mhen-y-bont ar Ogwr
am y penwythnos yn ymweld â theulu Sue. **7** Oes amser gyda chi i
alw yn y garej drws nesaf i'r siop ddillad? **8** Mae'n anodd gwybod

a gaf i gyfle arall. **9** Fe oedd y myfyriwr a gollodd y ddarlith ar
lenyddiaeth Gymraeg. **10** Roedd y tywydd yn ofnadwy a chawson
ni law drwy'r dydd bob dydd am bythefnos.

Unit 3

1 'r The film has started. **2** 'r They went to the swimming pool
before lunch. **3** 'r I saw him with the girl from the office. **4** yr The
hours were very long. **5** 'r We sold two horses to the man from
Carmarthen. **6** yr The time went too quickly unfortunately. **7** 'r
My favourite time of the year is the autumn. **8** 'r She enjoys the
programmes about Welsh history. **9** yr He won lots of prizes in
the Eisteddfod. **10** yr How many letters are there in the Welsh
alphabet?

Grammar in context
1 Music from the shows, i.e. London musicals. **2** Bois y Castell.
3 The Black Pig Company.

Test yourself
1 gwyliau'r Nadolig **2** i'r Bala **3** Afon Hafren (no article needed)
4 y ffliw **5** yr Eidal **6** mae Afon Teifi (no article needed) **7** mae'r, yr
haf **8** ar y bws **9** yr wythnos **10** rhyw ferch – always singular with
rhyw, y Pasg.

Unit 4

A caseg, athrawes, tafarnwraig, dafad, ysgrifenyddes, merch,
telynores, asen, Saesnes, siaradwraig.

B haelioni – masculine, cariad – masculine, derwen – feminine,
seren – feminine, porfa – feminine, barddoniaeth – feminine, gaeaf –
masculine, Cymru – feminine.

C 1 hen neuadd yr ysgol **2** dyfodol yr iaith Gymraeg **3** cartref cyntaf
Mair **4** merch chwaer y plismon **5** plant y Trydydd Byd.

Grammar in context

dyn–*man*–dynion; milwr–*soldier*–milwyr; gwraig–*woman*–
gwragedd; arweinydd–*leader*–arweinwyr; llaw–*hand*–dwylo;
plentyn–*child*–plant; derwydd–*druid*–derwyddon.

Test yourself

Symudodd Heledd, merch fy nhiwtor Cymraeg, i mewn i'r pentref
ychydig wythnosau yn ôl. Mae hi'n byw drws nesaf i neuadd y
pentref. Mae hi'n dweud bod ei chymdogion wedi bod yn garedig
iawn iddi hi. Mae llawer o dai gwyliau yn y pentref. Mae llawer
o bobl o drefi a dinasoedd mawr yn ymweld â'r pentref yn yr haf.
Maen nhw'n dod mewn ceir mawr sy'n llenwi'r ffyrdd cul. Saesneg
yw iaith y pentref yn yr haf ond Cymraeg yw hi yn y gaeaf. Mae'n
dda gweld person Cymraeg arall yn symud i'r pentref. Mae Heledd
yn athrawes Fathemateg yn ein hysgol gyfun leol.

Unit 5

A 1 unig blentyn **2** ddiddorol **3** hoff fwyd **4** hen bobl **5** gwahanol
6 sawl **7** felen **8** peth **9** meirw **10** fer.

B

```
G L E I S I O N D A
A D U S R R M I U H
C C R E F D A L O B
R T B L I F A I N C
O L E G A N C F E S
N O I M Y R T O W G
D N O M I N E W G Th
```

Grammar in context

She states the book is interesting (**diddorol**) and brilliant (**gwych**).
She thinks the series is excellent (**ardderchog**).

Test yourself

1 ffrog wen **2** yr unig blentyn unig **3** cryn densiwn **4** Cymdeithas
y Deillion **5** brawddeg seml **6** hen geir rhydlyd **7** hoff raglen fy
mrawd **8** gyda chalon drom **9** y tlodion **10** Arthur a'r Ford Gron.

Unit 6

A **1** f **2** d **3** e **4** a **5** c **6** b

B 1 Mae Abertawe yn fwy nag Aberystwyth. **2** Mae'r Wyddfa yn uwch na'r Preselau. **3** Mae Owen Glyndwr yn enwocach (fwy enwog) na William Morgan. **4** Mae Gwenllïan yn waeth na Bronwen. **5** Mae Gomer yn drymach na Watcyn. **6** Mae Wrecsam yn dlotach na Chaerdydd.

C 1 True **2** True **3** False **4** True **5** False **6** False **7** True **8** False.

Grammar in context
1 No, life is going to get better. **2** Their family and their friends, especially those younger than them.

Test yourself
1 fwyaf siaradus **2** gyflymach na **3** haws na **4** mor weithgar **5** waethaf **6** mor flasus **7** cystal **8** mwy cyffrous **9** mor gryf â / cyn gryfed â **10** wlypach.

Unit 7

A 1 Rhedodd e'n gyflym draw i'r siop. **2** Roedd y gwaith yn rhy anodd i mi. **3** Dylen nhw fod wedi gorffen erbyn hyn. **4** Roeddwn i ar fy ffordd adref pan welais i fe. **5** Mae hynny'n weddol rwydd i'w wneud. **6** Byddan nhw'n mynd bore yfory yn anffodus. **7** Ewch i weld os yw'r car ar glo. **8** Roedd y ffilm yn arbennig o araf.

B 1 erioed **2** byth **3** erioed **4** byth **5** byth **6** erioed.

Grammar in context
ofnadwy o siomedig, yn ôl (× 2), hynod o felys, rhy.

Test yourself
A 1 correct **2** incorrect **3** incorrect **4** correct **5** correct.

B John: Roedd y ffilm yn ofnadwy o wael.

Julie: Roeddwn i'n meddwl ei bod hi'n arbennig o ddiddorol.

John: Roedd dy lygaid di ar gau yn ystod y rhan fwyaf ohoni hi!

Julie: Doedden nhw ddim, mae hynny'n gelwydd! Dw i byth yn mynd i'r sinema gyda ti eto.

John: Dw i'n gobeithio y byddi di mewn gwell tymer ddydd Sadwrn nesaf.

Julie: Dw i wedi cael digon, dw i'n mynd adref. Nos da!

Unit 8

A 1 Mae e'n cysgu'n drwm. **2** Clywodd hi'r stori ar y newyddion. **3** Roedd hi eisiau ei ddarllen e. **4** Dwedon nhw eu bod nhw'n mynd i'w thalu hi. **5** Dyma ei gŵr hi. **6** Nid hi oedd ar fai. **7** Maen nhw'n mynd. **8** Ydyn nhw wedi ei bwyta hi i gyd?

B 1 Aethoch chi i glywed y cyngerdd? **2** Buodd e'n byw gyda fy mrawd. **3** Hi yw'r athrawes newydd yn yr ysgol. **4** Dafydd oedd yr unig blentyn na'm hatebodd. **5** Beth yw enw ei chi hi? **6** Rhaid i ninnau helpu mwy o gwmpas y tŷ. **7** Helpodd e ni yn y bore a nhwthau yn y prynhawn. **8** Sut mae dy rieni di? **9** Aethon nhw draw i'w thŷ hi y bore 'ma. **10** Dw i wedi byw ar fy mhen fy hun am flynyddoedd nawr.

Grammar in context
1 Eleri's brother. **2** Julie. **3** When she was at primary school. **4** Dafydd and Eileen. **5** They can't sell their house.

Test yourself
1 Mae ein plant wedi hen adael y nyth. **2** Aeth Steffan a'ch brawd i'r cyfarfod. **3** Fe'n ganwyd yn Lloegr. **4** Daethon nhw yn eu car eu hun. **5** Oeddech chi'n hapus yn byw yno ar eich pen eich hun? **6** Ni'ch gwelaf yr wythnos nesaf. **7** Ble mae eu hysgol nhw? **8** Dylai nhwthau ddeall y sefyllfa. **9** Chwychwi yw'r Pennaeth. **10** Fe'u harestiwyd yn syth.

Unit 9

A 1 c **2** f **3** g **4** j **5** h **6** b **7** e **8** a **9** d **10** i.

B 1 hon **2** hyn **3** hwn **4** hon **5** hyn.

C 1 hwnnw **2** honno **3** honno **4** hynny **5** honno.

Grammar in context

1 Pwy fyddai'n magu plant? *Who would bring up children?* **2** Sut bydd Ann yn ymdopi â bywyd coleg. *How will Anne cope with college life?* **3** Pam mae gŵr Mair mor awyddus iddi hi newid? *Why is Mair's husband so keen for her to change?* The demonstrative pronoun is **hyn** in the expression **hyn i gyd** – *all of this.*

Test yourself

1 Mae peth gwaith gyda fe i'w wneud cyn diwedd yr wythnos. **2** Yr anrheg hon yw fy hoff un. **3** At ei gilydd roedd y perfformiad yn ardderchog. **4** Hi yw'r athrawes sy'n helpu Catrin gyda'i mathemateg. **5** Aethon nhw i'r pwll nofio gyda'i gilydd. **6** Dw i'n cofio cael fy anfon i'r gwely am naw o'r gloch bob nos. **7** Byddai unrhyw blentyn yn hoffi hynny. **8** Pam nad yw Eluned yn hapus i fynd ar ei phen ei hun? **9** Mae amryw dafarnau da yn y pentref. **10** Faint dalodd y pris llawn?

Unit 10

A 1 bod **2** mai (taw) **3** y **4** fod **5** na **6** y.

B 1 Efallai y bydd e'n gwybod. **2** Efallai dy fod ti'n iawn. **3** Efallai na fyddan nhw yma mewn pryd. **4** Efallai y cei di'r llythyr yn y post yfory. **5** Efallai ei bod hi wedi clywed y plant eraill yn siarad ar ôl y parti.

Grammar in context

1 King Arthur **2** The light is very good. **3** The National Eisteddfod was held in St Davids.

Test yourself
1 Ydyn nhw wedi clywed bod Luned wedi colli ei swydd? **2** Roedden nhw'n siwr mai/taw Alun alwodd yr heddlu. **3** Efallai y dylwn fod wedi gofyn iddo fe. **4** Mae hi'n gwybod fy mod i wedi gorffen y llyfr. **5** Oeddech chi wedi clywed bod y Ficer ar wyliau? **6** Efallai na ddawnsion nhw i'r record olaf. **7** Dylai fe sylweddoli nad mynd heb fwyd yw'r ateb. **8** Roedden ni'n gobeithio y bydden ni'n cael y cyfle i'w wneud eto. **9** Efallai eu bod nhw'n tyfu llysiau ar gyfer y farchnad leol. **10** Roeddwn i'n meddwl ei bod hi wedi symud i Lundain.

Unit 11

1 ond (*It's late but I must finish the work before going to bed.*) **2** na'i chwaer (*She was more of an actress than her sister.*) **3** ac (*I will be going tomorrow and returning Monday.*) **4** nag (*I'm less nervous in the car now than I was.*) **5** na ddaeth (*She saw the child who didn't come on the trip.*) **6** a chasglu'r (*I must go and collect the children.*) **7** achos (*I should phone as he's sure to worry.*) **8** na theulu'r (*I know the groom's family better than the bride's family.*) **9** a (*He wrote to me every week and he phoned once a month.*) **10** neu ddwy'r (*One hour or two a week is sufficient.*)

Grammar in context
1 Yes **2** Good food, good beer and a good time.

Test yourself
1 Ysgrifennwch bopeth i lawr rhag ofn i chi anghofio. **2** Bydd e yno pan fydd e'n barod. **3** Mae hi'n drist achos bod y tywydd mor wael. **4** Gan ei bod hi'n gynnar galwodd e i weld ei fam. **5** Bydd hi'n rhy hwyr erbyn i'r bws ddod. **6** Er nad oedd e wedi dysgu llawer, roedd e wedi mwynhau'r profiad. **7** Gwell i fi fynd nawr, fel fy mod i yno cyn y plant. **8** Daethon nhw, er bod Owen yn teimlo'n dost. **9** Edrychodd Ellie ar ôl y plant er mwyn i mi wneud tipyn o waith. **10** Awn ni ddim oni bai i chi ddod hefyd. / Awn ni ddim oni bai eich bod chi'n dod hefyd.

Unit 12

A 17 + 3 = dau ddeg; 29 + 6 = tri deg pump; 7 + 5 = un deg dau;
44 + 13 = pum deg saith; 104 + 12 = cant un deg chwech;
357 − 30 = tri chant dau ddeg saith; 200 − 101 = naw deg naw;
78 − 8 = saith deg; 17 − 15 = dau; 1 − 1 = dim.

B 1 trydydd Cadeirydd **2** bedwaredd salm ar hugain **3** bumed
bennod **4** ail gân **5** unfed ferch ar ddeg **6** drydedd raglen **7** wythnos
gyntaf **8** pedwerydd dydd.

Grammar in context
Llanymddyfri pedwar deg dau **Bedwas** un deg dau; **Pontypridd** un
deg tri **Casnewydd** tri deg un; **Llanelli** un deg pump **Maesteg** un
deg dau; **Glyn Ebwy** pedwar deg tri **Cross Keys** un deg saith; **Pen-
y-bont ar Ogwr** dau ddeg un **Aberafan** tri deg wyth; **Castell Nedd**
dau ddeg tri **Glamorgan Wanderers** tri; **Abertawe** pedwar deg wyth
Caerdydd un deg wyth.

Test yourself
1 incorect, tair merch **2** correct **3** incorrect, saith ar hugain o bobl
4 incorrect, yr ail gwestiwn **5** incorrect, y pedwerydd tŷ ar ddeg
6 correct **7** correct **8** incorrect, yr ateb cyntaf **9** correct **10** incorrect,
deunaw / un deg wyth.

Unit 13

A 1 b **2** f **3** e **4** h **5** i **6** g **7** d **8** c **9** j **10** a.

B 1 pum munud ar hugain wedi wyth **2** deg munud wedi dau
3 chwarter i ddeuddeg **4** ugain munud i saith **5** hanner awr
wedi tri.

C 1 mlynedd **2** blwydd **3** flynedd **4** mlynedd **5** blwydd.

D 1 ddydd **2** ddiwrnod **3** ddiwrnod **4** dydd **5** ddiwrnod.

Grammar in context

Dydd Mercher y deuddegfed o Awst, Dydd Mercher 12fed Awst; Dydd Mercher y nawfed o Fedi, Dydd Mercher 9fed Medi; Dydd Sadwrn y degfed o Hydref, Dydd Mercher 10fed Hydref; Dydd Mercher y pedwerydd ar ddeg o Hydref, Dydd Mercher 14eg Hydref.

Test yourself

1 Mae hi wedi byw yno am dros chwe blynedd. **2** Mae fy mhenblwydd ar Ddydd Gŵyl Ddewi. **3** Maen nhw'n cael gwersi piano ar brynhawn dydd Sul. **4** Gweithiais i gyda fe am ugain mlynedd. **5** Maen nhw'n galw amdana i am chwarter wedi deg. **6** Prynodd Siân dŷ yng Nghilgerran ddwy flynedd yn ôl. **7** Mae'r trên nesaf am saith munud ar hugain i dri. **8** Arhosodd Gomer gyda'i ffrindiau yn Llanwrda echnos. **9** Bydd e'n hanner cant ym mis Awst. **10** Mae'r trip i'r pantomeim ar yr ail ar bymtheg o Ionawr.

Unit 14

A 1 mae wyth wedi'i luosi gan bump yn hafal i bedwar deg **2** mae dau adio naw yn hafal i un deg un **3** can medr **4** mae hanner adio chwarter yn hafal i dri chwarter **5** saith pwynt naw saith **6** mae dau ddeg saith tynnu naw yn hafal i un deg wyth **7** un deg pedwar litr **8** dwy ran o dair **9** mae chwe deg wedi'i rannu gan dri yn hafal i ddau ddeg **10** pedwar pwynt tri un.

B 1 f **2** e **3** g **4** h **5** c **6** b **7** d **8** a.

Grammar in context

Caernarfon gogledd-orllewin, naw mil chwe chant ac un deg un; **Wrecsam** gogledd-ddwyrain, pedwar deg tri mil; **Caerdydd** de-ddwyrain, tri chant un deg naw mil saith cant; **Llandudno** gogledd-ddwyrain, dau ddeg mil naw deg; **Aberhonddu** Canolbarth Cymru, saith mil naw cant ac un; **Tyddewi** de-orllewin, mil saith cant naw deg saith.

Test yourself
1 Mae'r walydd hyn yn drwchus iawn. **2** Beth oedd hyd y lori?
3 Roedd gormod o waith gyda fi i'w wneud. **4** Faint o docynnau
sydd ar ôl? **5** Roedd e'n pwyso dwy dunnell. **6** Mae'r dŵr yn fas
iawn. **7** Mae e wedi dysgu tipyn bach/ychydig o Gymraeg. **8** Beth
yw gwerth y tŷ? **9** Mae rhai o'r heolydd yng Ngorllewin Cymru yn
gul iawn. **10** Maen nhw'n byw llai na hanner awr o Gaerdydd.

Unit 15

A 1 hebddo fe **2** drostyn nhw **3** ynddi hi **4** wrthoch chi **5** amdana i
6 arnon ni **7** danyn nhw **8** ohono fe **9** rhyngon ni **10** trwyddi hi.

B 1 Dw i'n byw ar fy mhen fy hun. *I live on my own.* **2** Wyt ti'n
mynd yn ei lle hi? *Are you going in her place?* **3** Bues i'n byw yn
eu hymyl nhw am flynyddoedd. *I lived near them for years.*
4 Ofynnaist ti ar ei hôl hi? *Did you ask after her?* **5** Mae llawer o
ddysgwyr yn eu plith nhw. *There are a lot of learners among them.*
6 Mae'n poeni yn ein cylch ni. *He's worried about us.*

Grammar in context
cwtsho wrth, cysgodi o dan, cadw rhag, anfon at.

Test yourself
1 O ble mae'r plant yn dod? **2** Mae e wedi rhoi llyfr iddi hi.
3 Roedd y car y tu allan i'r tŷ. **4** Prynais ffrog newydd ar ei chyfer hi.
5 Dw i'n credu ei fod e wedi anfon y gwaith atyn nhw'n barod.
6 Roedden nhw'n arfer byw gyferbyn â'u hathrawes Gymraeg.
7 Es i i'r parti yn ei lle hi. **8** Doedd dim un ohonyn nhw'n medru
canu. **9** Daeth e er eich mwyn chi wrth gwrs. **10** I ble bydd y
teulu'n symud?

Unit 16

A 1 e yn **2** g wrth **3** f dros **4** h ar **5** j wrth **6** i i **7** d dros **8** b at **9** c o
10 a rhag.

B 1 o'i wirfodd **2** o ganlyniad **3** i'r dim **4** wrth y llyw **5** cael hyd iddo **6** wrth eu bodd **7** yn llygaid ei lle **8** heb yn wybod.

Grammar in context
Advert **1** – yng ngwres. This should be mewn gwres. Advert **2** – manylion pellach o. This should be manylion pellach oddi wrth.

Test yourself
Yn yr archfarchnad yn y dref neithiwr cwrddais i â merch o'r enw Carys a oedd yn fy nosbarth i yn yr ysgol. Dechreuodd hi siarad â fi wrth y stondin ffrwythau a doeddwn i ddim yn gallu dianc rhagddi hi. Aeth hi ymlaen ac ymlaen! Dwedais i wrthi hi fod rhaid i mi fynd ond doedd hi ddim yn fodlon gwrando arna i. Roedd hi'n ymweld â'i mam am y penwythnos. Mae Carys yn byw yng Nghaerdydd nawr a gofynnodd hi i mi anfon ebost ati hi os dw i'n penderfynu mynd i siopa yno rywbryd. Cytunais i er mwyn cael gwared â hi. Dw i ddim eisiau bod yn gas wrthi hi ond mae'n bosib y bydd rhaid i mi golli ei chyfeiriad hi. Gobeithio y bydd hi'n maddau i mi!

Unit 17

A 1 Dyw'r plant ddim yn gallu cofio. **2** Does dim llawer o arian gyda fi. **3** Dyn nhw ddim eisiau symud. **4** Dw i ddim yn darllen llyfr bob wythnos. **5** Does dim lluniau o'r ysgol gyda ni. **6** Nage, nid postmon ydy tad Sue.

B 1 dyn **2** dyn **3** does **4** dyw **5** wyt **6** dw **7** oes **8** ydy('r) **9** dyn **10** dych.

C 1 Mae fy mam wedi golchi'r dillad y bore ma. *My mother has washed the clothes this morning.* **2** Maen nhw wedi mynd i'r coleg yn Llambed. *They've gone to college in Lampeter.* **3** Wyt ti wedi deall y neges? *Have you understood the message?* **4** Dych chi ddim wedi gwneud digon o arian yn anffodus. *You haven't made enough money unfortunately.* **5** Dw i wedi rhoi'r lluniau ar y wal. *I've put the pictures on the wall.* **6** Dyn nhw wedi cael brecwast? *Have they had breakfast?*

Grammar in context

1 Gwraig Gethin yw hi / Mam Guto / Angharad / Mari yw hi / Mamgu Mared / Gruff / Olivia / Paul / James yw hi. **2** Brawd Mared yw e / Cefnder Olivia / Paul / James yw e / Mab Angharad / Huw yw e / Ŵyr Elin / Gethin yw e / Nai Guto / Mari / John yw e. **3** Guto yw brawd Angharad. **4** Mared yw cyfnither Olivia.

Test yourself

1 Ydy'r athrawon wedi bod i weld yr ysgol newydd? **2** Dyw hi ddim yn teimlo'n rhy dda. **3** Mae'r plant yn dysgu Sbaeneg am y tro cyntaf y tymor hwn. **4** Oes amser gyda chi i fynd i'r archfarchnad? **5** Dw i newydd orffen paentio'r ystafell fyw. **6** Maen nhw'n canu yn y cyngerdd yr wythnos nesaf. **7** Nac ydyn, dyn ni ddim wedi clywed oddi wrtho fe. **8** Ie, Teleri ydw i, mam Lowri. **9** Does neb eisiau mynd ar wyliau yno. **10** Nid fi yw'r unig un sy'n gobeithio ymddeol cyn hir.

Unit 18

A 1 Bydda i yn y gwaith yfory. **2** Byddwn ni yn Llandudno dros yr haf. **3** Bydd e'n canu yn y côr ddydd Sul nesaf. **4** Fyddi di yn y cyfarfod nos yfory? **5** Fydd hi ddim yn aros yn y gwesty. **6** Fyddan nhw ym mhriodas Elin y flwyddyn nesaf?

B 1 Bues i'n unig iawn am ychydig hebddo fe. **2** Buodd y dosbarth yn ymweld â'r Llyfrgell Genedlaethol yr wythnos diwethaf. **3** Fuon nhw'n siomedig? **4** Fuodd y Blaid Lafur ddim yno chwaith. **5** Buon ni'n siarad â'r heddlu eto ddoe. **6** Buest ti'n dwp i wrando arno fe.

Grammar in context

1 There will be a number of events for learners including two workshops. **2** The amount of Welsh used will depend on the ability and enthusiasm of those taking part.

Test yourself

1 Bues i'n dost / sâl iawn am bythefnos. **2** Fuodd e ddim yn hapus o gwbl pan glywodd e'r newyddion. **3** Byddwn ni'n galw am yr anrheg tua 10.00 o'r gloch. **4** Bydd hi'n cerdded y ci bob nos ar ôl swper. **5** Buon nhw'n garedig iawn iddo fe pan oedd e yn yr ysbyty. **6** Fyddi di'n perfformio'r ddrama eto cyn diwedd y tymor? **7** Fydd dim arian gyda chi ar ôl cyn hir. **8** Fuon ni ddim yn grac amdano fe, dim ond siomedig. **9** Bydda i'n dysgu tua deg gair Cymraeg newydd bob nos. **10** Fuodd e yn y fyddin yn ystod yr Ail Ryfel Byd?

Unit 19

A 1 b **2** f **3** d **4** a **5** e **6** c.

B 1 roedd **2** fuodd **3** oeddech **4** doedden (nhw) ddim **5** fuodd (hi) ddim **6** oeddech **7** fuodd **8** bues **9** oedden **10** fuost.

Grammar in context
1 She had passed her driving test having failed twice previously. **2** It can be expensive and trains can be late. **3** She was worried she might put the car in the wrong gear.

Test yourself
1 Doedden nhw ddim yn hoffi'r bwyd yn y gwesty. **2** Aled oedd yr unig un yn y gynulleidfa i gwyno. **3** Roedd hi'n heulog iawn yr wythnos diwethaf. **4** Doedd y plant ddim yn gallu mynd. **5** Oedden nhw wedi bod yno o'r blaen? **6** Doeddwn i ddim yn ei hadnabod hi pan oedd hi'n blentyn. **7** Roedden ni ar fynd pan alwodd ffrind fy mam. **8** Oedd ei thad yn gobeithio cael swydd yn y coleg? **9** Roeddwn i newydd gyrraedd adref pan dderbyniais eich neges chi. **10** Roedden nhw'n credu y byddai Gordon Brown yn ennill yr etholiad.

Unit 20

A eistedd, dibynna, etyb, erys, pery, bwyty, cwyd, yf, gwisga, meddylia.

B 1 Mae Dylan wedi dysgu ei eiriau e, anghofith e ddim ohonyn nhw nawr. **2** Newidian nhw ddim mo'r wers bore yfory. **3** Mae

Catrin yn caru'r tŷ, werthiff hi ddim ohono fe os yn bosib.
4 Chefnogwn ni ddim o'ch awgrym chi yn anffodus.

C 1 Wnewch chi esbonio'r sefyllfa iddo fe? **2** Wneith e ddim
gwrando arna i. **3** Gwneith hi alw heno cyn swper. **4** Wnân
nhw ddim dadlau nawr ei fod e wedi cytuno i fynd. **5** Wnawn ni
ganiatáu iddyn nhw gystadlu'r flwyddyn nesaf? **6** Gwnewch chi
gysgu'n dda ar ôl taith hir fel hynny.

Grammar in context
First proverb 1 gwneud 2 one swallow doesn't make a summer
(spring in Welsh). **Second proverb 1 gwêl** – 3rd person singular of
gweld. **2** in a parent's eyes his / her child can do no wrong.

Test yourself
1 Dysgiff e Ffrangeg i flwyddyn 7 yfory. **2** Chana i mo'r ddeuawd
gyda Carol. **3** Redan nhw yn Ras yr Wyddfa? **4** Chlywn ni ddim am
ychydig eto. **5** Gweli di'r gwahaniaeth yn syth. **6** Gwerthfawrogwch
chi'r amser gyda'ch gilydd. **7** Ddysgi di Astudiaethau Cymraeg yn y
coleg? **8** Chodiff hi ddim o'r post cyn 10.00. **9** Allwn ni fynd i gael
pryd o fwyd yn y bwyty newydd yng Nghaerfyrddin? **10** Tala i am
y bwyd os gofalith Adrian am y plant.

Unit 21

A Dydd Sadwrn prynodd e grys newydd. Dydd Sul ymwelodd e â
Nigel. Dydd Llun teithiodd e i Fiwmaris. Dydd Mawrth cerddodd
e'r arfordir. Dydd Mercher gyrrodd e i Gaerdydd. Dydd Iau
gweithiodd e gartref. Dydd Gwener darllenodd e lyfr John Davies,
Hanes Cymru.

Dydd Sul prynais i grys newydd. Dydd Sul ymwelais i â Nigel.
Dydd Llun teithiais i i Fiwmaris. Dydd Mawrth cerddais i yr
arfordir. Dydd Mercher gyrrais i i Gaerdydd. Dydd Iau gweithiais
i gartref. Dydd Gwener darllenais i lyfr John Davies, *Hanes Cymru*.

B 1 Prynwn ni losin o'r siop ar y gornel bob dydd ar ôl yr ysgol.
2 Ddarllenaist ti'r llyfr i waith cartref neithiwr? **3** Enillodd hi'r ras

am y tro cyntaf erioed. **4** Chymerodd e mo'r tabledi neithiwr wedi'r cyfan. **5** Teimlwn i'n drist iawn yn gwrando ar ei straeon e bob nos. **6** Fwytodd y plant eu cinio nhw i gyd?

Grammar in context
5 past tense forms cychwynnodd e – cychwyn, cyrhaeddon ni – cyrraedd, gwelon ni – gweld, mwynhaodd pawb – mwynhau, dychwelon ni – dychwelyd.

Test yourself
Roedd ein tŷ ni 'n dŷ bach ger yr orsaf. Gyrrai fe nhad lori a dysgai fy mam gerddoriaeth. Helpai Marged a finnau Mamgu i baratoi swper i bawb ar ôl yr ysgol. Cerddwn i'r ysgol bob dydd yn yr haf a'r gaeaf. Doeddwn i byth yn hwyr. Dw i'n cofio ein bod ni newydd gyrraedd yr ysgol un diwrnod pan alwodd Mrs Watkins, y brifathrawes, ni i mewn i'w swyddfa hi – roedd fy nhad wedi cael damwain ddrwg. Welon ni mohono fe byth wedyn. Bu farw yn y bore. Roedd hi'n amser trist ac anodd iawn.

Unit 22

A 1 gwyddai **2** ddaethon **3** chawn **4** wnaethoch **5** ches **6** est **7** wydden **8** ddoi.

B 1 aethoch chi **2** chân nhw **3** doen ni **4** awn ni ddim **5** gwnân nhw'r **6** wyddon ni ddim.

Grammar in context
Excellent – well worth listening to.

Test yourself
1 Aen i'w gweld nhw bob prynhawn tua phedwar o'r gloch.
2 Daeth hi yma'n gyntaf yn 1973 i ymweld â pherthnasau yn Sir Benfro. **3** Gawson nhw amser braf yn y parti? **4** Gŵyr fy mod i'n gobeithio symud tŷ cyn hir. **5** Ddeuai eu rhieni ddim i'w gweld nhw yn y sioe bob blwyddyn. **6** Chawson ni dywydd ofnadwy dros Ŵyl y Banc. **7** Gwydden nhw mai fe oedd ar fai am bopeth. **8** Ches i ddim o'r cyfle i siarad â nhw ar ôl y gwasanaeth. **9** Daw llawer o

bobl yma ym mis Awst i'r Eisteddfod. **10** Wnaethon nhw ddim byd i helpu gyda'r trefniadau.

Unit 23

A 1 agorwch **2** cer / dos **3** coginiwn **4** prynwch **5** ewch **6** ffonia'r **7** gofynnwn **8** dechreuwch.

B 1 Gadewch lonydd iddyn nhw **2** Gwnewch fel y mynnoch **3** Gad iddi hi fod! **4** Dos amdani!

Grammar in context

Heddwas:	Helo Mr Hughes **dewch i** mewn.
Mr Hughes:	Diolch.
Heddwas:	**Tynnwch** eich cot ac **eisteddwch** i lawr. Te ynteu coffi?
Mr Hughes:	Coffi os **gwelwch** yn dda. **Rhowch** ddigon o siwgr ynddo fe.
Heddwas:	Iawn. **Helpwch** eich hunan i fisgedi.
Mr Hughes:	Dim diolch.
Heddwas:	**Fedrwch** chi esbonio i mi beth ddigwyddodd ar y noson dan gwestiwn?
Mr Hughes:	Medraf, ond **peidiwch** â disgwyl i mi gofio popeth. Mae'n amser hir yn ôl.
Heddwas:	Wrth gwrs, **cymerwch** eich amser.

Test yourself

1 Meddylia amdano! **2** Tawelwch! **3** Caewch y drws! **4** Gwna dy orau! **5** Awn amdani! **6** Safed ar ei thraed! **7** Peidiwch â gwrando arno fe! **8** Daliwn ati! **9** Cymerent ofal! **10** Ysgrifenna at y Prif Weinidog!

Unit 24

A 1 Beth oedd lliw y llenni a gafodd eu gwerthu gan Tesco? **2** Eleri yw enw'r ferch sy'n byw ar waelod y stryd. **3** Cyrhaeddodd y trên a ddaeth o Lundain yn hwyr. **4** Dw i'n credu mai fe yw'r dyn na phrynodd mo'r tŷ. **5** Ble mae'r bachgen y rhoiais i'r arian iddo fe? **6** Hi yw'r ferch na chanodd yn y cyngerdd. **7** Dw i'n poeni am y plant y cafodd eu cartref ei losgi neithiwr. **8** Mae pentrefi hyfryd yng ngogledd Sir Benfro nad oes neb bron yn byw ynddyn nhw yn ystod y gaeaf. **9** Dyma'r merched o Ysgol Llansadwrn a oedd yn cynrychioli'r ysgol yng nghystadleuaeth nofio yr Urdd. **10** Stephen Jones yw capten newydd tîm rygbi Cymru sy'n chwarae Awstralia ddydd Sadwrn.

B 1 y cawn **2** yr enillan **3** a gollodd **4** a wnaeth **5** y cyfeiriais.

Grammar in context
1 The disaster that we can never forget. **2** negative relative clause **na allwn** – **ei** refers back to the antecedent, **y trychineb**, and agrees with it in number.

Test yourself
1 Pwy sydd biau'r llyfr ar ramadeg Cymraeg? **2** Oeddech chi'n adnabod y fenyw y bues i'n siarad â hi? **3** Pa nofelau dych chi'n mynd i'w darllen nesaf? **4** Ydy e'n cofio'r diwrnod y gwelodd e hi gyntaf? **5** Pwy yw'r bobl a gwynodd? **6** Beth oedd enwau'r plant na wnaethon nhw eu gwaith cartref? **7** Pwy oedd yr Aelod Seneddol a gollodd ei sedd yng Nghaerdydd? **8** Dych chi wedi clywed y bydd hi'n ymweld â ni cyn hir? **9** Weloch chi'r myfyrwyr na fynychan nhw'r ddarlith goffa. **10** Ble mae'r bocsys y daeth y cadeiriau ynddyn nhw?

Unit 25

A 1 Ganwyd / ganed fy mam yn Aberystwyth. **2** Gwerthir y cae. **3** Arddunid y tŷ bob Nadolig. **4** Nid arestiwyd y dyn. **5** Gwneir llawer o sŵn. **6** Ni ddefnyddir nifer o hen eiriau amaethyddol erbyn hyn. **7** Ysgrifennir y llyfr yn ddwyieithog. **8** Ni chynhaliwyd y parti wedi'r cyfan. **9** A gosbir y plant am dorri'r ffenestr? **10** Ysgrifennwyd y Beibl gan William Morgan.

B 1 Gweler tudalen saith. **2** Nac ysgrifenner ar y wal. **3** Na physgoter yn yr afon. **4** Na phoener. **5** Ysgrifenner mewn inc. **6** Na thynner.

Grammar in context

1 Examinations. **2** A woman out walking her dog found a body in a forest near Swansea (Abertawe). **3** Over 4,000 pounds for the intensive care unit in Singleton hospital. **4** six: **cynhaliwyd** – cynnal, **gohiriwyd** – gohirio, **daethpwyd** – dod, **darganfuwyd** – darganfod, **codwyd** – codi, **trefnwyd** – trefnu.

Test yourself

1 Disgwylir glaw trwm heno. **2** Cynhaliwyd y cyfarfod er gwaethaf y gwrthwynebiad. **3** A ddangoswyd y ffilm mewn du a gwyn? **4** Dywedir mai Sir Benfro yw'r sir bertaf. **5** Nac ysgrifenner o dan y llinell hon. **6** Ni ddysgir y pynciau drwy gyfrwng y Gymraeg. **7** Aethpwyd / awd â'r milwyr i'r ysbyty mewn tacsi. **8** Ni wnaethpwyd digon o waith er mwyn sicrhau llwyddiant. **9** Gweier tudalen 40 an ragor o enghreifftian. **10** Cyhoeddid llawer mwy o lyfrau i blant y llynedd.

Unit 26

A 1 dylech **2** meddai **3** farw **4** ddylid **5** gorfu iddi **6** genir, meddan.

B 1 Dylasai gyrraedd erbyn hyn. **2** Ni ddylwn chwerthin am ei ben. **3** Dylem geisio codi'n gynharach. **4** A ddylaset ddod â'r gwaith adref? **5** Ni ddylid eu beirniadu am ddweud hynny.

Grammar in context

1 On top of a large clock. **2** Put some pepper where its tail should be.

Test yourself

1 Ddylai fe ddim yfed a gyrru. **2** Dylwn i fod wedi sylweddoli fod problem gyda hi. **3** Bu farw ei frawd e o gancr. **4** Ganwyd / ganed llawer o blant mewn amgylchiadau trist iawn. **5** Dylai lefel uwch o wasanaeth gael ei ddarparu. / Dylid darparu lefel uwch o wasanaeth. **6** Oedden nhw'n gorfod mynd? **7** Mae'n haws dysgu Ffrangeg na Chymraeg meddan nhw. **8** Ddylen nhw ddim bod wedi gwrando arno fe. **9** Gwedda'r papur wal blodeuog i'r hen dŷ hwn. **10** Ddylech chi ddim fod wedi mynd heb ei chaniatâd.

Unit 27

A 1 Pe byddai fy mam ddim yn gallu gyrru byddai hi'n symud i
Abertawe. **2** Pe byddai'r tocynnau i gyd wedi'u gwerthu byddai'r
plant yn gwylio'r cyngerdd ar y teledu. **3** Pe bydden nhw ddim yn
gallu dod nos yfory byddwn i'n gohirio'r cyfarfod. **4** Pe byddai hi'n
bwrw eira bydden nhw'n aros gartref o flaen y tân. **5** Pe byddwn i
ddim yn deall byddwn i'n chwilio am yr ateb yn fy llyfr gramadeg.
6 Pe bydden ni'n gallu ymddeol y flwyddyn nesaf bydden ni'n
mynd i Awstralia am chwe mis.

B 1 os bydd **2** os dych **3** pe byddwn **4** os yw **5** pe byddai
6 pe bydden.

Grammar in context
1 bod – po **2** gallu – gallech.

Test yourself
1 Pryna i'r tocynnau nawr tra bydd cyfle gyda fi. **2** Hoffen ni fynd
yno eto yn y Flwyddyn Newydd. **3** Gwell iddyn nhw aros yno nes
bo'r glaw yn peidio. **4** Gallech chi fod wedi dod i'n gweld ni yn
y ddrama. **5** Hoffai hi ymweld â ni eto cyn hir? **6** Ddylai fe ddim
fod wedi ymateb fel hynny. **7** Pe bydden nhw wedi cael gwybod
beth i'w wneud, bydden nhw wedi'i wneud e'n syth. **8** Allai'r plant
henach ymuno â ni am swper? **9** Gofynnodd y fam a fyddai'r pwll
nofio ar agor ar ôl yr ysgol. **10** Mae mwy o adnoddau ar gael i
ddysgwyr Cymraeg y dyddiau hyn, heb os nac oni bai!